WE ARE EACH
OTHER'S HARVEST

WE ARE EACH OTHER'S HARVEST

CELEBRATING AFRICAN AMERICAN FARMERS, LAND, AND LEGACY

NATALIE BASZILE

AMISTAD

An Imprint of HarperCollinsPublishers

HarperCollins books may be purchased for educational, business, or sales promotional use.
For information, please email the Special Markets Department at Spsales@harpercollins.com.

FIRST EDITION

Designed by Matchbook Digital

Library of Congress Cataloging-in-Publication Data is available upon request.

ISBN 978-0-06-293256-3

21 22 23 24 25   LSC   10 9 8 7 6 5 4 3 2 1

ALSO BY NATALIE BASZILE

Queen Sugar

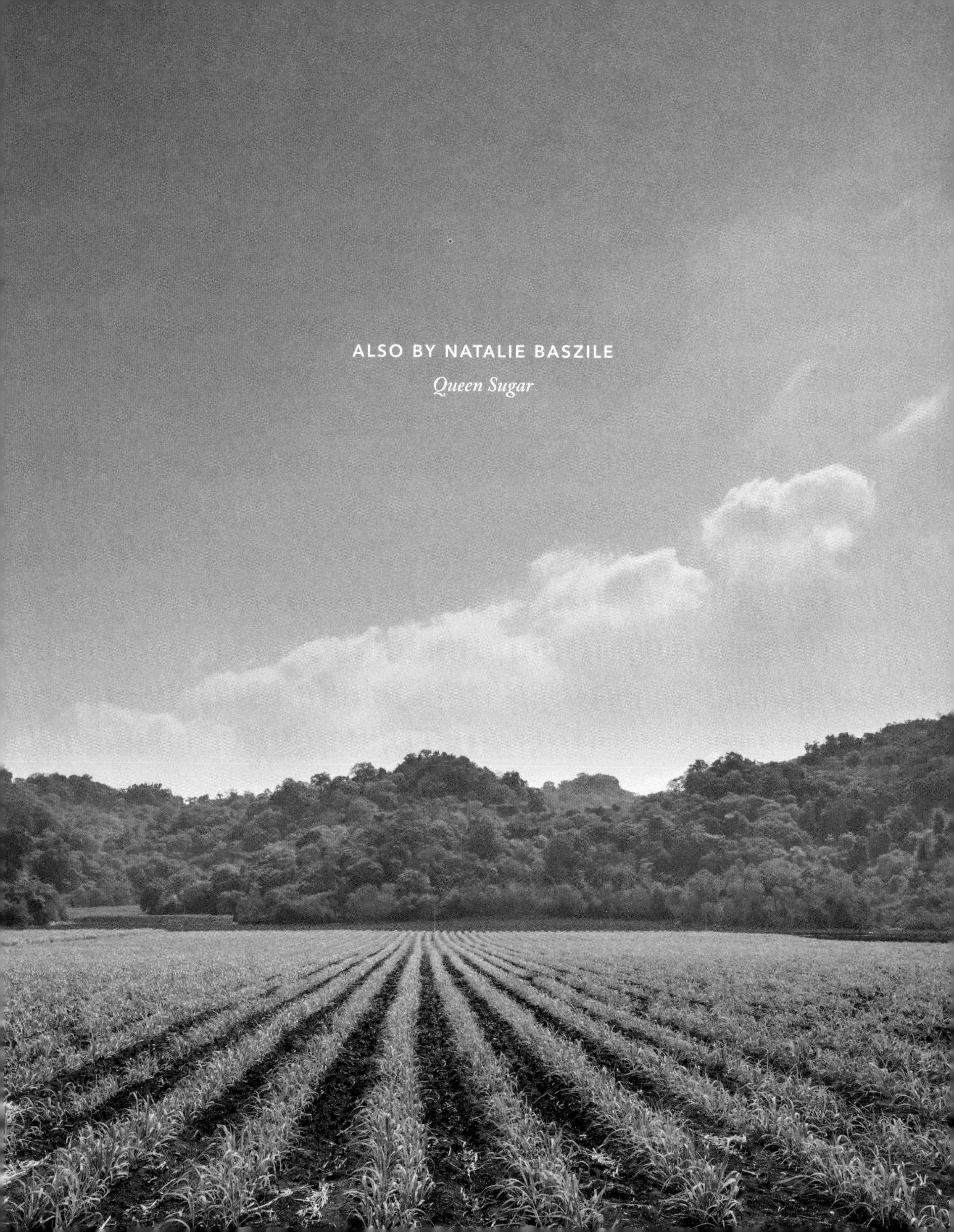

We are each other's harvest; we are each other's business; we are each other's magnitude and bond.

—GWENDOLYN BROOKS

African-American history is not somehow separate from our larger American story, it's not the underside of the American story, it is central to the American story. [O]ur glory derives not just from our most obvious triumphs, but how we've wrested triumph from tragedy, and how we've been able to remake ourselves, again and again and again, in accordance with our highest ideals. I, too, am America.

—PRESIDENT BARACK OBAMA AT THE
DEDICATION OF THE NATIONAL MUSEUM OF
AFRICAN AMERICAN HISTORY AND CULTURE, 2016

Contents

The earth does not belong to man, man belongs to the earth. All things are connected like the blood that unites us all. Man did not weave the web of life. His is but one strand of it. Whatever he does to the web, we do to ourselves. All things are bound together. All things connect.

—CHIEF SEATTLE

Foreword

BY NATALIE BASZILE

Drive east along Interstate 80 from San Francisco toward Sacramento, past vast acres of alfalfa, watermelon, and rice, and you'll eventually come upon a two-story mural of a solitary figure squinting out across the land. Dressed in a plaid shirt, jeans, and work boots, a tuft of gray hair peeking out beneath a baseball cap, the figure kneels in a patch of sunflowers. With one hand, the figure cradles a husky yellow Labrador. The other hand points out to the horizon.

The figure is a farmer.

He is a middle-aged man . . . and he's white.

The artist who painted the twenty-by-twenty-foot mural titled *Stewards of the Soil* says that she meant to pay tribute to the farmers in her community. I don't fault her for wanting to honor them—farming is difficult work—and I acknowledge that her mural reflects the picture most people have in mind when they envision the American farmer.

And yet, every time I drive past it, I can't help but think it tells only part of the story. Surely, somewhere across the thousands of acres there must be a handful of Black and brown farmers. Who are they? What stories might they tell if given a chance?

My passion for the stories of Black farmers and my interest in the related issues of land stewardship and food justice were first sparked one morning years ago when I was a student at the University of California, Berkeley. Once a month, usually on a Saturday, I bought groceries for my paternal great-uncle Lewis Baszile. He was one of the few members of my father's family to have migrated to California from Louisiana in the 1940s, and one of only two who'd settled in San Francisco. In his early seventies by the time I enrolled in Berkeley, Uncle Lewis looked forward to my monthly visits. He was usually standing in his doorway waiting for me when I pulled up in front of his house on Lyon Street.

That particular Saturday, I was running late. Rather than shop for Uncle Lewis's groceries at my local supermarket in Berkeley, I stopped at a supermarket a few blocks down Telegraph Avenue in Oakland. I was appalled by what I encountered. Worse than the dismal lighting and dingy tiled floor was the poor quality of the produce: a few limp bunches of collards and withering mustards, shrunken heads of cabbage, bushels of shriveled green beans, and apples and pears that were dented and bruised. The inequity between the two markets—this one in Oakland, and my neighborhood market in Berkeley—was glaring. I was infuriated and offended. How, I wondered, could the produce in the market near campus where all the white students shopped be so bountiful while the produce in the *same* supermarket chain just a few blocks away where the Black people shopped be so inferior?

Back then, no one I knew spoke of food justice and food sovereignty. The term "food apartheid" wasn't part of the lexicon. I had no outlet for my frustration, no place to express my outrage. But the memory of picking through those bins of substandard produce stuck with me.

Years later, I learned that my maternal great-great-grandfather, Mac Hall (b. 1845), arrived on one of the last slave ships and was sold twice before landing on the Stamps Plantation in Butler County, Alabama. After Emancipation he settled in the tiny rural settlement of Long Creek, near Georgiana. He was a merchant, blacksmith, beekeeper, and farmer, and eventually owned 680 acres of land thick with peach orchards. The family homeplace was only fifty miles from the Tuskegee Institute. Five of Mac Hall's grandsons, whom everyone referred to as the Hall Brothers, learned carpentry and brick masonry at Tuskegee. Years later, they carried those skills with them when they migrated to Detroit, Michigan, where they built two-story brick houses for themselves and their family members in Royal Oak Township. Like their grandfather, they cherished their connection to the soil and understood the value in owning and taking care of land.

Their cousin, my grandfather Mamon, and his wife, Willa Mae, continued the same tradition of property ownership. They bought eleven lots around Royal Oak Township. After Mamon was killed in a car accident, Willa Mae sold the lots when she needed extra money. In the end, she sold all but one, which she kept for her vegetable garden. To this day, my mother, an avid gardener, grows collard greens in a corner of her backyard. "Staying connected to the soil," she likes to say, "is in our DNA."

It's no surprise, then, that years after I graduated from Berkeley, news coverage of Black farmers converging on Washington, DC, to protest against the USDA's discriminatory practices reignited my passion for Black farmers' stories. I followed the proceedings of the famous class-action lawsuit *Pigford v. Glickman*. That passion and a growing curiosity about the lives of today's Black farmers led me to write *Queen Sugar*, which is set in the sugarcane belt of South Louisiana. In writing *Queen Sugar*, I wanted to tell the story of a Black farming family like the one from which I'd descended. The novel was my attempt to stop the clock, to remind readers that Black people have always had a deep connection to the land. I wanted to celebrate farming as a noble endeavor and encourage readers to continue to pass their families' land down through generations. *Queen Sugar* is a declaration that Black land matters. It reminds us that if we can remember our history, we can reclaim the legacy that our ancestors fought and sacrificed for.

Today, those same passions and curiosities have led me to help preserve and celebrate the voices of the Black and brown farmers and land stewards who remain. Every week, it seems, a new article hits the newsstands sounding the alarm about Black land loss and the dwindling numbers of Black farms and landowners. I believe it's not enough to name the problem: we must solve it.

Thankfully, hope is not lost. Black farmers continue to persevere, often in spite of the obstacles and discrimination they've faced. And a new generation of Black farmers and farmers of color has taken up the mantle, determined to carry us forward. They call themselves "the returning generation," and they are fierce and unapologetic in their quest to reclaim their legacy. Like their forefathers and foremothers, they understand the value of land stewardship. They are building community and appreciate the opportunity farming provides to pursue entrepreneurship and to assert a new level of independence and sovereignty.

This country was built on the free labor of enslaved people whom carried their agriculture expertise with them when they arrived on America's colonial shores. Black people's labor and knowledge of agriculture built this country. Farming is part of our national identity; it is central to America's origin story. *We Are Each Other's Harvest* is my attempt to elevate Black and brown farmers' voices and stories; to celebrate their resilience, ingenuity, and creativity; and to honor people like George Washington Carver, Fannie Lou Hamer, Booker T. Whatley, who started the community-supported agriculture (CSA) movement, and Booker T. Washington, who understood farming and agriculture as a path to liberation.

Plenty of Black and Indigenous people of color have devoted their lives to this movement, and they have far more experience and knowledge about farming than I do. Dozens of organizations, local and national, urban and rural, as well as activists and forward-thinking policy makers, continue to work tirelessly on behalf of Black farmers, veterans, and farmers of color.

I have tried to gather stories from a range of people—old and young, rural and urban, southerners, westerners, and northeasterners, landowners and stewards—who encourage us to remember our roots and reclaim our legacy. I could easily spend the next five years crisscrossing this country, meeting people and chronicling their experiences. Perhaps, one day, I'll do that.

For now, as we find ourselves reeling with the devastating effects of climate change, wealth disparity, and global pandemics, it's my hope that this work contributes to the ongoing conversation about farming, sustainability, food justice and food sovereignty, land stewardship, intergenerational wealth, and community. I hope it shines a light on the systems that continue to rob Black and brown people of their birthright; that it encourages people of color to reclaim our legacy and reinvigorates our commitment to self-determination; that it motivates people to devise solutions to the ongoing challenges farmers face; and that it resets the narrative around labor, inspiring communities of color to reimagine what it means to be connected to the soil.

"You see?" the farm said to them. "See? See what you can do? Never mind you can't tell one letter from another, never mind you born a slave, never mind you lose your name, never mind your daddy dead, never mind nothing. Here, this here, is what a man can do if he puts his mind to it and his back in it. Stop sniveling," it said. "Stop picking around the edges of the world. Take advantage, and if you can't take advantage, take disadvantage. We live here. On this planet, in this nation, in this country right here. Nowhere else! We got a home in the rock, don't you see! Nobody starving in my home; nobody crying in my home, and if I got a home you got one too! Grab it! Grab this land! Take it, hold it, my brothers, make it, my brothers, shake it, squeeze it, turn it, twist it, beat it, kick it, kiss it, whip it, stomp it, dig it, plow it, seed it, reap it, rent it, buy it, sell it, own it, build it, multiply it, and pass it on—can you hear me? Pass it on!"

—TONI MORRISON,
SONG OF SOLOMON

Introduction

BY DR. ANALENA HOPE HASSBERG

Virtually all Africans come from food-growing societies. As migrant peoples do, they brought their agricultural expertise with them across the Atlantic: heirloom seeds concealed in locks of hair through the treacherous Middle Passage, and a deep, ancestral knowledge of how to plant and cultivate yams and chiles, mustard greens and peanuts, melons, coconuts, and a host of medicinal roots and herbs. Although a centuries-long system of unprecedented brutality, bondage, and discrimination has threatened to extinguish African descendants and their foodways since 1619, they are a people of faith, resilience, poetry, and patience. Forcibly carried across oceans and seas, their spiritual connection to land endures.

For African-descended people, particularly those who trace their ancestry back through legacies of enslavement, resistance has been constant. Their subversive acts have been as grand and visible as organized rebellions and social movements, and as humble as keeping small garden plots on cash-crop plantations. Popular reductions of Black foodways to mere scraps from a master's table miss the fact that many enslaved Africans also grew an array of vegetables, legumes, and fruit to supplement their insufficient diets, and as a result, they often had higher vitamin, mineral, and protein levels than poor whites who also struggled to survive in the face of starvation. Food and farming have long been a form of resistance and ritual: a gift from people

who believed in a hereafter that would someday know freedom from the horrors of
slavery, though they themselves would never live to see it.

The end of the Civil War brought formal emancipation of the enslaved, and
many believed that freedom had finally come. They shouted, sobbed, and dropped to
tired knees in prayer, gathered what little they had acquired, and walked off of plantations en masse. They would quickly learn, however, that their freedom was sym-
bolic and nominal at best. Multiple laws were immediately passed to restrict Black
mobility and landownership. Lynchings, beatings, and other forms of anti-Black
violence escalated alongside mass incarceration as part of a wide-scale campaign to
maintain the racial and economic order. Free by definition only, emancipated people
were forced back into vulnerable land-tenure arrangements like sharecropping and
tenant farming, which would ensure that they remained in perpetual debt to plantation owners, banks, and other outside lenders through systems of credit, mortgages,
and liens on crops and property. Many returned to the same plantations they had left
only days before, with no choice but to once again perform backbreaking labor on
land that was not their own.

There has been an unshakable conviction among Black people that true liberation requires landownership: a sentiment echoed by the Black ministers who advised
General William T. Sherman to provide forty acres and a mule to freedmen along
the South Carolina and Georgia sea coast after the Civil War. It reverberates through
the teachings of Black nationalists like Malcolm X, who proclaimed land as the basis
of independence, revolution, justice, and equality. The millions of formerly enslaved
Africans knew they could sustain and reproduce themselves if given the chance and
a parcel of earth. After all, it was their farming and agriculture skills that had built
the massive wealth and global power of the United States. A testament to their skill
and resilience, the number of Black family farms rose steadily until the early twentieth century, when the mass exodus of Black people from the rural South to the urban
cities began.

Over six million Black Americans left the southern United States between 1916
and 1970 in search of jobs and better livelihood.[1] Waves of people, at once migrants
and refugees, traveled north and west seeking wartime work in the naval shipyards of
coastal cities, as well as deliverance from white supremacist violence. These regions
appeared to be a land of milk and honey for those fleeing the terror of lynching and

starvation in the South, but a different kind of racism pervaded these places: it pulsed through overcrowded tenements and police batons; it was embedded in low wages and coded as red lines on real estate maps. Black people in cities like New York and Chicago found themselves severed from the soil and estranged from generations of traditional foodways and growing practices. Industrialization also brought the rise of processed foods, which had a lasting impact on food purchasing and preparation in Black urban communities. For people with such a rich agricultural history both in the United States and throughout the African Diaspora, the urban environment was drastically different. Within just a few short decades, city dwellers were disconnected from the land and subjected to new perils—like substandard housing and food-related illness—that would impact Black health outcomes, life chances, and livelihood for years to come.

Those who remained to farm in the rural South struggled to stay viable as the number of large and corporately owned farms grew and as agricultural technology and crop production became more advanced and expensive. Small farmers seeking to maintain or expand their operations often turned to the US Department of Agriculture (USDA), whose loan agencies were designed to provide economic support for farmers impacted by low crop yield, natural disasters, or other such setbacks. However, Black farmers seeking USDA support would find that working with unsympathetic loan officers in southern counties and local parishes was futile at best, a nightmare at worst. Over the course of several decades, tens of thousands of Black farmers sent hundreds of complaints per week to the USDA's Civil Rights Office until it was officially closed in 1983. In 1984 and 1985, the USDA lent $1.3 billion to farmers to buy land. Of the roughly sixteen thousand farmers who received loans, 209 of them were Black.[2]

Black farms had declined by as much as 98 percent by the end of the twentieth century, and it is estimated that Black farmers cultivate less than half of 1 percent of the country's farmland today.[3] Still, being no strangers to struggle or hard work in the face of discrimination, Black farmers survived, and some even thrived without the institutional assistance that their white counterparts received. They made ways out of no way by growing what little food they could on land generally reserved for cash crops. They foraged and fished, and they preserved perishables through the winter by canning and pickling. Black farming (and Black life more broadly) is based on an economy of sharing and collectivity. Black farmers developed cooperatives to share food, economic resources, and farming equipment. They created democratically owned credit unions to build financial independence, and farmers' unions to organize and protect farmers' rights. Many came to own huge swaths of their own farmland, which has remained a source of equity and esteem in their family lineage.

Farming has been a revolutionary act—both as a means of sustenance in the face of dehumanization and constant erasure, and also as a full-circle return. In recent years, the latent seeds of Black agriculture have begun to sprout again as Black and other oppressed people are returning to agrarian identities that have been suffused with stigma and trauma, and reimbuing them with honor and pride. In cities, they are reclaiming urban space and developing new relationships to food and farming. They are rediscovering land where there seemingly was none: in the parkway dirt between the sidewalk and the street, in pots on porches, and in the tracts of empty, blighted lots. There are also the stirrings of a reverse migration from the city back to the countryside, where a new generation of Black farmers are reclaiming traditions and relearning lost skills to survive the end of the (modern) world.

This volume is a reminder that, just as the abundance of the earth is still here (even in dying cities choked by concrete), so too are Black farmers. The rich narratives, interviews, photographs, and poems throughout these pages offer a sweeping and expansive view of Blackness and resilience through the lens of the land. Like Natalie Baszile's novel *Queen Sugar*, this project traces a regional and ideological return to agricultural ideas that have been resurrected and supplemented with innovation and creativity. It demonstrates the versatility of Black agriculturalists who, in addition to growing fruits and vegetables, are cultivating fiber, raising animals, blacksmithing, woodworking, and protecting the future of the food supply through apiaries and beekeeping. More than just a celebration of the tenacity of Black farmers (which would in itself be enough), this book also complicates the importance of ownership to a people who were themselves owned, and explores their struggle to live in right relationship with land stolen from Indigenous people who believed in nonownership. It captures the ways that farming still lives in the bones and bodies of Black people and how the recent resurgence of the soil can be both balm and suture for new generations seeking to repair ancestral connections, heal generational trauma, and develop livable futures.

The voices amplified in this book are those who are prioritizing landownership to build intergenerational wealth and sovereignty, who are seeking redress and reparation at long last for descendants of the enslaved. They are the ones whose dreams of freedom have been denied, delayed, and derailed by structurally racist policies. They are spearheading efforts to combat food apartheid, poverty, and poor health and are staking claim in a country that their own labor, blood, and sweat have historically created. The stories gathered here are about enslavement and migration, dispossession and displacement, and the ways that, in spite of old obstacles and new forms of oppression, Black has always been green and sustainable by necessity. The reader is invited to reimagine the image of "farmer" with women and people of color in mind, and the notion of "home" as the places and ways of being that our spirits remember even if our bodies have never visited. This project takes stock of what has been lost and damaged while also asking, Who is still here?

In these increasingly uncertain times, marked by pestilence and mass confusion, fears of an unstable future lead some to isolate themselves and withdraw, to stockpile and hoard enough for whole neighborhoods while hiding in their homes. But these times call for the exact opposite response. Farming is the past, and it is also the future: the key to sustenance and reproduction in the city and the countryside. Cooperation is at the center of community building, and growing food together creates an alternative system that will sustain us when grocery shelves are bare. We can find respite in the soil, and abundance in times of scarcity. Just as we do not plant seeds for immediate harvest, we may not see the fruits of our labor in this lifetime, but like the ancestors, our job is to sow the seeds and prepare a place for the ones who will inherit the world. It is time for a collective reimagining that pairs ancestral knowledge with twenty-first century skills and that places Black and other oppressed people at the helm of new ways forward.

1.

*T*hose Winter Sundays

BY ROBERT HAYDEN

Sundays too my father got up early
and put his clothes on in the blueblack cold,
then with cracked hands that ached
from labor in the weekday weather made
banked fires blaze. No one ever thanked him.

I'd wake and hear the cold splintering, breaking.
When the rooms were warm, he'd call,
and slowly I would rise and dress,
fearing the chronic angers of that house,

Speaking indifferently to him,
who had driven out the cold
and polished my good shoes as well.
What did I know, what did I know
of love's austere and lonely offices?

2.

*E*veryone Beneath Their Own Vine and Fig Tree: A Remembering in Seven Parts

BY MICHAEL TWITTY

GENESIS

This is a remembering.

On the land, we wrote in seed a coded language centered in the archive of hidden knowledge planted in the soul of each and every African who managed to arrive alive on these shores. On earth, in water, and in sky, we passed from one generational era to the next an incredible lore, ancient yet new. We knew which trees were elevators of spirit, which soil enriched our blood, what water stood between us and the dead, and which constellations had the power to emancipate. The music of the Universe and the dance steps it dictates were birthrights, not mysteries. We were forced . . . coerced into not only raising a nation from its infancy, but walking the Atlantic world into modernity, leaving behind what blood we hoped we would not miss.

EXODUS

This is a remembering.

One day there will be no one who remembers or who lived the life of those who left bondage and went into freedom with a dream and a plow. There will be a permanent amnesia.

Before freedom came, some of us ran away to survive. We dreamed of a boat ride back to Guinea, a red carpet to respond to the red flag that brought us. Some made it. Some went north to Canada and put tobacco in the ground, just out of reach of a killing frost. Some went south and east to the islands and cast a net, others went southwest and herded cattle with hides as varied as blossoms and fingerprints. Many, without choice, stayed through the worst years of "the slavery."

The nightmare ended in a hail of blood. The day of Jubilee arrived in five acts: 1862 to 1863 to 1864 to the Surrender to Juneteenth; the day of liberation did come, winding its way from autumn to summer. Chains rusted and broke.

The people I celebrate who occupied the land between slavery and civil rights splashed on Florida water cologne and crushed dark bricks for blush because no makeup existed for them. They chose their children's names by Bible prophecy or by season or day of the week. Planting and harvest were the birth rhythms. They resisted white supremacy by making irresistible music genres and food and words and dances. Their doors were painted "haint blue" to keep the evil off.

Their grandparents were the Antebellums. They had hog bladders for firecrackers. Names were based on whispers from Africa. Jesus wasn't official, and spirits in the trees weren't obsolete. Cotton, tobacco, rice, and sugar defined life but not for their own sake. They fought and prayed in ways too subtle for us to appreciate. They paid an enormous price for our freedom.

Their great-grandparents were the African exiles. They were America before America. They brought the light of the supposed "Dark Continent." They seeded a civilization with other untouchables. They left treasure maps in words, ingredients, DNA, names, and talk of pots silencing laughs.

Their great-grandparents were the last generation to be untouched. They only knew gods that looked like their reflection in the streams. They dreamed their children into the cosmos. They understood the language of the dwarves in the rainforest. They did not fear death. They were free.

No book or page will do the trick. All the voices will be gone. We will lose more than we know. We will lose the knowledge of who was where, what seeds they planted, what animals they raised, how they made a life from no life, how they made a set of rules meant to kill them into seeds of change, how they made bricks, how they made mortar, how they made churches and praise houses and big houses and outhouses and grape arbors, peach orchards, wells and dipper gourds, tobacco barns and headstones and porches and swings and life from no life.

Like the generations before them who knew different fates, a book will be closed on a certain people. They were an agrarian people who marched out of slavery and into semi-freedom. These were the children of Jim Crow's time, a people who built their lives out of the red clay dust and muck of loam and gritty sand. They are dwindling, and we, those who remember the shadows of their ways, are dwindling. We scramble to remember faces in early photographs; we go to courthouses to see which graves are under which mall or gated development or gas station. We work because we know the night is coming and someone needs to have a light. This is a remembering. Now is the time to remember.

We have already begun to forget. The plows are gone. The millions of acres have shrunk. We wax nostalgic about "they." "They used to." "They," never "we."

SOIL

Take your finger, place it on the Mason-Dixon line, and start to trace your way back. Let your digits get wet in the brackish tides of Chesapeake Bay, go to the appendages of land sticking out into the water, the place where it all began, all of this inherited strife. Go against the Piedmont spine, feel the tops of the pines and oaks, dip down to the clay, and soil your fingers with the iron within. Move down the coastal line, and mash yourself into the sand. Dance over to the loam, the Black Belt, the long rich belt where once an ancient sea stood and Yemonja swayed while her lullabies became fish. Push toward the Mississippi out against more mountains down to the bayous and melting coastline. This borrowed place, now partly made of your ancestors, is your old country.

Some of us were sharecroppers, others tenants, but many were landowners. Everyone saw themselves as living a verse of Bible, beneath their vine or fig tree. Here we waited for the good times, prayed against the inevitable bad. On mattresses of corn husks or Spanish moss we planted the next generation. In the bottoms we planted sweet potatoes and melons; but where the land would not yield, we planted the bodies that became the ancestors.

ROOTS

Before Georgia, there was Guinea. There were dawns that went back to the very beginning of time. Just before our leaving, the dawns were the same as they were after we left. Two hours before light, came the first crowing. Then came the barking of dogs and prayers carried up in circles and the sparking of fires and the sound of the mortar and pestle giving the day its heartbeat.

When we danced, we moved according to the tasks of the field and farm. We began to live with the seasons and master the patterns of mounding earth, carving the land into plots, shifting earth for rice paddies, singing songs to the dry-time, making sun by stringed instrument, letting our songs drip in alternating patterns until our souls were soaked when the rains came.

We knew every tree, mushroom, fruit, and their uses. We had middens and used ashes, chicken and goat manure to keep the ancient soil fertile from year to year. Over millennia we practiced to near perfection the art of living on and with the land. We the Fulani ranged our cattle; we the Kongo climbed the raffia palm; we the Asante and Igbo brought yams out of the earth; we the Mende and Temne threshed rice; and we the Bozo set our nets out on the Niger. We fed ourselves and made a life to dance by.

THE GROANING TABLE

From the gardens and our fields came our groaning tables. Springtime brought mustard and turnip greens and rabbits and young chickens to be fried, shad in some rivers and herring in others. There were dandelion greens, lamb's-quarters, and poke salad, and they would clean you out from the top of your head to the bottom of your feet. Crawfish came out of hiding, and our plates were filled. Late spring brought new potatoes and green onions. Summertime was what everyone waited for. Supper on the grounds in the summer meant lemonade and iced tea, sometimes with mint, punches and shrubs made from crushed berries, tomatoes and bell and hot peppers, cantaloupes and watermelons, fresh field peas and more potatoes. We had potato salad, fried chicken, deviled eggs, coleslaw, skillet-cooked squash, and rice a thousand ways. Blue crab time became barbecue time, and with it green corn time, until the harvest of the crops and corn and sweet potatoes brought their own glories. Winter moved us from hog killing time to the oyster months and possum and yams, turkeys, venison. Dried field peas, cabbages and turnips and sweet potatoes in banks, jars of put-up spring and summer produce—this is what got us through the winter.

Remember the orchard? Clingstone peaches, Chickasaw plums, Stayman Winesaps, and Seckel pears planted when we first knew freedom: life-giving, sustaining fruit. Those vines in the grape arbor were muscadines and scuppernongs and fox grapes that your great-great-grandmother put the good store-bought sugar loaf to so she could make the communion wine. Nobody ate the fruit off the tree without threats of sickness. Once the summer treats of cobblers and the fall treats of pies were made, crocks and jars formed a rainbow in the pantry. A few cloves here, broken cinnamon sticks there, allspice, nutmeg, bits and pieces of worlds they would never see.

FORCES OF NATURE

My great-grandfather planted forked sticks in the soil—said a prayer, thrust it in the ground at a crossroads, didn't look back. In his time, when you found an "Indian" arrowhead, you said it came from thunder in the sky, and put it around your neck to keep from being lynched. These were the men who threw seed in paths to guarantee a healthy newborn. These were the women who chose names by divination from the Scriptures. These were the ancestors, with pockets filled with cottontail feet, John the Conqueror root, and the good witch hands of sassafras. Their necks were strung with asafetida bags to keep off sickness. They pierced dimes to hide them from the evil eye. They smelled of crushed basil planted by the front door to keep the devil and the men without skins away.

The injustice was ugly, but the fields were gorgeous. Nobody hated green. Ever seen a field of pretty tobacco? Sap-swollen leaves masquerading faintly of mint on a hot Maryland or Virginia or Carolina afternoon? When cotton was in blossom, the flowers would be born and die in the same day, changing colors like costumes until the bud was left that would become in time a boll and everything from Carolina to Tennessee to Texas knew snow in boiling heat. Rice fields had a shimmering green and later a golden husk that battled birds for survival, and cane grew as tall as the tallest man could not grow down in Louisiana, Georgia, and Florida, promising syrup and liquor after the rest of the crop was sold.

OUR OWN KIND OF FREEDOM

From our homesteads in Oklahoma and Kansas to our cabins in West Virginia and Pennsylvania, we knew how to take care of each other. That was the number one dictate of the land: love the others on it just as you love the land and those who gave it to you in trust. Our values were there—to work and celebrate cooperatively, to have humor when it felt like there was none, to decorate our lives with the love we never received outside. In our spaces we were Father not boy, Mother not gal, Elder not uncle or aunt. We took the labels off of racist products. We made a world in our image. From our image we knew our Creator.

3.

Handed the Rain

BY ED ROBERSON

given to
look into   the bowl
of sky

for it to fill
with future
see it turned

upside down on the grass
see the ladle pass

hear the god underneath
calling his inside
the heavenly vault   eternal

how that bump
reminds me   how we saw it
once

from the underside of
Nut   a mother's belly

see dissolve
against her vast ground
the drowned cloud of black

lives   the solution's population
of rain crowding the city
in the belly

see it now as the sea extended
the drowned city   lit   in this sky

see our sky
the bone clouds casting
African

tomorrows   only
an arm   black balletic cloud
extends itself

dark nimbic
invertebrate squall

I am handed rain
by a portuguese man-o-war
These are

new skies
once we absorb the seas'
solution as the bodies lost

the sting
fire of lightning   flesh

the water
body
air

we drown together
in our living
to drink

from this
bone

4.

Writing Queen Sugar

BY NATALIE BASZILE

Often, in offering advice to young writers, more seasoned authors will say, "Write what you know"—which means, write about and from your experience. I was born in a Los Angeles suburb and have spent my entire life in California. So, when people learn that I wrote *Queen Sugar*—a novel about a young African American woman who inherits eight hundred acres of sugarcane land in South Louisiana—they're curious to know how that advice applies. How could I possibly have written about a world so different from my own?

The answer is that my father, the late Barry Baszile, was born and raised in South Louisiana. He is my connection to my southern heritage. And so, to understand what lies at the heart of *Queen Sugar*, you have to know something about my dad.

He was born in 1937, during the height of Jim Crow segregation, and lived with his family in Elton, a tiny town in the southwest corner of the state near the Texas border. But unlike the rest of his family, who somehow managed to make peace with the place, my dad hated Louisiana and couldn't wait to escape.

He frequently told my sister and me a story illustrating how motivated he was to leave. As a teenager in Elton, my dad worked at the town's only gas station after school and in the summer. Occasionally, when it was hot, he went to work without shoes. On his breaks, he went inside the garage, where it was cool. He'd prop his bare feet on a spare tire or a toolbox. Once, when he fell asleep, the white boys who worked in the gas station with him slathered his feet with liquid rubber and set it on fire, then fell over themselves laughing as he stomped out the flames. They called the game "Hot Foot."

It's no surprise, then, that for my dad there was nothing romantic or compelling about the South. California was the land of opportunity, the place where he could realize his dreams free of the limitations the South imposed. And so, the night of his high school graduation, he packed his single suitcase and caught a ride to California with a woman from Elton who needed someone to help pay for gas and share the driving. He was part of the last wave of the Great Migration. He settled in Los Angeles and never looked back. He never lived in Louisiana again.

While many African American parents send their kids "back home" to the South each summer, my parents never did. As a result, my sister and I grew up in Southern California not really knowing our southern family. For the most part, Louisiana was a mystery, a place we knew only from my grandmother Miss Rose, her occasional letters and phone calls, and the boxes of Louisiana delicacies—dried gulf shrimp, homemade pralines—that arrived on our doorstep once a year around the holidays.

And yet, as much as my father despised the South and most of what it stood for, he maintained a strong connection to his family. Once a year, usually in April or May before the humidity became unbearable, he traveled back to his hometown to take Miss Rose on a road trip. His rule was that he would take her wherever they could drive to and from in four days, believing that after four day's time the ghosts of his past would start to haunt him. He flew into Lake Charles and drove the few miles

to Elton. Miss Rose was usually waiting on the porch, her pink suitcase packed and ready by the time he pulled up. "Mother, where would you like to go?" he'd ask. Sometimes they drove to Grand Isle. Other times they drove to New Orleans. If Miss Rose felt ambitious, they drove to Little Rock, Arkansas.

I was a college sophomore when I first accompanied my father and Miss Rose on one of their road trips. By then, I'd declared English as my major and had taken my first African American literature class, Barbara Christian's "Black Women Writers." Professor Christian, tall, slender, and brown-skinned, with a dozen gold bangles stacked along each forearm, had introduced me to the Grand Dames of African American literature: Zora Neale Hurston and Toni Cade Bambara; Gloria Naylor, Alice Walker, Nella Larsen, Gayle Jones, and Toni Morrison. There was something majestic about their novels, something elegant about their characters' lives, even if their circumstances were humble. Those authors captured what I knew was true and dignified about the Black experience, and I'd started to imagine what it might be like not just to *read* those books, but to *write* books of my own, to be part of the conversation and find my place in African American literary tradition.

Now, as my father drove and Miss Rose sat in the passenger seat nursing her bottle of Coca-Cola, I sat in the back listening as they recounted stories of my father's childhood or gossiped about what was happening in town. Through their stories, Louisiana—the place that was so different from everything I'd known—came to life. As a budding storyteller, I found the pull of the people and the place impossible to resist.

July 15, 1999, marked my birth as a writer. That was the day I resigned from my father's business—a company that sold aluminum sheet, plate, rod, and bar to the aerospace and aircraft industry—and began my life of words. Years earlier, when I was twelve or thirteen, I'd promised my dad that when I graduated from college, I would work for him. He had a saying: "My word is my bond." It was a sentiment he lived by, and he had passed that sense of personal accountability on to me. So even though I dreamed of writing, I kept my word. For eleven years after graduating from college, I tried to love aluminum. For eleven years I forced myself to care about B-1 bombers, space shuttles, and Joint Strike Fighters built by the defense contractors who were our customers. But by 1999, I couldn't take any more. I was miserable. My dad was starting to talk of retiring and passing the business along to me. I knew that if I didn't quit and take a chance on pursuing my dream, I never would. If I stayed, one day—maybe not the next day or the next year, but eventually—I'd wake up and not care about the business my dad had spent most of his adult life building. I couldn't disrespect his legacy. The best thing was for me to leave.

Toni Morrison says, "If there is a book you want to read, but it hasn't been written yet, you must write it." And so, on June 15, 1999, inspired by the novels I'd read in Professor Christian's class and with a story idea in mind, I resigned. Bumping over the railroad tracks that crisscrossed the industrial section of town where my dad's business was located, I was both thrilled and terrified. On one hand, I'd finally broken away! On the other, I'd cut the safety net and was immediately flooded with the anxiety of knowing I couldn't turn back. The only thing I could do was get to work.

Every day for the next four years I wrote the story that would eventually become *Queen Sugar.* Those early drafts told the story of Charley, a young African American woman who leaves her relatively privileged life in Los Angeles and, with her young daughter, Micah, in tow, relocates to the tiny town of Saint Josephine—a fictitious version of Miss Rose's town.

In 2003, my husband and I moved from Los Angeles to San Francisco. Every morning I walked our young daughters to the corner bus stop, then went straight to my writing desk. Soon word spread among the school families that I was writing a story set in Louisiana.

As it happened, there was another Louisianan at our school. Her name was Stephanie Shea. Our daughters were in the same kindergarten class. Stephanie's personal story was similar to my father's, only a generation later: she was the only member of *her* family to leave Louisiana and migrate to California. We became fast friends, bonding over our Louisiana roots.

In San Francisco I'd joined a writing group and shared chapters of my story, but early readers didn't understand Charley's motives. "Why," they asked, "would someone leave a life of ease in a bustling metropolis like Los Angeles to live in a tiny southern town?" For months I couldn't answer their question.

In 2005, Stephanie invited me and some other parents from school to celebrate her fortieth birthday in her South Louisiana hometown. By then, I had decided that my character, Charley, would inherit some land—possibly a farm—and was returning to the South to manage it. It was a creative decision that tapped into my old passion for the stories of Black farmers and my long-held belief in Black landownership. The problem was I didn't know what type of farmland Charley would inherit.

Days before Stephanie's party was scheduled to begin, I flew down to Louisiana determined to find a crop for Charley. I visited half the rice fields and crawfish ponds in the small towns near Elton, but no location struck me as interesting or visually poetic. Discouraged, I headed off to Stephanie's town, where people had started gathering for the festivities.

"How's the book coming along?" Stephanie asked as we sat on her front porch.

"Not good," I said. "I can't find a crop for my character."

Stephanie thought for a moment. Then, casually, she said, "My mother owns some sugarcane land. Let's go for a drive."

What I didn't know was that Stephanie's town, New Iberia, was located in the heart of South Louisiana's sugarcane country. I'd never heard of New Iberia before I stepped onto her porch. I had no idea sugarcane *grew* in South Louisiana. We climbed into Stephanie's car and drove down Highway 182 toward St. Martinville. She pulled off the road into the middle of her mother's sugarcane field.

My favorite novels are set in locations with a strong sense of place. I rejoice when a writer paints a picture with words that capture the beauty and magnificence of the

landscape. I wanted the landscape of my novel to evoke a sense of awe and wonder—the same sensation I felt when I read my favorite books. The moment I stepped out of Stephanie's car, I knew I'd found my crop. It was the middle of July. The sky was a glorious turquoise blue. The sugarcane was ten feet high, and the cane leaves rustled in the light afternoon breeze. I didn't know how sugarcane grew or how it was harvested, but I knew sugarcane's history stretched all the way back to the Caribbean, where people had fought for it and died over it. I knew that sugar was one of the three crops—along with cotton and tobacco—that built the American South and, by extension, built this country. Standing in the middle of that sugarcane field, I felt my novel take on greater significance. I wasn't just writing about one woman's struggle; I was writing an American story. I turned to Stephanie. "This is it," I said. "Charley is going to inherit sugarcane land."

"When the student is ready," the saying goes, "the teacher will appear." My teacher was René Simon. He was a classmate of Stephanie's from Louisiana State University and, to my delight, was an actual sugarcane farmer. By the day of Stephanie's party, word had spread among the guests that I was writing "a sugarcane book." René approached me on the edge of the dance floor and offered to answer any questions I might have as I began my research. "Give me a call anytime," he said and handed me his card.

When I got back to San Francisco, I called him: "If my character inherits land," I asked during our first phone conversation, "how much would be enough to present a challenge, but not too much that it would be unrealistic?"

René thought for a moment. "She'd probably have about eight hundred acres."

I hung up and folded that information into the story. A few days later I called back: "If my character doesn't have a lot of money, what kind of equipment could she afford?"

"She'd probably have an old tractor and a couple busted-up cane wagons."

Soon, I was calling René once a day. Then I was calling two or three *times* each day. René's knowledge and expertise were invaluable. The information he shared about sugarcane farming found its way into the novel, expanding and deepening the story. Finally, one Friday in late October, after my twenty-fifth or thirtieth call, René said, "You need to come back down to Louisiana to see this world for yourself." I booked a ticket and flew back to New Iberia in early November. It was "grinding," the term sugarcane farmers use to describe the sugarcane harvest season. For three days, René and I drove the back roads of sugarcane country, dodging tractors pulling wagon loads of sugarcane to the mills. The air smelled of burnt sugar. As we drove, René explained how sugarcane grew and how it was harvested. We talked  about his life as a farmer and my life as a writer. We shared stories about our families, the challenges of raising children, our hopes for the future. From the looks we received when we stopped for lunch at the local watering holes, I'm sure some people wondered what a white sugarcane farmer and a Black woman from San Francisco could possibly have to talk about. There were times when I wondered, too. I thought about my dad—the stories he'd shared about his southern boyhood and how hard he'd worked to escape the South. "Be careful," he'd warned when I told him that I was writing a book set in Louisiana. And yes, there were moments when I was reminded, sometimes bitterly, that I was far from home and understood, to my core, exactly why my father had escaped. But my curiosity about South Louisiana, the people and the culture, was mostly positive and ultimately overshadowed any concern for my personal safety.

Over the next four years, from 2005 until 2009, I returned to South Louisiana as often as I could. René became one of my dearest friends. Together, we wandered the floors of some of the largest sugarcane mills in the state. He arranged for me to ride on tractors and combines, and when I called once to ask how sugarcane grew, he arranged for me to plant sugarcane early one humid August morning alongside migrant workers.

New Iberia and the string of small towns along Highway 182—St. Martinville, Breaux Bridge, Jeanerette—became my second home. I loved South Louisiana and devoted myself to telling the story of her culture and her people—not a story of moonlight and magnolias, but instead a story that portrayed Louisiana in all of her complexity—one that celebrated her beauty but didn't turn away from her ugliness.

By 2009, ten years after I walked away from my family business, the manuscript was finished. I had written and revised the novel more than a dozen times. It was the moment to look for an agent and a publisher. But writing a novel and getting it published are two different things, and finding a home for the book proved to be harder than I anticipated. Literary agents who  read the manuscript loved the characters and the sense of place. They loved the family drama and the world of sugarcane. They loved the details about farming and Charley's struggle to find her place. They just didn't love it enough to represent me. The summer of 2009 proved to be one of the most challenging periods of my life. The rejection letters from agents flooded my in-box. Some of the agents to whom I'd been introduced by writer friends in San Francisco didn't even bother to acknowledge receiving the manuscript, let alone read it.

A freelance editor who'd previously worked at one of the big publishing houses read the novel. We met at a café in San Francisco where I looked forward to her feedback. "Well, at least you have this," she said, pushing the manuscript across the table. "Now you can throw these pages out and start over." That was the day I sat on my front steps and wept. I'd invested ten years of my life trying to tell a nuanced story about Black people—a story that honored and celebrated what I knew to be the richness and vitality of the Black experience. But no one seemed to understand my vision. No one seemed to understand what I was trying to say.

"I don't think this novel is going to happen," I said to René over the phone.

That same summer I'd been awarded a residency at the Ragdale Foundation, an artists' colony north of Chicago. I packed my bags and got on the plane with the latest version of the novel—the same version the editor told me to scrap—tucked in the bottom of my suitcase. I was so discouraged I couldn't bear to look at what I'd written; it was too painful. I had given the book everything I had, and I'd failed.

Every now and then, the universe intervenes and sends you a message. In the cab on the way to Ragdale, still exhausted and discouraged, I was slumped over in the back seat when I noticed a magazine wedged between the cushions. Flipping through the magazine, I came across a small article profiling a young woman. She was a musician, and in the article she talked about how hard she was willing to fight for her art. She didn't care what obstacles she faced, or how many rejections she received; she was determined to keep going. Nothing could stand between her and her artistic vision.

I read the article and thought, "Well . . . *shit* . . . If she can fight for her art, so can I."

At Ragdale, five days passed before I was able to wade back into the story. Eventually the world I'd created on those pages came alive again. I reconnected with the characters and heard the rhythm of the prose. I rewrote the novel again. Then again. Then again.

In 2011, almost two years after those first rejections, I sent the manuscript back to the agents. This time, I also included a new agent who'd been recommended by a friend. That agent read the novel in twenty-four hours and called me. "I love it," she said, and she offered to represent me.

Two months later, we had a contract with a publisher. The novel was published in 2014.

As painful as parts of my publishing journey were, I learned invaluable lessons about determination and perseverance. Time and again I found myself drawing on reserves I didn't think I had. There were moments of tremendous joy accompanied by moments of crushing doubt. But my struggle was no different than that of people who labor every day to move their lives forward: waitresses, professors, artists, farmers—*especially* farmers, who, perhaps more than anyone, have a vision of what can be; who, with enough hard work and sacrifice, produce something where there was nothing but the kernel of an idea, a seed of hope. In all the years it took me to write *Queen Sugar*, I drew inspiration from Black farmers whose lives I worked hard to imagine and whose stories of struggle, perseverance, and resilience I was determined to honor.

I can only speak for myself. But what I write and how I write is done in order to save my own life. And I mean that literally. For me, literature is a way of knowing that I am not hallucinating, that whatever I feel/know is.

—BARBARA CHRISTIAN (1943–2000), AUTHOR AND PROFESSOR OF AFRICAN AMERICAN STUDIES, UNIVERSITY OF CALIFORNIA, BERKELEY

5.

Excerpt from *Black and White: The Way I See It*

BY RICHARD WILLIAMS

Lightning almost stopped nineteen-year-old Julia Metcalf that stormy day in 1942, as she raced the old mule cart down the muddy dirt road. Jagged forked streaks tore across the big dark Louisiana sky and the thunder that followed pounded into her like a hammer. The labor pains were coming increasingly fast, spreading from deep within her swollen belly. She was thoroughly soaked, her clothes plastered to her body. She drove the mule harder. She had to get to Charity hospital, miles away. It was the only hospital close enough that would treat Negroes.

She flicked the reins harder. "Gettie up, Midnight."

She had first heard the distant thunder that meant a storm was coming earlier this cold and dark February day.

She grabbed the cardboard box she used to collect her wash from the clothesline and lit out back before it hit. Without warning, the first labor pains crashed through her body. She grabbed the clothesline for balance and struggled to stay on her feet. A second wave of pain hit but she continued to take her wash in, folding each piece carefully before placing it in the cardboard box.

A sharp pain hit her in the stomach. She dropped the box and fell to her knees with a shriek. Contraction subsiding, she picked up the laundry and made it into the old house. Puddles of rainwater had already formed on the floor. She was accustomed to leaks in the tin roof. She always put pots and tins beneath them to catch the water. Later, she would use it to wash clothes, or heat it on the stove for cooking or bathing. Rainwater was welcome in the house because it meant she wouldn't have to carry heavy buckets in from the well.

Julia's life had never been easy. Her father, Harold Metcalf, had been born to sharecroppers in 1895 in Nachitoches, Louisiana, just south of Shreveport. When he was twenty-one, he married Julia's mother, the former Julia Thompson, who had moved to Shreveport with her parents in 1924. They had four sons and four daughters, including Julia, who was named after her mother. The Metcalfs worked hard to make sure their children knew the word of prayer. Faithful believers, they put their trust in God and relied on him to fill their needs. Harold read the Bible aloud every night, and even as a baby, Julia liked best to climb up on her father's lap and read along with him. She was his favorite, maybe because she saw things differently

than the other kids. When white people set Harold's barn on fire and it burnt to the ground, everyone screamed and cried. Not Julia. She shrugged.

"Why y'all crying? Ain't nuthin' we can do about that barn."

Maybe, Julia thought as she ducked a tree branch swept by the wind, *that's why I was so calm when the first pains hit*. She had gasped as a stream of water burst from between her legs but just sat down in the rocking chair and rocked. She wasn't ready for the baby. She had no clothes, no diapers, nothing. Well, she thought, *she* wasn't ready, but the baby sure was, so she went to hitch up the mule without another word.

She drove the mule hard, feeling the rain hit her, ducking flying leaves and dirt from the cotton fields around her. Years before, after half a lifetime of picking cotton, her father had decided to quit and make his living as a sharecropper. He made a deal with a Mr. Richmond to work his fields, part of his earnings going to pay off his right to own the land outright. Harold did not know he was making a deal with the devil. After years of paying for the land, Harold assumed the land was rightfully his, and decided to go to Mr. Richmond to ask for the deed.

His wife was frightened. She begged him not to go. "If you make a big deal about it, they might tie you to a tree and whip the flesh off your back till you die."

A proud man, Harold's only response was, "I want what's mine."

Harold fought for composure as he went up to the big house. He held in his hand yellowed pieces of paper that showed each time he had made a payment, and for how much. The deal was he could buy the land for $150. Harold's records showed he had actually paid that sum off years before. He knocked on the big white door and a female house servant came and told him to wait outside while she fetched Mr. Richmond.

Mr. Richmond was very tall, over six feet, his black hair streaked with gray. He had sharp eyes, one blue and one green, and a gaunt face with high hard cheekbones. He limped because his right leg was shorter than his left, and he wore boots with a special heel made to even it out. Mr. Richmond loved his black boots. They went all the way up to his knees. The boots were famous because he had a reputation for using them to kick Negroes in the head. He was proud of that. He used to tell people he could kick them in the head and the blood wouldn't even leave a stain.

"Mr. Richmond," Harold began, polite but firm, "I was wondrin' when you gonna give me the papers for my land. I done paid you all the money I owe you, suh."

Richmond's laugh held no humor. He looked Harold right in the eye and brought his face close. "Now, Harold. You know a nigger can't own land, don't you?"

Tears of anger and frustration welled up in Harold's eyes. He held up his papers. "But, suh, I paid you—"

Richmond cut him off. "My records show you still owe me fifty dollars. As soon as you pay me the rest of what you own me, I'll be glad to give you those papers. Now, be a good boy and go back to the fields. We don't have to cause no hard feelings, do we?"

"No, suh."

"You been working for me too long for us to be enemies. I let your family live on my land for practically nothing and you come to me with some nonsense about *I owe you*? Get out of here before I have your Black ass whipped to death."

"Yes, suh, Mr. Richmond. I didn't mean no harm. We still friends, suh?"

Mr. Richmond smiled a cold smile and slammed the door in Harold's face.

Harold was never the same after that. When he wasn't working, or reading his Bible, all he talked about was leaving. A man can't go round lettin' people cheat him. It ain't right.

"It just ain't right."

But he couldn't just ride off the Richmond land without a plan. It was surrounded by a fence, and both the front and back roads were blocked by gates. At night, Mr. Richmond put a lock and chain on them. When his family saw Harold was determined, fear set in. What if Mr. Richmond found out? What if he called the sheriff with his guns and dogs? But Harold would hear nothing about that. Every night he vowed to his wife, "Mama, I'll die before I stay on this land another day."

"But, Harold, we got a home and you just want to up and leave? That's crazy."

"We ain't got nuthin' and we don't own nuthin. We don't belong to ourselves. We belong to the white man. Now, I'm gonna take the children and go. If you don't come with us, we gonna leave you here."

It was dark the night the Metcalf family packed up to go. There was no moon, no stars, no nothing to betray them. They took only what they could carry and headed for the back gate. The Metcalf farm was pretty far from the main house but the whole Richmond place was over twenty acres. Every sound startled the family. Every dog's bark seemed like it was meant for them. Two Black men in field hand's garb were waiting with a wagon on the other side of the back gate. Harold and his family squeezed their belongings through a hole in the fence and the men helped them lift their few pieces of furniture over it and into the wagon. They helped the children over, too. They wanted to ride in the wagon but there was no room except for their mother.

The family walked for hours on dark and lonely roads.

Excerpt from *Black and White: The Way I See It*, a memoir
by Richard Williams with Bart Davis (Atria Books)

6.

*R*esilience and Reinvention

STANLEY HUGHES AND LINDA LEACH

Pine Knot Farms
Hurdle Mills, North Carolina

Stanley Hughes's blue baseball cap is the only thing standing between him and the pelting rain as he steps down from his white pickup truck and makes his way up his driveway. He doesn't hurry. Instead, he walks at a deliberate pace—fast enough not to get completely soaked, but slow enough not to slip. It's a pace that comes with having lived long enough not to be troubled by a summer rainstorm, while also being sprightly enough to suggest a certain youthful vigor. Hunkered down in my car where I've been anxiously waiting for the rain to let up, I feel a surprising calm settle over me as I watch Stanley stamp the mud off his boots and step through his screen door. In thirty seconds, he has taught me a lesson in patience and perseverance: Life, his pace seems to say, is about the long game. Don't sweat the small stuff.

The Hughes house sits on a rise overlooking a gravel road and acres of vegetable and tobacco fields. A tin-roofed log structure the size of a small cabin is a short distance away, and down the road is a larger two-story farmhouse reminiscent of North

Carolina's antebellum past. It's the family homeplace, where Stanley was born and where his sister, Peanella, still lives.

Pine Knot Farms, located in the unincorporated community of Hurdle Mills, is a Century Farm, meaning that it was established over a hundred years ago. I've come here because I've heard that the Hughes family grows organic tobacco. I've also heard that, like so many Black farmers, they've had problems with the Farm Service Administration (FSA).

Linda Leach, Stanley's wife, welcomes us into their kitchen. She has a heart-shaped face and wears bright red lipstick. Her jet black hair is pulled tightly away from her face, gathered into a long braid that's wrapped into a bun. Her eyes glisten as she clears a spot for us at the kitchen table. Her manner is warm but reserved—which makes sense given her former career as a teacher, school administrator, and businesswoman. She is her husband's biggest champion and fiercest protector—and she doesn't suffer fools.

Stanley emerges from a bedroom down the hall and slides onto a stool. He wears a crisp plaid shirt and jeans. The family's dog, Lola, settles herself at Stanley's feet. Outside, rain continues to drum on the roof.

Stanley begins by explaining that he comes from a long line of farmers on both sides of his family. His maternal grandfather, Ira Tapp, was believed to have been a free Black man from the Caribbean. He started buying land in 1911. Over time, he purchased more than four hundred acres, which he eventually divided between his seven children. Stanley's paternal grandfather, Fletcher Hughes, bought 125 acres of farmland in Hurdle Mills for $2,000 in 1912. Stanley recalls the days when his mother, Addie, managed to put three meals on the table every day and made all her family's clothes. Like so many farming families at the time, she made her own soap, flour, molasses, and cornmeal, and managed to generate enough income from annual tobacco sales to keep the taxes paid on her own fifty-three-acre farm as well as her husband's 125 acres—all without ever working outside the farm.

Listening to Stanley narrate his life story, one can't help but feel the weight of history. At seventy-one, he's old enough to recall the days when Black people had no choice but to rely on each other for their daily survival, when information was passed along by word of mouth and generations worked side by side. One can't help but think of Stanley Hughes as a bridge between two worlds. His memories stretch back to a time that's almost forgotten, yet his feet are firmly planted in the present and his eye is trained on the future.

"I was born in 1948," he begins. "I grew up going to school and farming. Once I got grown, maybe eighteen or nineteen, I wanted a car so I got odd farm jobs. I wanted a little extra money so I started farming with my daddy. When I grew up, we didn't have nothing but mules. You plowed with a mule, you cut wood with an ax. They used to have things called "choppings," where a bunch of neighbors would come in and help you cut wood. You'd go from farm to farm chopping wood to take people through the winter months. Most times when they'd cut it, then they'd stack it in the teepee shape so if it rained, it wouldn't really hold water. Later on, if you had a mule and wagon, or if you had a tractor with a homemade trailer, you'd throw the logs on the wagon and bring them to the house and stack them up again."

Stanley's recollections confirm Black farmers' long history of innovation and creativity. For generations, denied access to capital to purchase equipment, Black farmers honed their blacksmithing skills and made their own. Self-taught inventor and free man of color Henry Blair patented the first seed planter in 1834 and a cotton planter in 1836. Many others, whose names will never be known, invented a whole host of tools and implements out of sheer necessity, only to have their designs reproduced by white farmers and equipment manufacturers who then patented and sold those inventions for enormous profits.

"Then, just like we had a 'wood chopping,' we'd have a 'wood sawing.' Everybody didn't have a tractor. One man might have a tractor and a saw. He'd go around and saw his neighbor's wood. Later on, my daddy bought a chain saw. The first chain saw I ever knew of was a two-man chain saw. It took two men to handle it.

"They had 'wood choppings' and 'corn shuckings.' With tobacco, you'd harvest it with your own family, but when you'd get ready to harvest your corn, you'd have fifteen or twenty people. You'd shuck the corn and throw it in a pile. Some of them would be shucking corn, then they'd pick it up and haul it to the crib. A crib was like a smokehouse where you'd put your meat.

"Your reward for choppings and shuckings was a Sunday dinner. It would never be like a Sunday meal—say you go to church and you'd have a homecoming meal or something like that. This would be with extra things you didn't ordinarily eat during the week, like sweet potato pie, banana pudding, or a grated sweet potato pudding with raisins. Different things like that. Little extra treats.

"I was the youngest of twelve children. Most of my siblings were a lot older than I was. Two or three of them left the farm in 1961. That's what really caused my daddy to buy a tractor. It was a whole 360-degree turnaround. There was such a thing as a 'riding plow' where you hooked to a mule, but we didn't have that. I think my uncle bought one because he couldn't afford a tractor." Stanley traces his finger in a line along the table to demonstrate the difference between how a mule-drawn plow and a tractor functioned. "If this is your crop, with a mule you had to come up this side and go back down this side, then you had to have somebody else run the middle. With a tractor you could do it all in one pass. The early tractors went on from plowing one row to two rows. Now they're doing four, six, eight rows.

"In 1972, my daddy lost his leg to diabetes. They took it off in October, and believe it or not, by March or April he was back to cutting wood with an ax, working the crop with a hoe. Later on, he had to have his other leg amputated so he couldn't do anything else. But he could sit at the house and very well tell you what to do. I had an older brother; we'd be doing something and my daddy would say, 'When y'all finish that you need to be doing so-and-so.' We come up the Black way—wasn't nothing easy.

"This farm has always been organic, but back then they didn't know to call it that. They had no clue about the word 'organic.' We pulled tobacco. You had to raise your own plants. Each year you started a plant bed so there'd be less grass. Our thing was using a mule and a hoe to chop grass. That kept us going over all those years. Basically, they didn't have the money to buy fancy fertilizers. If there were any chemicals used, it took my daddy years to adapt to use anything like that. . . . In the spring when we cleaned the stable where we kept the cows and mules, we'd throw that manure out on the land. We were just like the Indians. Think about it: they used to put a fish under the plants; they fertilized with fish."

I ask Stanley about being a hog farmer.

"I got into hogs when my daddy got his leg amputated. A lot of times Mama was there and needed help. I would work the hogs and be able to stay on the farm and help her. That was going to be my second job. In other words, I would be the overseer—take my mama to town and my daddy to the doctor." Stanley's mother had inherited fifty-three acres, part of the four hundred acres originally purchased by her father, Ira Tapp. "My mama let me have the farm. I mortgaged the farm to put hogs in.

"Around 1979, all the economists started predicting what farmers' futures would look like. They kept saying hog farming was going to be a lucrative business. Hog farming was going to be one of the better things to get into if you wanted to continue farming. If you got a good price, you could take a hog and make more money than you could with a cow. A cow wouldn't have but one litter a year, but a hog could have three. If you did a weaning average of eight pigs per litter, that's twenty-four pigs. At the time they were saying hogs would bring in sixty to eighty cents per pound. You couldn't beat it. You can't grow and pick that. I wanted to build a field pig operation. I was going to expand it to go from fire-to-finish, from baby pig to where it could go straight to the kill floor." Stanley borrowed money from the FSA to start his operation. He needed funds to design the hog houses, to buy the livestock and equipment.

A baby pig is ready for sale at eight weeks. But if Stanley could keep his pigs longer—up to six months—and fatten them himself, a process called "finishing," he could make more money. He noticed that hogs finished with corn feed were more solid than hogs finished with oat or wheat feed. There was another benefit to feeding with corn: the pig was ready in four and a half months rather than six.

Stanley calculated that if he could grind his own corn for feed, he could take the thousands of dollars he was spending to purchase commercial feed and use that money to pay back the mortgage he'd taken out on his mother's land. "The commercial dealers' prices were only going to get higher. By me making my own feed, I could have saved $20 to $25 a ton." But first, he needed a mill to make the feed and a grain bin to store it. He'd already come out of pocket to purchase some of the equipment, but he needed an additional $150,000. He took his business plan to his local FSA office and outlined his plans for expansion with the hopes of borrowing money. The local agents rejected his plans and denied his application.

Two years after Stanley mortgaged his mother's farm to invest in his pig operation, the market was saturated. "Everyone was into hogs. There was too much competition." The bottom fell out of the market. Farmers couldn't get the prices per pound that they'd counted on. Suddenly, they couldn't make their loan payments. "When the price dropped, I couldn't finish the hogs. I didn't have any income. I couldn't make the annual payments."

Like many of his white counterparts, Stanley turned to the US Department of Agriculture (USDA) for debt relief. This is when his trouble began. "I believe Ronald Reagan was president. He shut down the government loans, wouldn't let us restructure. That really squeezed me out. I couldn't make the payments. I was out. They came up saying I could make a settlement. They said I had so many days to come up with $100,000."

All told, Stanley owed the federal government $265,000. "We went to bankruptcy court, but the FSA said my farm plan wouldn't work. I had different professional people who said my plan *would* work. We went back and forth two or three times." In the meantime, Stanley joined the class-action lawsuit *Pigford v. Glickman*, filed on behalf of Black farmers who had lodged discrimination complaints against the USDA. For a while, his case was suspended while the government conducted its investigation. "I was part of *Pigford*, but I was never compensated. In the end, the FSA got to where they didn't want to do it. We had an eight- to ten-year ride before they dropped the hammer." Adding insult to injury, one day an FSA official told Stanley's lawyer, "I've been after this fucking guy a long time." With no way to come up with the $100,000 to settle his debt, Stanley had no choice but to file bankruptcy. The government seized the fifty-three acres his mother had inherited from her father.

As Stanley shares his story, Linda, sitting across from him at the table, has occasionally added minor details but has otherwise let Stanley do the talking. But now, as she listens to him recall his struggle and the discrimination he faced, her anger boils over.

"At that point," she says, "Stanley and I were engaged. He had his mother's farm and she gave permission to put the hog houses on it. When he couldn't make the payments, the FSA didn't work with him." Linda's fiery spirit is evident as she explains the FSA's long history of discrimination and the racist tactics local agents deployed to prevent Black farmers from getting loans.

"Black folks would go to the FSA to submit an application to borrow money so they'd have enough money to farm for a year. When they would go in, the FSA or the FHA [Farm Home Administration] agent would give them the application to more or less take home and fill out by themselves and tell them they needed maybe one document. The farmers would go home, fill out the application and bring back that one document.

"When the farmer would get to the agency, that Farm Service agency employee would tell them, 'Oh, well, you don't have form C,' for example. 'And you don't have your certificate of your farm number, and you don't have your form 578.' Well, first of all, the farmer didn't know what a 578 or a farm number was. The Black farmer would have to ask someone, 'What is a 578? What is a farm number?' Then the Black farmer would have to come back to the FSA office with someone the FSA agent trusted, meaning a Caucasian male or female who owned farmland and who had taken the Black farmer under their wing, and they would explain what a farm number and a 578 was.

"You'd apply for your loan in October, and they'd tell you it would be approved by December. You go back in December, and they'd say, 'Well, bring this other paper; it's going to be February.' In other words, the door kept swinging back and forth, back and forth. The agents had the Black farmer going back and forth, thinking the they would get tired and give up.

"Crop planting time would come, and Black farmers still wouldn't have their money. Meanwhile, white farmers put in for their money in September, they had it by October or November."

"In our local FSA office," Stanley says, "we had to make sure the money we borrowed was paid back *before* we could get another loan. A lot of deals we could have capitalized on would have gotten away. A farmer would say, 'Stanley, I got a tractor and all this equipment. I'm going out of business. I'll let you have it for $3,500,' which was a good deal. He'd already have cut the price on it because he knew me well. I'd say, 'I'll let you know what I can do in a few days.' I go over there and talk to the loan officer. He'd say, 'Yeah, that's a good deal. We can work that for you.' I come back, the loan officer would say, 'I can have the money in two weeks.' That two weeks would turn into a month. The other farmer would say, 'Stanley, I can't wait no longer. I got to have my money.' The deal would be gone. We lost a lot of deals.

"A lot of Black farmers would rent land. They'd say to the landowner, 'You going to rent me this farm?' They had to pay him by a certain time. The owner needed the money because they had to pay taxes on the land. The Black farmer would go back to the owner and he'd say, 'I can't wait no longer. I'm going to rent to somebody else.'

So, they'd have lost that farm. Whole lot of Black farmers who could have expanded and gotten bigger had to get smaller. All that made it harder to meet their other obligations. All that killed us."

"And that is true to this day," says Linda.

The story of Black farmers has often been a story of hardship and struggle, but it is also a story of determination and perseverance and reinvention. Stanley explains how they managed after Stanley's mother's farm was seized.

"I was renting other land," he says. "I continued to farm."

Linda shifts in her chair as she narrates the story of how she helped her husband reinvent himself. "We weren't married at the time, but when Stanley told me the story, I was going to go in and buy the farm back. The hog farm is back down the road. You turn down another gravel road, and there it is. The hog houses are all still there. But then, Stanley's first cousin who owned *this* twenty-five acres decided to sell. It stretches up this way and goes around the bend and joins to Stanley's daddy's portion. This is 125 acres of certified organic land. So, I decided to let the hog farm go and buy this land. I made the decision just that quick. I bought this land because another white man was after it because it's certified organic.

"There's a huge wooden school on this land, on the back of this property called a Rosenwald School that the kids in this community attended. Rosenwald Schools were financed by Sears and Roebuck and were built all across the South 'for colored children only'. The roof has fallen in, but we have some of the chairs and desks at our homeplace across the road."

The white man Linda mentioned who was interested in their property turned out to be the Realtor who was supposed to be representing Stanley's cousin. One day, he appeared on the property. "The Realtor walked this land and took pictures of everything. He said, 'Stanley Hughes is staying here, right? Isn't this land certified?' I said, 'Certified what?' He said, 'You know what I'm talking about—certified organic.' I said, 'Yes, it is.' He said, 'Well, that ups the asking price. I can go ahead and put my sign out front.' I thought about the Rosenwald School being on this land. I thought about all the history. I said, 'Let me ask you something before you put your sign up. Are you going to put in your write-up in the description that the individuals who buy this land must seek permission from Stanley Hughes and get it in writing that Stanley will give them access to the road into this house? Because otherwise, they're going to have to build themselves a [new] road up here.' He said, 'Well, I didn't know all that. I'm going to put the sign up, but technically, I'm going to be the one buying this land.' I said, 'Do you realize what you just told me is unethical? What you need to know is, you're not talking to a dummy. I will take care of you.' I told him, 'I should have been here when all this *mess* happened with the hog farms because *I would have done the talking.*'

The next morning I called the North Carolina Real Estate Commission in Raleigh and I reported his butt. I sure did. He had met Miss Queen Bee—*me*. He didn't lose his license, but I reported him anyhow. In the end, *I* bought this land; I sure did. It's in my name and my name only. With someone else, what that man said would have flown over their head, and under their chin, and through their ears. But not me. This happened in 2014, and I'm just telling you how this is still happening. From North Carolina all the way down to the Mississippi Delta." Linda she shakes her head, almost too furious to speak. "All those other Black farmers—all eight of them—they were all hog farmers and every last one of them lost their farms. They were also tobacco farmers."

"The FSA put a lot of Black farmers out of business, and it is still happening today," Stanley explains. He reflects on how badly FSA agents treated Black farmers when they came to the office. "Farmers would go to the FSA office and sit all day. They'd never get called."

Linda sits back in her chair. "We saw a documentary by Land Loss Prevention. It told how in the southern states—Georgia, North Carolina, South Carolina, Alabama, Mississippi, Arkansas—all the southern states—Black families have lost millions of acres of land because of racism in America. When I saw that documentary, I just cried and boo-hooed. I was so full of anger after watching that documentary, I said, 'Someone has to do something.' I mean *really*."

"A whole lot of folks have gotten swindled out of land because of leases," says Stanley. "White people would come up and bring a lease that says, 'I'm going to lease your farm.' The Blacks were older people who didn't know how to read. The lease was actually a purchase agreement. They didn't know what they were signing. The lease would say, I'll lease your farm from you for $1,000 per year. In a year or two the whites would go back to the Black people and tell them, 'Y'all got to move because I own this land.'"

"I'm telling you some horrifying things have happened to Black folks in this country," Linda says. And for a few minutes we sit together in silence, struggling to contain our shared outrage.

In the end, Stanley and Linda have prevailed. With a combination of hard work and innovative thinking, they have built an impressive organic farming operation. Stanley is the only Black farmer selling certified organic tobacco in the state of North Carolina. He is also one of the twelve original growers of the Eastern Carolina Organics company.

In addition to organic tobacco, Stanley and Linda grow an impressive variety of produce. They concentrate on greens growing three varieties of kale and two varieties of collards, in addition to fennel, squash, tomatoes, beets, carrots, and five varieties of sweet potatoes with an eye toward adding a sixth variety. In fact, it's their sweet potatoes that have catapulted them to relative stardom. Cured with Stanley's secret methods, passed down from his grandfather, Hughes sweet potatoes have been featured in over forty local, state, and national publications, including *Eating Well*, the *New York Times*, and *Gourmet Magazine*. Word of their sweet potato greens' cancer-fighting qualities has spread, and researchers from Duke University and the University of North Carolina have contacted them for samples. Even as they look forward to semi-retirement, they want to keep expanding their farming operation with plans to grow organic hemp.

Like the generations who came before them, Stanley and Linda are committed to helping their community. There is a garden in front of their house that Linda calls the Agape Love Garden, from which the family's six employees harvest fresh produce for weekly distributions to the sick and elderly. There is a small pile of tote bags emblazoned with the Pine Knot Farm logo in the corner of her kitchen. "They got tote bags like this yesterday that were filled to the brim. They got sweet potatoes, corn, yellow and green squash, onions, yellow and green zucchini, string beans, okra, German Johnson tomatoes. I want people to eat healthy."

Stanley continues to farm his 125 acres, but he also farms all of his first cousin's land.

Their story is an inspiration. When I tease Linda for downplaying the fact that they've been featured in so many newspapers and magazines, she smiles modestly. "We're plain and simple folks. We let the work we do speak for us."

If the racial wealth divide is left unaddressed and is not exacerbated further over the next eight years, median Black household wealth is on a path to hit zero by 2053—about 10 years after it is projected that racial minorities will comprise the majority of the nation's population. Median Latino household wealth is projected to hit zero twenty years later, or by 2073. In sharp contrast, median White household wealth would climb to $137,000 by 2053 and $147,000 by 2073.

—FROM PROSPERITY NOW,
THE ROAD TO ZERO WEALTH, 2017

7.

*L*ittle Farm, Big Dreams

KAMAL BELL

Sankofa Farms
Cedar Grove, North Carolina

The two-lane road to Sankofa Farms in Cedar Grove, North Carolina, winds through seemingly impenetrable walls of pine trees. In the distance, the sky threatens rain, but on this overcast morning, just after 7:00 a.m., it's strangely fitting that the skies above Sankofa are clear.

In the three brief years since Kamal Bell founded Sankofa Farms, he's managed to make a name for himself. He has a friendly face and an easy smile that radiates light and positivity. He's the kind of guy you'd want as a neighbor. The average age of the American farmer is sixty-five years old. If farming, and especially Black farming, is going to continue, the industry needs to attract more young people like Kamal to take up the mantle.

Bell grew up in Durham, where his earliest lessons in community organizing came from his experience in Catholic school where he observed the Catholic community coming together to support ideas that push their community forward. "If they need a school, they come together and do whatever it takes to add value—from individual family donations to fundraisers."

Kamal attended North Carolina Agricultural and Technical University (A&T), where he planned to major in animal science until his passion for Black studies made him reconsider. "I would go to the Black section of the library to read when I was supposed to be studying for class. I read all the Black leaders—Martin Delany, Malcom X, Booker T. Washington, W. E. B. DuBois—and I started asking myself how I could give back to my people and push our race forward." One day, he came upon Elijah Muhammad's *Message to the Black Man*. "I asked myself, 'What was I going to do for my people?' So, instead of me thinking, 'I'm going to graduate and get a good job,' I thought, 'I like agriculture.' Both Elijah Muhammad and Booker T. Washington stressed that the farm could be an engine to help retool the Black community, so I thought, 'I'm going to try to be a farmer.'"

The very next day, Kamal changed his major from animal science to animal industry, which focuses on farm production and livestock. Realizing he needed experience, he connected with a professor who specialized in swine production and worked in the swine unit at A&T for a year and a half. "I got a lot of management experience. I got to work up close with animals, but I knew I needed to work with plants, too."

Fast-forward two years, when Kamal met his future wife, Amber. "We had a child when I was a senior and she was a junior. I thought, 'Alright. I'm having a kid. . . . You can't run from your responsibilities.' So, I asked myself, 'How can I always make sure I have a structure to support our child?'" His first idea was to start a dehydrated pineapple and apple chip business in their apartment kitchen. He called the business Unity Farms. Soon, Kamal found himself balancing engagement, parenthood, saving money, and running a business. "That business went really well. I saw a real transformation in consciousness with our customers. When I went to events and conferences, people asked, 'Do you have a farm?' I'd say, 'No, but I'm working on it.'"

As Kamal took the first steps to convert Unity Farms from a home-based business to an actual farm, he encountered the same obstacles as did so many Black farmers before him. The first came as he applied for a Farm Service Administration (FSA) loan to buy a piece of property. "The FSA agents wouldn't return my calls or provide clarity on the farm loan process. But the universe worked in my favor," Kamal says. While searching for the local FSA director's contact information, he came across the name and number of an agent who was a fellow North Carolina A&T graduate. "She was supposed to have been listed for another county, but she was listed by mistake." The agent helped Kamal with his application, which should have guaranteed its acceptance. But when he submitted his application, the local loan officer, Dock Jones, told him that his Unity Farms wasn't registered in North Carolina. His application couldn't be processed. "I went back to the drawing board," he says.

"I happened to listen to a lecture by Amos Wilson in which he said we need to accept our African identities and build institutions using our culture. We need to stop using other people's culture and gravitate to our own because there's power there. I'd taken an 'African history to 1800' course at A&T as an undergrad, so I thought, 'I'm going to name my farm 'Sankofa,' which means 'go back and get' and derives from the Twi language in Ghana. It has a meaning to American Africans, and it also has a tie to the old *Muhammad Speaks* newspaper, which showed hands uniting from Africa and America. When our brothers and sisters in Africa, especially West Africa, see the symbol, they see that we haven't forgotten our ancestry. The symbol represents a bridge bringing us together." Kamal changed the business's name and registered again with the state. But then the FSA agent informed him he needed a crop enterprise budget and an offer to purchase land.

Luckily, the mother of Kamal's close college friend was a real estate agent. "She's the bomb. We found this property by universal design. I'd never heard of Cedar Grove." But Kamal's fight wasn't over. Once he located the piece of property he wanted to buy, he prepared his loan application, but once again, the FSA agent wouldn't return his calls. "I'm persistent if I really want something," Kamal says. "I put everything I had into getting this land." He drew strength and inspiration from an article in online magazine, *The Counter*, about the famous class-action lawsuit *Pigford v. Glickman* and knew how the US Department of Agriculture (USDA) handled Black farmer's complaints and applications. "Just knowing that little bit of history was encouraging."

Kamal turned in his application and was encouraged when the agent told him it was one of the best applications he had ever seen. So, Kamal was stunned when the agent called later to report that his application had been denied because his managerial experience couldn't be verified. He was working on his master's in agricultural education by that time. "That didn't make sense because I'd worked on a swine farm for a year and a half. I'd done organic research with A&T through my master's for a year. I'd worked with a Black farmer in McLeansville for a year. I had letters of support from everyone I'd worked with saying I had managerial experience. They wanted to discount all of my farming experience." Kamal's only choice was to appeal the decision.

"I like to research. I like to read. I have an idea of how things have worked historically in this country. When I presented my case to the executive director, I'd gathered all the information I'd found—the quote from the US secretary of agriculture, Tom Vilsack, saying he wanted young people to come back to farming. I included the article that talked about how five white men own more land in this country than forty million Black people combined. The agent looked at me. He was like, "Whoa. We're going to try to work this out."

The morning of the appeal, Kamal arrived early at the FSA office in Oxford, North Carolina. "I tore them up in the appeal. I asked on what grounds they felt they could discount my managerial experience given that I had the letters of support verifying that I had it." Kamal's appeal meeting lasted thirty minutes. A couple of days later, he received word that his application would advance to the next level. Soon after, his loan was approved. But there were more obstacles to overcome. The day Kamal was set to close on the property, the agent forgot the check. "How do you forget a check for $60,000?" A process that should have taken only three to four months, took eight.

Kamal and Amber finally closed escrow on Sankofa Farms in March 2016—a challenging time to start planting. "We did not have time to plant for the year. We still needed to purchase a tractor, ground working implements, and a shed to store materials that were needed for our operation." Meanwhile, the first installment on their loan was coming due in January, but they didn't have any way to generate revenue to make the first $10,000 payment—nine short months after they had been approved for it. The loan officer had repeatedly encouraged Kamal to buy a home to use as collateral, but he had read about Eddie Wise, another Black farmer in North Carolina whose pig farm and home had been seized by the USDA. "That's how they get people," Kamal said. At the time, he was still teaching and was able to use his teaching income to pay the loan in the first year.

It was as he reflected on the obstacles he'd encountered during the application process and the ways he'd prevailed that Kamal decided to start a program for young Black men. Early in his teaching career, he'd started a garden at the middle school and saw how Black youth gravitated toward it. With that program's success in mind, he invited young Black teens ages twelve to sixteen out to Sankofa Farms. Three days a week, he drives one hour and forty minutes to pick up his students. Currently, he has six young Black men in his year-round program. Two have been with him for four years. "This is an escape and a healing place for them. This is a place where they can solve the issues in our community. We just don't talk about food deserts. We talk about imperialism, our identities, who we are. This is a space where they can better themselves and change what they see in their communities. It's a tool of empowerment."

Now, Kamal surveys the boundaries of his twelve-acre property, which stretches out to a line of distant trees. "The whole farm looked like this when we started," he says, pointing to a nearby section of rocky Orange County red clay covered with pine, cedar, and sweet gum trees. "We've been battling this terrain for the last three years. My students are usually out here with me. We cleared all this land by hand." Together, Kamal and his students have laid the irrigation system and installed tunnels, which will eventually function as greenhouses. "We've had to learn how to do everything from the ground up. When my students are finished here, they'll know enough to go out and get their own farms."

In addition to growing vegetables, Kamal trains his students on beekeeping. When the Bee Keeper's Association in Durham learned that he was working with youth, they invited him to visit the association's apiary. Kamal was reluctant at first. "I was scared of bees," he says, but one of his students, Kamron, was curious. "It's the students' farm, too, so anything they suggest we get, I say, alright." Now his students are certified beekeepers. Their original three hives have grown to eighteen. His small batches of Sankofa Farms honey sell out as quickly as he's able to bottle them. The beekeeping adventures he offers on Airbnb have become one of the most popular experiences in the area. He also has an observation hive that he takes on the road to show students.

Most of Sankofa's funding comes from grants. Through them, Kamal pays for everything from equipment and infrastructure to cover crops, with more funding on the way that will enable him to grow leafy greens year-round. He has also received equipment donations from Bayer Crop Science to dig a well.

"It's funny. In college, people tried to ding me for wanting to be a farmer," Kamal says. "When I'd talk to them about wanting to be a farmer, they'd say, 'What are you going to do with that? You're going to be a poor-ass farmer. You need to get another job.' They even made jokes about my dehydrated chips. Some people I knew in college wanted to work for Microsoft. One of my classmates got a corporate job. He was excited about his paychecks. Four of my classmates planned to be corporate executives. They said, 'Kamal is going to be his own CEO, but he's going to be poor.' Fast-forward to now. Some people have had job transitions. Now they're asking me how they can work with Sankofa Farms."

Kamal is currently growing squash, cowpeas, and watermelon. "My main goal with Sankofa Farms is to get food to people in food deserts." He wants to partner with local churches to distribute the food he grows. "That's going to take time to develop." Kamal says. "I didn't take the traditional route. But to be able to keep this going for generations to come, that's going to take a whole lot more effort." Ever the student of history, Kamal is determined to learn from the older generation. "We put the farm in a trust. We have a will to execute. This will ensure the farm is here beyond me." His eventual goal is to have a school on the farm.

"Everybody is stuck on technology, but I'm looking at the people. I want to invest in the people. People are the innovation. I don't mean to make this sound easy. To keep the students inspired, to set up a model that's centered around youth and educate them so they can tell people in their community how to do this? That's where the power is."

8.

*B*lack to the Land

BY LEAH PENNIMAN

Our ancestral grandmothers in the Dahomey region of West Africa braided seeds of okra, molokhia, and Levant cotton into their hair before being forced to board transatlantic slave ships. They hid sesame, black-eyed pea, rice, and melon seed in their locks. They stashed away Amara kale, gourd, sorrel, basil, tamarind, and kola in their tresses. The seed was their most precious legacy, and they believed against odds in a future of tilling and reaping the earth. They believed that we, Black descendants, would exist and that we would receive and honor the gift of the seed.

With the seed, our grandmothers also braided their ecosystemic and cultural knowledge. African people, expert agriculturalists, created soil-testing systems that used taste to determine pH and touch to determine texture. Cleopatra developed the first vermicomposting systems, warning citizens that they would face harsh punishment for harming any worm. Ghanaian women created "African dark earth," a compost mixture of bone char, kitchen scraps, and ash that built up over generations, capturing carbon and fertilizing crops. African farmers developed dozens of complex agroforestry systems, integrating trees with herbs, annuals, and livestock. They built terraces to prevent erosion and invented the most versatile and widely used farming tool: the hoe. Our people invented the world's initial irrigation systems five thousand years ago and watered the Sahel with foggaras that are still in use today. They

SOUL FIRE FARM IS A BLACK-, INDIGENOUS-, AND PEOPLE-OF-COLOR-LED COMMUNITY FARM IN PETERSBURG, NEW YORK, FOUNDED BY LEAH PENNIMAN AND HER HUSBAND, JONAH VITALE-WOLFF.

domesticated the first livestock and established rotational grazing that created fertile ground for grain crops. Our ancestors created sophisticated communal labor systems, cooperative credit organizations, and land-honoring ceremonies. Our ancestral grandmothers braided all this wisdom and more into their hair and brought it across the Middle Passage. It is our heritage.

Despite the colonial projects of chattel slavery, sharecropping, convict leasing, redlining, lynching, and systemic discrimination, our people held tight to the seeds and cultural wisdom they inherited. They are our rememberers, and we celebrate them. We give thanks to Dr. George Washington Carver for reminding us to regenerate the soil with leguminous cover crops and thick mulches. We offer gratitude to Fannie Lou Hamer for carrying on the cooperative tradition with the establishment of Freedom Farms. We acknowledge Booker T. Whatley for bringing us the farm-to-table marketing strategies of "pick your own" and community-supported agriculture. We pay homage to Shirley and Charles Sherrod for their role in creating the first-ever community land trust on fifty-seven hundred acres of Black-owned land in Georgia. And to Hattie Carthan for urban farms, and to Ira Wallace for seed keeping, and to all the rememberers we have not named, we offer our thanks.

My grandmother Brownie McCullough Smith was one of these rememberers. The Great Migration carried her from rural North Carolina to the dense neighborhoods of greater Boston, yet she maintained her relationship to soil. Grandmommy kept a strawberry patch and a crabapple tree, and I remember harvesting and making preserves at her side as a small child. Amid a stormy sea of racialized bullying and familial trauma, I clung tight to this relationship with plants and land as an anchor throughout my early years.

As soon as I was old enough to be paid for my labor, I took a job with the Food Project in Boston, learning to tend vegetable crops and run farmers' markets in formerly redlined neighborhoods. I was hooked. Sustainable farming lived at the intersection of my passionate love for the earth and my commitment to social justice. I could tend the soil and feed my people. I went on to work at several other farms in the northeast, including Many Hands Organic Farm and the Farm School, and eventually I started a youth urban farming program in Worcester called YouthGROW. I attended every organic farming conference that I could and read dozens of books on sustainable agriculture, convinced that life on the land was my destiny.

Doubt threatened to become disillusionment by the time I had circled the sun twenty-one revolutions. At the time I did not know about Carver, Whatley, Hamer, or any of the other Black agrarian rememberers. All of the conference presenters, book authors, and farm owners I encountered were white. I had been fed images of only white people as the stewards of the land, only white people as organic farmers, only white people in conversations about sustainability; the only consistent story I'd seen or been told about Black people and the land was about slavery and sharecropping, about coercion and brutality and misery and sorrow. I had been bombarded with messages that our only place of belonging on land is as slaves, performing dangerous and backbreaking menial labor. I wondered if my perception of my own destiny was misguided and if my skills and talents would be of greater use in the movements for education justice, prison abolition, or any of the myriad struggles that seemed more relevant to Black people. I wondered if I was a traitor to my ancestors in choosing to be a farmer, if I was undoing generations of effort to get our people *off* of the land and into urban spaces.

And yet, hidden from me, there was an entire history, blooming into our present, in which Black peoples' expertise and love of the land and each other was evident. I needed to uncover the truth that our twelve-thousand-year history of noble, autonomous, and dignified relationship to land as Black people far surpassed the 246 years of enslavement and the seventy-five years of sharecropping in the United States. As Black farmer Chris Bolden-Newsome explains, "The land was the scene of the crime." I would add, "She was never the criminal."

Just to cover my karmic bases, I became a high school teacher, working predominantly in urban public schools over a seventeen-year period and rabble-rousing for relevant curricula, racial equity, and the dismantling of the school-to-prison pipeline. Still, destiny has a tight grasp, and I never managed to skip a single growing season on the land, which meant a life of second and third shifts to get it all in.

After years of working on other people's farms, my partner, Jonah, and I realized it was time to start our own project. The seminal moment came when we were living in the South End of Albany in 2005 with our two young children and could not, despite our college degrees and "farmy" skills, access fresh food for our family. Our apartment was in a neighborhood under food apartheid, that system of institutional racism that populates certain zip codes with fast food and liquor stores, and other zip codes with upscale farmers' markers and high-end groceries. When our neighbors learned that we knew how to grow food, they demanded, "When are you going to start the farm for the people?"

We took that challenge seriously and started exploring the lands around Albany, New York, to see which parcel would claim us as friends and stewards. In 2006, we signed "white man's papers" to wed eighty acres of eroded and degraded mountainside land that would become Soul Fire Farm. We spent years investing in the soil and basic infrastructure, building a straw bale home by hand, and installing a driveway, electricity, septic, and water well. The farm grew over the years from our family's project to a community farm with a staff of eight people and an extended family of thousands of volunteers, alumni, and members. It shifted from a parcel that was privately owned by our family to a cooperative model where all residents have a voice in decision making and the land herself has veto power through divination.

In the Krobo language of Ghana, there is a proverb that guides our work, "Three stones make the cooking pot stand firm." The three "stones" of our work are the farm, the training programs, and the reparations organizing.

Our first and most important "stone" is the farm. We intensively cultivate five acres of vegetables, fruits, herbs, eggs, and pastured poultry using Afro-indigenous regenerative practices that leave the land with more organic carbon and biodiversity each year. We also care for seventy-plus acres of wildlands, which are sustainably harvested for fuel and medicines, while maintaining habitat for our nonhuman relatives. All that nutrient-dense food gets boxed up weekly and delivered to the doorsteps of the hundred-plus families who are members of our Ujaama farm share and pay whatever they can afford on a sliding scale. Many of these members are our neighbors who asked us to start Soul Fire Farm back in 2005.

Our second "stone" is the training programs. Many Black folks do not have the luxury to attend remote agricultural schools or work for free at a so-called apprenticeship. So, we attempt to "skill up" our community through the BIPOC FIRE (Black-Indigenous-People of Color Farming in Relationship with Earth) fifty-hour residential course, which weaves together farming, carpentry, organizing, and trauma healing in a culturally relevant and supportive space. We also embody "each one teach one" through our youth workshops, advanced farming 2.0 sessions, books, videos, articles, lectures, and other free dissemination of knowledge on Black agrarianism.

Our third "stone" attempts to address the structures that prevent Black farmers from thriving. It is no accident that 98 percent of the rural land is owned by white people, that Black farmers comprise only 1.5 percent of the farmers, and that our people are more likely to suffer from diet-related illnesses and hunger. Reparations are due for a history of enslavement, dispossession, and discrimination. We catalyze reparations through our Uprooting Racism training program, a regional land trust for BIPOC land stewards, and a reparations map that matches those with inherited wealth to Black farmers who need resources. We are also working in solidarity with Turtle Island indigenous communities whose land was violently wrenched from them and who deserve immediate and unequivocal sovereignty in their unceded territories.

Soul Fire Farm is a precious and powerful place, but it is far too rare. We need hundreds of BIPOC-led agricultural training and healing spaces if we are to survive as an agrarian people. The seed is passed to you, Black child of Black gold. If we do not figure out how to continue the legacy of our agricultural traditions, this art of living in a sacred manner on land will go extinct for our people. Then the KKK, the White Citizens' Councils, and Monsanto will be rubbing their hands together in glee, saying, "We convinced them to hate the earth, and now it's all ours." We will not let the colonizers rob us of our right to belong to the earth and to have agency in the food system. We are Black Gold—our melanin-rich skin the mirror of the sacred soil in all her hues. We belong here, bare feet planted firmly on the land, hands calloused with the work of sustaining and nourishing our community.

9.

cutting greens

BY LUCILLE CLIFTON

curling them around
i hold their bodies in obscene embrace
thinking of everything but kinship.
collards and kale
strain against each strange other
away from my kissmaking hand and
the iron bedpot.
the pot is black,
the cutting board is black,
my hand,
and just for a minute
the greens roll black under the knife,
and the kitchen twists dark on its spine
and I taste in my natural appetite
the bond of live things everywhere.

10.

*T*he Last Plantation: The USDA's Racist Operating System

BY PETE DANIEL

White male supremacy became an essential element of the US Department of Agriculture's default ideology, part of an operating system that dominated offices, dictated decisions, and often barred African Americans, women, Native Americans, Hispanics, and even poor whites from its agenda.[4]

The USDA was established during the Civil War, but its young white fingers did not touch rural issues generated by Emancipation or the transformation of labor relations that emerged after slavery, especially the crucial questions of labor control and ownership of crops. Its agenda grew, and its reach gradually expanded as the 1887 Hatch Act gave it dominion over state experiment stations, and two years later the USDA gained cabinet status. The Smith-Lever Act of 1914 created the Cooperative Extension Service that placed USDA employees in counties throughout the country at the same time that the Woodrow Wilson Administration segregated the civil service, basically sanctioning racism throughout the federal bureaucracy.

Mistreatment of Black farmers degenerated into jocular racism epitomized by Secretary of Agriculture Earl Butz's demeaning racist joke in 1976, which the *Christian Science Monitor* viewed as "an obscene characterization of Black Americans." Butz's comfort in cracking a racist joke among USDA employees suggests that such demeaning humor often bounced off headquarters walls and was echoed in distant agency outposts.[5] Overt racist statements such as Butz's joke riddled the white male culture of the USDA, and discrimination typified departmental policy.

It had taken seventy years since its founding for the USDA to gain control of the countryside, culminating in New Deal farm programs that made rural America eligible and magnified opportunities to tilt programs to favor white male farmers and to push others either into agribusiness or out of farming. To execute acreage reduction, loan policies, and the extension service mission, the USDA compiled records on every farm in the country, heightening the possibility of favoring white male farmers who could afford mechanization at the expense of all others, in particular sharecroppers, African Americans, women, Hispanics, and Native Americans.

This revolutionary agenda occurred in the context of a long historical continuum. The emergence of a free labor system after Emancipation produced a body of new legislation as landlords insisted on labor laws to bind sharecroppers and tenants to annual contracts and lien laws that defined crop ownership. Litigation between owners and tenants in county and state courts created a complex body of decisions and precedents that varied from state to state and changed over time. Resourceful African American farmers negotiated this legal minefield, and by the first decade of the twentieth century held title to some sixteen million acres of land. By 1920, there were 925,000 African American farmers. While many of the nearly one million Black farmers were tenants or sharecroppers, the landowning class was substantial and had acquired farms during some of the worst years of discrimination and violence.[6] Despite their numbers, Black farmers had no voice in shaping legislation and USDA policy, which were controlled by white male politicians and bureaucrats in Washington and by county USDA employees in the hinterland. With hard work and sagacity, African Americans acquired land, but holding on to it in the face of racist government policy proved increasingly difficult after the Great Depression.

In 1933, Congress created the Agricultural Adjustment Administration (AAA) to carry out numerous programs aimed at helping farmers control surplus commodities and raise prices. Acreage allotments—that is, how much land a farmer could plant to a commodity—became the AAA's centerpiece; to execute allotments, county committees across the country relied on data collected on every farm. The Washington AAA office decided on a commodity's national allotment and apportioned each state its share, and then each county was awarded acreage to be assigned to farmers based on previous production formulas. This program changed names over time but is most familiarly known as the Agricultural Stabilization and Conservation Service (ASCS).

The three county ASCS committeemen were elected by local farmers, prompting the USDA to boast that these committees were the epitome of grassroots democracy. In practice, though, farmers usually voted, if at all, for better-educated white men who could understand opaque USDA rules.[7] While a few tenants may have been elected to these committees, no sharecroppers or African American farmers gained a seat, although they were sometimes allowed to vote since the only candidates were white men. A farmer disgruntled with a committee's decisions could appeal to a county review committee composed of another three white men, or to Washington, or finally to a federal court. Few farmers had the resources to carry a fight very far, and county committee decisions were usually the last word. The white committees often favored friends, relatives, and office help and punished those who were not white men.

In the early years of the New Deal, the division of federal payments for acreage reduction created major issues between landlords and sharecroppers. In 1934, the USDA Office of the General Counsel produced a remarkable study of lien laws that revealed a legal niche that would award a portion of ASCS payments to sharecroppers, many of whom were African Americans. USDA leadership evidently considered the study a violation of its emerging agenda favoring landlords and fired the "liberals" who produced and supported the study.[8] Allowing a landlord to keep the entire ASCS payment demonstrated not only USDA class bias but also its determination to subsidize landlords who could use federal payments to mechanize their operations and dismiss sharecroppers. USDA policy thus defined sharecroppers out of federal payments even though legally they were eligible. William R. Amberson, a professor at the University of Tennessee Medical School in Memphis in 1934, gave a succinct account of how AAA policies turned eastern Arkansas into a battlefield as landlords and sharecroppers struggled for supremacy. In his opinion, federal policies made a bad situation worse.[9]

Laws regarding liens and tenure had usually favored landlords, but before the New Deal, disputes had been interpreted by judges and tried before juries, a step removed from local politics, and precedents were recorded in county and state reports.[10] A Mississippi case illuminates not only an example of the complexity of lien laws even as the USDA instituted county ASCS committees but also African American sharecroppers' access to the courts. In 1933, tenant W. R. Jenkins rented Mrs. M. E. Jackson's farm and agreed to pay her $1,000 standing rent and received from her an advance to finance his operation. Then Jenkins contracted with four African Americans and made sharecropper arrangements to furnish them and, after deducting their furnish, divide the crop proceeds equally. When Jenkins sold the crop, he turned all of the money over to Mrs. Jackson who, after settling with Jenkins, took the sharecroppers' portion and applied it to Jenkins's outstanding $2,300 debt to her. The sharecroppers brought a case that traveled to the Mississippi Supreme Court, which ruled the croppers had a lien on the crop for their labor "paramount to all liens and encumbrances of rights, of any kind created by, or against Jenkins, except the lien of Mrs. Jackson for her rent and supplies furnished to Jenkins." The court ordered that the sharecroppers receive their share plus 6 percent interest.[11]

Contracts became more complex when a USDA program allowed farmers to rent part of their land to the federal government. In Mississippi County, Arkansas, a case similar to *Jackson v. Jefferson* arose when, in 1935, a renter kept rental money that by contract should have gone to the landlord, who then seized the croppers' share. The dozen sharecroppers sued and won back their share of the crop proceeds.[12] State courts were bound by lien laws that applied equally to landlords, tenants, and sharecroppers. Increasingly, ASCS committees decided such cases, thus removing disputes from courts where juries and precedent offered legal protection to all citizens. Industrious Black farmers took advantage of the USDA rental program. An East Baton Rouge official in Louisiana indignantly complained that a Black farmer rented land and "is sub-renting that same land to the United States Government, collecting the rent in cash and spending it as he pleases." The USDA replied that any tenant, regardless of race, could accept and dispose of the rental money. His contract gave him control over the rented land.[13]

In 1956, the Soil Bank program opened another cash window for those who controlled cropland, whether they farmed it or not. Historian Linda Flowers, who grew up in North Carolina, wrote of a farmer who rented "every available acre a big landowner had for twenty-five hundred dollars" and the next day put it in the Soil Bank for $6,000 without ever even cranking his tractor. "If the decimation of tenantry was not the purpose of the Soil Bank," Flowers judged, "it was certainly its effect."[14] Landowners could bank their most unproductive acres and intensively farm the remainder using machines and chemicals.

After ASCS committees intruded into disputes over allotments, tenure disagreements, and government programs, state and local court cases involving landlords, tenants, and sharecroppers, such as in the *Jackson* and *Dulaney* cases, decreased drastically. Disputes increasingly arose not over sharecroppers' portions (they were becoming extinct) but over government benefits and acreage allotments, new elements introduced into farming that offered broad territory for disputes. By the 1950s, ever-shrinking allotments triggered fierce disputes within counties and states complicated by agricultural policy so abstruse that even judges puzzled over its logic.[15] Most disputes, however, were settled administratively at the local, state, or federal level, where no records of precedents were kept, and only a Freedom of Information Act search could uncover decisions since few county ASCS committees archived decisions. Thus, decisions remained encrypted and unavailable to the public. Moving disputes from courts to committees was revolutionary but attracted little opposition.

The allotment stakes rose higher as agribusiness marched across the land and allotments not only became crucial to farm survival but were also commodified and could be rented, bought, and sold. By the 1960s, a tobacco farm took additional value of $7,000 per acre of allotment, while cotton and rice farms ran from $500 to $1,000.[16] Thus, a government program intended to control surplus commodities attained monetary value, giving landowners a windfall. Distrust of local committees is documented in the approximately six thousand review proceedings in 1954 and fourteen thousand a year later.[17] To combat being allotted into oblivion, some farmers suggested that those with small allotments should not be cut in the same proportion as those with more. Tobacco farmers, for example, had plows, mules, barns, slides, and packhouse space to handle their customary acreage, and reductions threatened their farming operation. The USDA replied that a program that preserved small acreages would be impossible to implement, a dubious claim given its data on farms. It was as if acreage policy targeted small farmers for extinction. In a larger sense, complex and opaque USDA programs controlled the countryside but were largely hidden inside complex legislation and cumbersome officiousness, puzzles that confounded even the most diligent critic.

In the early 1960s, as the USDA operating system grew increasingly into a tool for discrimination, Morton Grodzins, a University of Chicago political science professor, served on a committee that evaluated the ASCS. He submitted a minority report that concluded that rather than epitomizing grassroots democracy, as often claimed, the ASCS structure was actually authoritarian. Among other issues, he questioned the power of committees to rule on "quasi-judicial matters" that earlier had been settled in courts of law, and he faulted the USDA for not addressing this alarming grasp of power. Grodzins recommended that the ASCS committee system be abolished, but his minority report languished as the study's majority supported the ASCS. A *Columbia Law Review* article in 1967 put the issue succinctly: the ASCS election procedure used by the USDA "permits to exist, and by its neglect of its duties encourages, a system which gives white southern farmers vast power over the economic well-being of their Negro neighbors." By this time African American challenges for seats on ASCS committees had produced a catalog of authoritarian behavior. Yet neither Grodzins's report nor the *Columbia Law Review*'s analysis gained traction, and the issue faded.[18]

A poor farmer's only affordable recourse to AAA discrimination, unfortunately, lay in the USDA's Washington bureaucracy, and in the mid-1930s, some four hundred letters per week poured into the USDA mailbox. In many cases, Washington bureaucrats simply sent the complaints back to the county, in some cases to the very people complained of, and this bureaucratic custom endured at least into the 1980s, when the USDA civil rights office either ignored, destroyed, or sent complaints back to the county office.[19] In the first six years of the Reagan administration, the USDA civil rights office had eight different directors and a new reorganization plan each year. The USDA lagged behind nearly all government departments in the number of African American and female employees.[20]

Several years after the New Deal began in 1933, a prominent southern citizen of a rural county counted twenty-seven federal agencies among people who, he observed, had formerly tolerated no federal intrusion.[21] Some of these agencies helped stabilize rural life, but others contained seeds that would transform the countryside. The number and complexity of New Deal agencies visited on rural communities offered not only opportunities but also temptations for manipulation and pelf. By the end of World War II, the USDA had shed most programs intended to aid poor farmers, such as the Farm Security Administration and the Bureau of Agricultural Economics, and instead preached efficiency and favored larger farm operations.[22] The USDA grew into agrigovernment, a Goliath composed of the headquarters bureaucracy, experiment stations, research facilities, regulation units, acreage policy divisions, land-grant universities, state agricultural offices, and county agricultural employees and committees. Its companion, agribusiness, included farming operations and the manufacture and distribution of farm commodities. These powerful conglomerates cooperated to reshape the country's rural life by controlling policies, research, regulation, farm structure, and the products of science and technology. The personnel both of agrigovernment and agribusiness were overwhelmingly white men, certainly the leadership positions, and they cooperated to replace labor-intensive with capital-intensive farming operations. This revolution came about at the confluence of the Great Depression, World War II, the civil rights movement, and the USDA's increasing support of science and technology, the firms that could provide it, and the farmers who could afford it. That it discriminated against Black, female, Native American, Hispanic, and poor white farmers was imbedded in the operating system.

Throughout this radical transformation, no African Americans were consulted about policy, there were no Black ASCS county committeemen, and the Negro Extension Service was segregated and demeaned. Capital-intensive agriculture crushed small farmers across the nation, but in the South the confluence of mechanization and the beginning of the civil rights movement proved especially brutal. In January 1956, Medgar Evers and Mildred Bond, two NAACP field workers, toured eight hundred miles of the Mississippi Delta and reported that mechanization was the engine accelerating desperation among sharecroppers and tenants. Landowners made sharecroppers into day laborers to avoid sharing any of the crop or federal money. "Various tales were related to the field workers how these families are being driven from plantation to plantation as each owner resorts to cutting down on the cost of labor by getting cotton picking machines, planters, etc."[23] The USDA often blamed Black farmers for being inefficient, for having acreages too small to utilize large machines, and for being inept, and after blaming the victim set Black farmers adrift to sink or swim.

After World War II, the USDA moved belligerently toward support of capital-intensive agriculture and contemptuously abandoned concern for small farmers whose affection for annual routines often did not promise wealth but did provide satisfaction. Tilling the soil meant observing seasons and understanding when to plant and cultivate and then harvest and sell the crop. Many African American farmers worked a modest acreage and did not expect great wealth, but they did hope to plant each year. For these small farmers, the USDA emphasis on efficiency, machines, and chemicals challenged their resources. Even a farmer with a small acreage needed seeds, fertilizer, and pesticides and even hoped for a tractor. Land-grant schools failed to study how to bring small farmers along in this transformation. While ASCS committees reduced acreage in efforts to control surplus commodities, experiment stations and land-grant universities conducted research to increase production that was often sponsored by corporations that specified topics and wished-for research results.

During the crucial years of the Eisenhower administration, the USDA increased pressure on African Americans. After the *Brown v. Board of Education* decision in 1954, Black farmers who belonged to the NAACP, registered to vote, or sent their children to white schools were denied federal support and harassed by local whites. The more African Americans insisted on equal rights, the more ruthless the white response. USDA leadership did nothing to protect activist Black farmers from the racist decisions of county ASCS committees. Tellingly, former Secretary of Agriculture Ezra Taft Benson did not even mention African Americans in his 1962 autobiography, *Cross Fire*.

The US Commission on Civil Rights report in 1965, *Equal Opportunity in Farm Programs: An Appraisal of Services Rendered by Agencies of the United States Department of Agriculture*, found discrimination throughout the USDA, and a follow-up report in 1982 did not remark on notable progress. The 1965 study observed that, except for some custodial positions in ASCS offices, "there were no Negroes employed in professional, clerical, or technical position in the South, either in State or county positions."[24]

Secretary of Agriculture Orville Freeman, responding to the commission's report, in 1965 issued a memorandum demanding equal treatment for African American farmers. He hired William M. Seabron, an African American who had held a leadership position in the Urban League before joining the USDA, as his assistant for civil rights. Freeman also appointed several African American farmers to state ASCS committees and established the Citizens Advisory Committee on Civil Rights. Seabron was buried in the white bureaucracy with hardly any staff, reported to an unsympathetic assistant secretary, and liaised with twenty civil rights offices throughout the country that may or may not have supported equal rights. His decisions were sometimes reversed, ignored, or contested. Seabron's office files in the National Archives catalog how racist bureaucrats not only undermined civil rights but also concurred with discriminatory decisions detrimental to Black farmers. Seabron battled almost alone against discrimination. When Republicans came to power under Richard Nixon, USDA bureaucrats cynically blamed Seabron for not achieving more for civil rights. Even as landmark civil rights legislation made its way through Congress and the movement gained headlines, discrimination persisted throughout the USDA bureaucracy, and the press mostly ignored the alarming demise of Black farmers. Secretary Freeman personified good intentions that blanched when confronted with deeply imbedded racism.

Despite commission reports, studies by concerned organizations, and occasional newspaper articles chronicling discrimination, few people learned about or cared about what happened to Black farmers and, in a larger sense, to rural America. Farmers did not fare well in the age of civil rights activism. Southern white farm ownership in that decade fell from 515,283 to 410,646, and white tenants from 144,773 to 55,650, while Black owners declined from 74,132 to 45,428, with an alarming decline of Black tenants from 132,011 to 16,113.[25] Whatever else the Great Society achieved, its programs did not favor African American farmers. Rural life no longer held the charm it once did—except in nostalgic visions of white yeomen farmers or idyllic images of well-kept farmhouses and vast fields. The USDA had almost stealthily grown into a huge and needlessly complex bureaucracy that served and rewarded conflicting interests and courted a vast constituency covering congressional districts that demanded funding for experiment stations and land-grant school projects. Its operating system had grown so complex that only specialists could decipher it, all the better to cloak racism, and bureaucrats utilized a vocabulary that pledged equal rights while carrying out discrimination.

By the end of the Eisenhower administration, the rural table had been set to serve the white male elite and to remove farmers deemed small and inefficient, including an initiative to remove as many remaining Black farmers as possible. That this purge occurred during the civil rights movement with scant public interest or awareness is an example both of how invisible USDA policy had become, especially what went on in localities run by a white male elite, and the public's disinterest in the issues of Black farmers. Discrimination had become regularized to the extent that it no longer registered as remarkable. USDA headquarters ignored racist behavior in states and counties and seldom issued a discouraging word of protest. Lacking oversight, county committees assumed enormous power to shape the development of capital-intensive agriculture. These three thousand committees allotted acreage, administered price support programs and conservation grants, and disbursed an enormous sum of federal dollars.[26]

The 1965 commission report was based on extensive interviews throughout the South, and the transcripts that survive in the National Archives provide a damning view of USDA perfidy. Interviewers talked with Black extension workers, county ASCS committeemen, FHA employees, farmers, and others involved with agriculture. The interviews barely mentioned the Student Nonviolent Coordinating Committee (SNCC) or organizations involved in voter registration and other civil rights initiatives, but as the sun set on Freedom Summer in 1964, civil rights activists focused on federal programs that at least theoretically guaranteed a just distribution of federal funds. The challenges in Mississippi in 1964, and in Georgia, Louisiana, Arkansas, and Alabama in the following years, alarmed white ASCS leaders and prompted them cynically to encourage violence, intimidation, fraud, and purposeful ineptness to divert Black voters.[27] The ASCS establishment stooped to any tactic to protect the federal largesse from African Americans.

Bitterly disappointed by the Democratic National Convention's refusal to seat the entire Mississippi Freedom Democratic Party (MFDP) delegation, the civil rights groups that had worked under the umbrella of the Council of Federated Organizations (COFO) evaluated their work in the autumn after Freedom Summer. COFO workers, many of them in their late teens and veterans of SNCC projects, examined the ASCS structure and hastily organized to challenge ASCS committee seats in twenty-one Mississippi counties, including Holmes County. There, eight hundred Black farmers owned their land, many of them taking advantage of a Farm Security

Administration project that divided some nine thousand acres into 106 farms available to Black farmers. SNCC canvassers were well received by these independent farmers, who shared their homes and stories of resistance to white chicanery, and there were promising signs of support in other counties. Worried ASCS bureaucrats began a campaign of disinformation or no information that included failing to send notification letters to Black farmers or directing them to the wrong polling place. More violent opponents to Black voting shot into houses.

The 1964 Mississippi ASCS elections were held primarily in rural stores or buildings owned by whites, an uncomfortable setting for Black farmers who understood the economic power not only of the store owners but also of planters who menacingly stood around as votes were cast and counted. Penny Patch, an eighteen-year-old white SNCC veteran, and a young Black woman observed voting in a small country store in Panola County. "It was terrifying to be so totally isolated in that little store surrounded by people who hated us," she recalled. Some white teenagers threw a live snake at their feet that slithered under the wood stove. "We were young, we were living in wartime conditions," she recalled. Poll watchers at other sites were ordered to leave, and some were arrested.[28] ASCS offices unconvincingly distanced themselves from intimidation and arrests by sheriffs.

COFO workers were adept at reporting abuses. William H. Forsyth Jr. wrote biting letters of complaint to, among others, USDA Secretary Orville Freeman, the USDA inspector general, the US Commission on Civil Rights, and local ASCS officials, chastising the ASCS for not holding reelections in all Madison County communities, instead of just two. Washington ASCS leaders spent some time drafting an evasive reply. "Forsyth, I understand, is a 17-year-old boy and is getting mail to & from almost everybody," an outraged official wrote in the margin to a draft, which did nothing to answer Forsyth's erudite criticisms.[29] Frustrated ASCS leaders at the state and county levels denied improprieties and absurdly accused COFO workers of breaking rules. ASCS officials in Washington, DC, Mississippi, and contested counties washed their hands of any blame. Despite ASCS efforts, fourteen African Americans won seats on six community committees, but none were elected to the powerful county committees.

As the reaction to Forsyth's letter indicated, white USDA leaders not only lacked sympathy with the passion for equal rights that flowed from the 1960 Greensboro sit-ins but also denigrated young African American civil rights activists whom one USDA leader labeled "the younger, more radical elements of the Civil Rights movement." It was easier to placate the NAACP or the US Commission on Civil Rights, so USDA leaders sought to discredit young COFO workers to prevent their "ridiculous statements," which no doubt included challenging ASCS elections.[30]

As ASCS elections approached in 1965, SNCC, the Congress of Racial Equality, and the National Sharecroppers Fund explored ASCS voting regulations, eager again to challenge all-white county committees in Mississippi, Louisiana, Georgia, Arkansas, Tennessee, and Alabama. Even as civil rights workers invented imaginative diagrams that unlettered Black farmers could understand, ASCS officials marshaled illegal ways to prevent Black farmers from voting. What comes across most strongly in challenges both in 1965 and 1966 is the competence of articulate civil rights workers and the bumbling and lying incompetence of ASCS officials who devised barriers to Black voters in a desperate effort to maintain control of the substantial federal funds that went through the county committees. Fighting white power ultimately exhausted the ardor of many civil rights workers, and after 1966, challenges to ASCS dwindled.

In December 1966, a community development worker shared his concerns with a Mississippi National Sharecroppers Fund worker. "Tenants, sharecroppers, and renters are getting tossed off the land right and left," he warned. Mechanization had a major impact on farming, he wrote, "but the immediate reason for throwing the people off the land is their increasing activity and interest in sharing in federal programs they're entitled to." In a Hinds County ASCS election, Blacks won all five contested seats, making "the local whites pretty mad." Invigorated Black farmers were challenging furnishing merchants and demanding receipts and refusing to sign away their share of USDA payments, and they were met with increasing white hostility. He concluded that "things are going to hell in a handbasket."[31] A litany emerged of African Americans contesting federal programs, local whites resisting, and state and national USDA leaders fecklessly taking no action. African Americans were seldom invited to sit in on meetings that discussed reform and were often demeaned or ignored when they did attend. In three chapters of my book *Dispossession*, I discussed this battle over federal programs, which vividly documented USDA racism.[32]

One of the USDA's historic duties was keeping farmers up-to-date with the latest research on better farming methods generated by experiment stations and land-grant universities. In 1892, long before any federal program, Booker T. Washington initiated the Tuskegee Negro Conference and later added farmers' institutes, courses in agriculture, a farm newspaper, and leaflets. Around the turn of the twentieth century, demonstrations to teach farmers to combat the boll weevil infestation gained popularity, and as the idea spread, Black farmers participated. Tuskegee's Thomas M. Campbell became not only the first African American extension agent but also a legend for his work among Black farmers.[33] White land-grant schools established during the Civil War not only taught horticulture but also, after the Smith-Lever Act of 1914, administered the federal Cooperative Extension Service that spread across the country. Since land-grant schools were segregated, Congress in 1890 established Black land-grant schools, the so-called 1890 schools, that housed Black agents who were closely supervised by whites. The Negro Extension Service was underfunded, like the 1890 land-grant schools, but despite discrimination Black male and female agents did heroic work among Black farmers.[34] Experiment stations and land-grant schools through the extension service provided information to farmers to improve husbandry, but the Negro Extension Service was the last link in this chain and shared neither adequate funding, personnel, nor information.

As I have observed in earlier work, the Cooperative Extension Service resembled an octopus that from Washington wound its tentacles around land-grant schools and county extension personnel. Because its budget contained a mix of federal, state, and county funds, it used its vague status both to invade all levels of government and, when challenged, to shield itself from responsibility. White male county agents and female home demonstration agents distributed information from experiment stations and land-grant schools intended to improve husbandry and homemaking. Male and female agents of the Negro Extension Service worked under the supervision of white county agents, were paid substantially less, were often housed in shabby offices with sparse furniture and second-hand office machines, and were demeaned by the white county staff. In 1948, for example, John B. Jordan, the Black agent in Evergreen, Alabama, reported to the state Negro Extension Service leader that he paid office rent and for electricity, fuel, water, and telephone out of his own pocket. The annual expenses came to $360 a year. "I sweep and clean the office myself," he wrote.[35] USDA headquarters in Washington and white land-grant schools ignored such discriminatory treatment. Numerous articles and books document not only discriminatory treatment but also the hard work and accomplishments of Black men and women in the Negro Extension Service.

In a 1951 article complaining that Black youngsters were excluded from national 4-H events, such as the National 4-H Congress and the International Youth Exchange, and had never won a national 4-H scholarship, Revella Clay cited the difference in Black and white extension agents' annual salaries. Nationally, whites averaged $4,904 and Blacks $3,138, and the difference was even more stark in Alabama (where whites were paid $5,331 and Blacks $2,872 per year) and in Arkansas (whites, $4,478, and Blacks, $2,855). The 46,000 African American 4-H members were segregated from the 330,000 white members.[36] As the civil rights movement arrived, pressure increased to integrate camps and events, and whites fought every effort to grant equal access.

As the civil rights movement gained support in the 1960s, pressure increased to integrate the extension service. It turned out to be a one-way street, for in every case African American extension staffs were transferred from Black to white land-grant schools where they were usually ignored and given no responsibilities, as if their former work were negligible. The intent, of course, was to eliminate African American executives and agents and preserve white control.

When the order came down to integrate the Alabama extension service, Negro Extension Service executives—including office head Bailey Hill, editor Willie Strain, and head of girls' 4-H Bertha M. Jones—moved from Tuskegee University to Auburn University. Willie Strain had risen from a county agent to edit *The Negro Farmer*, a newspaper that reported on farming, 4-H activities, general news, and advice, and he also worked with agents on improving farming methods and publicity. Both Bailey Hill and Bertha Jones were assigned little work at Auburn, and Strain's supervisor saw no need to continue *The Negro Farmer*, as if Black farmers no longer needed news and advice. Given nothing to do, Strain arrived at his office each morning and was shunned as whites turned their backs. He would quickly leave his office for the library.

Restless, he went back to graduate school at the University of Wisconsin, but when he returned he was passed over for promotion to a job for which he was highly qualified. He sued. Auburn investigated every aspect of Strain's career, attempting in vain to undermine his credibility. The case, *Strain v. Philpot*, expanded to include Auburn's efforts to evade integration throughout the state's extension service. After Judge Frank M. Johnson had digested the depositions, hearings, records, and five briefs, he saw no need for a jury trial and wrote a decision castigating Auburn's evasions and calling for reform across the state.[37] Alabama's efforts at manipulation were replicated throughout the South as civil rights programs were twisted to allow white control, so similar cases were brought throughout the region as white land-grant schools tried desperately to defeat equal rights. Having Black female agents conduct sessions that included white women became extremely contentious, as did having Black agents in charge of white women in county offices.[38] The *Strain* case demonstrates the unintended consequences of integration; school integration followed a similar path when Black teachers were often dismissed and Black schools closed. As Greta de Jong has eloquently observed, whites ruthlessly contested government programs intended to benefit African Americans.[39]

In 1946, the Farmers Home Administration (FHA, later FmHA) was founded almost as if to atone for the Farm Security Administration programs that sometimes aided poor farmers but had fallen from the grace of agribusiness and politicians who no longer supported its programs. Although still tasked with providing last resort loans to poorer farmers, the FHA in the South entrapped Black farmers with unnecessarily large loans, cleaned them out (sold their possessions) when they could not pay off the loans, misinformed them of loan programs, refused to explain complex application forms, and treated them rudely at county offices.

The National Sharecropper Fund Papers in Detroit and William Seabron's files at the National Archives bulge with documentation of FHA racism, and US Commission on Civil Rights investigators in 1964 uncovered discriminatory FHA behavior throughout the South. County FHA supervisors were appointed, not elected, and they reported to area supervisors who served under a state FHA director. Eighty African Americans worked for the FHA in the South, serving Black farmers from segregated offices; they were barred from FHA committee meetings, and only two served on state advisory committees. No matter how egregious the behavior of FHA county supervisors, they were protected by their white superiors.

The seasonal routine for farmers began with spring planting, and they customarily borrowed enough money to buy seeds, fertilizer, and pesticides for the crop year and paid off the loan when they marketed their crop. When poor farmers could borrow from credit merchants or banks, they dealt with local people who knew them and could judge their competence without intrusive oversight. Farmers who had no other credit options applied to the FHA and endured an intrusive eligibility test to determine if they were creditworthy. If approved, they signed documents indicating interest rate, the FHA's right to accelerate the loan, a description of the property backing the loan, and a financial plan. Unlettered farmers faced with sheaves of forms depended on FHA office staff to explain loan programs and help with filling out forms, but offices were often run by petty and racist men and abetted by a staff of women who were often impolite and unhelpful to Blacks. The FHA increasingly failed to fulfill its intended role, for state and county offices twisted the loan programs to favor larger farms and ultimately to fund segregated community projects. When it came to African American farmers, FHA officials became as arbitrary, capricious, and insulting as the meanest planters and supply merchants. They relished refusing credit to deserving farmers, as the 1952 case of Alabama farmer Joe Henry Thomas demonstrated. Thomas owned an eighty-five-acre farm, rented other land, and tended nine acres of cotton. He owned a pickup and livestock, and his wife did public work. They hoped to build a modern house and consolidate their debts with an FHA loan. The county supervisor turned down the loan request without even visiting the Thomas farm.[40]

The voting rights initiative in Tennessee's Haywood and Fayette Counties in 1960 vividly illustrated the intersection of civil rights, mechanization, and FHA duplicity. When sharecroppers and tenants attempted to register to vote, many were evicted and replaced with machines and chemicals. The NAACP and other groups supported the evicted farmers, and the US Justice Department prevented some evictions, but the arrival of machines and of the civil rights movement created a grave crisis. A Memphis attorney, James Franklin Estes, complained of another issue: credit. His office had received complaints from more than five hundred Black landowners, tenants, and sharecroppers complaining that those who attempted to register "will not receive any form of credit for crop planting, cotton producing or other purposes as a form of reprisal." Estes's letter was addressed to President Dwight D. Eisenhower, and it was bounced to the FHA, which fretted over a reply before declaring there was no discrimination. There were no keys on FSA typewriters that could spell out "discrimination," no matter what the evidence.[41] The NAACP, the National Sharecroppers Fund, and other organizations supported the evicted farmers but could not finance their farming or block oncoming machines and chemicals.

A widespread FHA tactic granted Black farmers large loans that would prove difficult to pay off. In the spring of 1961, for example, Georgia county FHA supervisor Carl Grant persuaded Fred Amica to take out a larger loan than usual. Amica had a good crop year and was paying off the loan when Grant arrived at his farm with a judgment against the unpaid balance and removed Amica's farm equipment, including a tractor that he had nearly paid off. When the sale of Amica's property did not satisfy the full amount of the loan, Grant garnished the future cotton crop and spread the word that Amica had not paid off his FHA loan, ruining his credit.[42]

Persuading a Black farmer to take on more debt and seizing property for the unpaid balance became a common practice among FHA supervisors. It resembled the landlord/credit merchant practice of "cleaning out" farmers each season that Booker T. Washington had complained of at the turn of the twentieth century. FHA supervisors also lied to Black farmers, promising them a loan and then waiting until the farmer became indebted for seeds and fertilizer to announce that the loan did not come through, leaving the farmer in debt and unable to finish his crop. Other supervisors told farmers that the loan they hoped to apply for did not exist. Office staffers often treated Black applicants with contempt, telling them to come back later or sending them home with unexplained forms. Such sleazy and, indeed, unethical behavior brought no reprimands from Washington.

In 1962, South Carolina attorney Ira Kaye observed that a number of Black farmers were facing failure with debts so large that even a good harvest would not pay them off. These Sumter County farmers applied for FHA loans in a "very dinky, dingy office," Kaye reported, that "was no less than a national disgrace." That was bad enough, but as long as the FHA supervisor and committee were all white men and the ASCS committee continued to cut tobacco and cotton allotments, these farmers were doomed. Investigations throughout South Carolina found poor farmers on the verge of extinction, unable to purchase expensive machines and chemicals or to access funds to farm even on a modest scale.[43]

The US Commission on Civil Rights carefully scrutinized FHA employment of African Americans throughout the South and found only two on state advisory committees, a few serving as alternate county committeemen, and twenty assistant county supervisors who worked with Black farmers. Commission investigators talked both with white FHA supervisors and African American assistant supervisors. T. T. Williams interviewed assistant county supervisor John S. Currie, a 1938 graduate of Tuskegee Institute, who handled cases for Black farmers in Hinds and Rankin Counties, Mississippi, from his dingy office across the hall from the white FHA office. Currie's office had no telephone, but he could obtain supplies from across the hall, although he had to walk two blocks to a federal building to use a restroom. Many of the Black farmers, he explained, sought only small operating loans, knowing that their acreages could not utilize large machinery and that raising beef cattle on their small farms was impossible.[44]

The FHA operated with malevolent efficiency to track Black farmers, carefully monitoring and punishing any contact with civil rights activists. An Alabama farmer who owned eighty acres and rented an additional sixty-nine secured $2,600 to plant twenty-eight acres of peanuts. When the white man he contracted with to dig his peanuts discovered he was active in civil rights, he removed his machinery, and the FHA office refused the farmer a loan to hire help to dig the crop. The USDA's William Seabron intervened and requested an inspector general investigation of the Barbour County FHA office, but that did nothing for the farmer, who had lost twelve tons of peanuts.[45] When an Alabama farmer asked the FHA supervisor about a $2,500 loan to improve his house, he was told he must get recommendations from three white people, an impossible request since the farmer was active in civil rights.[46]

John D. Pattillo, the FHA supervisor in Greene County, Alabama, along with his staff, personified coarse, insulting, dismissive, and unhelpful bureaucrats. Using coarse language, he misinformed Black farmers that there was no such thing as an economic opportunity loan, suggesting it was "something they heard about in the jungle." He was duplicitous when ordered to appoint a Black alternate committeeman, misleading him about his responsibilities. FHA office help treated Black applicants rudely, often sending them away without forms or threatening that even if they qualified, they would not get loans. A Black pastor argued that Pattillo's actions were racist and that he should be fired. In 1966, Pattillo was transferred out of Greene County but not disciplined.[47]

Even as the FHA denied loans or used other tactics to ruin Black farmers, it supported loans that would transform rural land into golf courses, shooting ranges, and tourist attractions solely for the use of whites.[48] Even as Congress passed the Civil Rights Act and the Voting Rights Act and the federal government, at least in theory, advocated equal rights, USDA leadership mouthed support for equal rights while turning on African Americans with vengeance.

When one looks through the papers of the US Commission on Civil Rights, the National Sharecroppers Fund, the Records of the Secretary of Agriculture, the papers of the NAACP, SNCC papers, and other collections, USDA racism emerges as a major theme. During the age of the Civil Rights Movement, roughly from 1954 to 1980, the USDA announced that it carried out programs that ensured equal rights, but instead its racism sharpened until, by the turn of the twenty-first century, there were but eighteen thousand Black farmers left of the nearly one million three-quarters of a century earlier. This was not an accident but rather the result of a USDA operating system that threatened not only Black farmers but small white farmers and women, Native Americans, and Hispanics.[49]

Over the years since the 1950s, nearly every secretary of agriculture has offered platitudes about improving the department's civil rights record, but none discovered a tool that could excavate racism either in Washington or throughout the country. Racism hid behind a vocabulary of euphemisms and compliance, but during the Reagan administration, policies became so overtly racist that they created documentation that ultimately informed the *Pigford v. Glickman* decision in 1999 and successful suits by women, Indians, and Hispanics. Despite these expensive settlements, nonwhite and female farmers still complain of USDA discrimination.

As I concluded in *Dispossession*, "The tracks of discrimination led from local committees and agriculture offices to state offices, to underfunded Black land-grant schools, to flush white land-grant schools, to experiment stations, and on to Washington to disappear into the trackless bureaucratic wilderness where untamed prejudice flourished and staff alienated from the land punished the clientele they were hired to help."[50]

At the very same time that America refused to give the Negro any land, through an act of Congress our government was giving away millions of acres of land in the West and the Midwest—which meant that it was willing to undergird its white peasants from Europe with an economic floor. But not only did they give them land, they built land grant colleges with government money to teach them how to farm. Not only that, they provided county agents to further their expertise in farming. Not only that, they provided low interest rates in order that they could mechanize their farms. Not only that, today, many of these people are receiving millions of dollars in federal subsidies *not* to farm, and they're the very people telling the Black man that he ought to lift himself by his own bootstraps. This is what we are faced with, and this is the reality. Now, when we come to Washington in this campaign, we are coming to get our check.

—MARTIN LUTHER KING,
"WE ARE COMING TO GET
OUR CHECK," 1968

American society made the Negroes' color a stigma. America freed the slaves in 1863 through the Emancipation Proclamation of Abraham Lincoln but gave the slaves no land or nothing . . . to get started on. At the same time America was giving away millions of acres of land in the West and in the Midwest, which meant that there was a willingness to give the white peasants from Europe an economic base. And yet it refused to give its Black peasants from Africa who came here involuntarily in chains and had worked free for 244 years any kind of economic base. So emancipation for the Negro was freedom to hunger; it was freedom to the winds and rains of heaven; it was freedom without food to eat or land to cultivate; and therefore, it was freedom and famine at the same time. And when white Americans tell the Negro to lift himself by his own bootstraps, they don't look over the legacy of slavery and segregation. I believe we ought to do all we can and seek to lift ourselves by our own bootstraps, but it's cruel jest to say to a bootless man that he ought to lift himself by his own bootstraps. And many Negros by the thousands and millions have been left bootless as a result of all of these years of oppression and as a result of a society that deliberately made his color a stigma and something worthless and degrading.

—MARTIN LUTHER KING, INTERVIEW WITH SANDER VANOCUR OF NBC NEWS, 1967

11.

*F*ather and Daughter

HARPER AND ASHLEY ARMSTRONG

Armstrong Farm
Bastrop, Louisiana

Harper Armstrong points to a large, multicolored map of the African continent hanging on the wall outside his farm office. A Ghanaian flag, a three-masted ship, and cutout shapes of Mississippi, Tennessee, and Louisiana float in the space where the Atlantic Ocean should be. Harper's uncles took a DNA test and were able to trace his family's roots. Now Harper pushes his baseball cap back and scratches his forehead as he explains what we're looking at. "This shows the journey my family took to get here." As he reads the narrative neatly printed along the map's lower half, his manner is surprisingly calm for a man who has experienced the highs and lows of farming. "The Armstrong family originated in Ghana, Africa, 1800. From there they moved to Tennessee in 1812. James Armstrong, our great-great-grandfather, was born in 1812. At some point around 1910, his descendants moved to Mississippi."

Harper goes on to explain that in 1920, James's son, Andrew, and his family moved to Mer Rouge, Louisiana. They arrived in their mule-drawn wagon and began sharecropping alongside other tenant farmers. Andrew died in 1943, and the farm passed to his thirty-year-old son, Joe Willie, Harper's father. The oldest of twelve siblings, Willie understood that his entire family looked to him to carry on the family tradition, so he took up the mantle. He sharecropped until 1948, then bought 120 acres.

It's one thing to trace one's family roots back to the African continent; it's another to wake up every morning and work the same soil that your forefathers worked, to walk in their footsteps. Harper grew up on his family's farm and began farming himself in 1963, when he was still in high school. He farmed for two years, then moved to Detroit briefly to work at RailCrew Xpress. In 1965, the same year he got married, he was drafted into the army. In 1966, soon after his return, Harper's mother died. He received a hardship discharge in 1967 and came home to help his father with the farm. "That sort of sealed it. I've been farming and working other jobs at the same time ever since."

Farming is a full-time endeavor. Between planting, harvesting, and repairing equipment, there's enough work to keep a person busy around the clock. But talk to enough Black farmers, and you start to hear similar stories of determination and sacrifice, the lengths they've had to go to in order to keep their farms afloat.

"I always did two or three different jobs in addition to farming," Harper says. "I sold pots and pans for a sideline hustle. I sold trees. During the '70s my brother started running a café, and I went into the jukebox, pool table, and vending machine business. When Ms. Pac-Man came out, I even got into selling that, putting machines in the different Black locations." Harper's employer, Natural Gas, closed its plant in Bastrop, Louisiana, and he was transferred to Pearl, Mississippi, but he injured his back on the job in May 1988 and was forced to retire. Through it all, he continued to farm.

Harper gradually expanded from his father's original 120 acres to 300 acres and kept growing. "Back in 1973, we were farming fifteen hundred acres. After that, a cousin of mine who was farming a thousand acres died, so I took over his land. That older generation was farming but started giving up their farms because their children weren't farming. I bought or leased their land." By 1992, Harper was farming three thousand acres, growing cotton, soybeans, and grain. "I came along at a good time, I guess."

Harper and his wife, Lois, became parents later in life. "After twenty-three years of marriage, my wife and I were blessed and our daughter, Ashley, came along. We've been attached to her. I've been farming and farming and farming. Now she's out here with me. My wife says I'm trying to make a boy out of her, but I always say it's not about a man thing. It's about making a living and not letting nobody say you ought not to be out here doing this. Because if you can make a living at it, you can be successful. Women do everything. Ashley can do anything on this farm—she can drive a tractor and operate any of this equipment."

While it's true that the average American farmer is white, male, and in his sixties, the April 2019 agricultural census reveals that there are more women in agriculture than ever. According to the census, "Over the last five years, the number of male farmers fell, while the number of female farmers rose: Female producers now make up 36 percent of farmers, a 27 percent increase from 2012. Although only 38 percent have a female primary producer, the person who makes the most decisions on the farm, . . . now 56 percent of farms have at least one female producer."

"Farming has always been a part of my life," Ashley says. "I have baby pictures of me in cotton fields. It's all I knew. When I was younger, I didn't understand much about farming. I just knew whenever I was out of school, I had to go to the farm with my dad. I can remember being twelve or thirteen when I started driving tractors—the smallest ones, of course—but as I got older, I was able to operate more advanced equipment. By the time I was twenty-two, I could operate any piece of equipment we had, from front loader tractors to the eighteen-wheelers we used to haul grain. The new tractors have GPS systems. You can't just throw anybody out there.

"I fought the idea of farming for a long time. I didn't think I really wanted to be here. I wanted to venture out and see what was out there. But even while I was at University of Louisiana, Monroe, I was always out here. I'd have class two or three days a week, and when I got out of class, I'd come back here."

In 2016, Harper, his wife, and Ashley each secured $125,000 contracts to grow watermelons, peas, squash, and peppers. With the uncertainties of farming in mind, they purchased insurance under the US Department of Agriculture's NAP program, which provides financial assistance for producers of noninsured crops when low yields, loss of inventory, or prevented planting occur due to natural disasters. Just to be safe, Harper paid for an additional premium so that, should disaster strike, 85 percent of his contract would be guaranteed.

Toward the end of April, a tropical depression dumped softball-size hail across the region and caused catastrophic flooding. Harper's crops were destroyed. His office and his fields were under four feet of water. "We almost lost everything—between the crops and everything, we lost almost $1 million." Harper believed that his NAP crop insurance would cover some of his losses. Following protocol, he notified his local FSA office, alerting them to the damage. But instead of sending an adjuster out to Harper's fields to assess the damage, the local FSA agent told him to replant his crop and "keep his records." No one came out to assess the damage until after his second crop was harvested. "You all get through and finish what you've got, then they say they'll send an adjuster. Nothing in between. Just at the beginning and at the end. What do you need adjusting when you get through with everything?" When Harper filed his claim at the end of the season, he was denied. The same FSA office that had instructed him to keep his records now argued that he hadn't filed his claim in a timely manner. They also argued that he hadn't followed the planting guidelines outlined in the handbook, but they'd never provided one. "All of a sudden, they didn't pay us nothing. The supervisor at FSA was supposed to tell us what to do. We just went off of what he said. We ought to have had at least $250,000 to $300,000. We didn't get paid nothing. I lost maybe $500,000 in that crop. It's simple. If I'd have been white, I'd have got paid. They don't think Black folks should be paid."

The Armstrongs' experience with the USDA is part of a long and ongoing history of discrimination. Black farmers continue to be denied access to information and capital that would allow their farms to thrive.

With the losses that the Armstrongs sustained, most farmers would fold up shop. But Harper and Ashley are determined to continue farming. "We're not going to give up," Harper explains. "We're going to keep on. We're going to reinvest. Like I said, I've been at this for seventy-some years. I started running this farm with my daddy when I was fifteen."

As disastrous as the flood was, Harper recognized an opportunity. For months, USDA advisers in Washington, DC, had encouraged farmers to switch from growing row crops to produce.

"Over the last couple years, I came to the conclusion that I had to reinvent myself. My fields were scattered. I was going fifty miles farming grain, cotton, and soybeans. Looked like all we were doing was spending money. It looked like we were *almost* making money. When I was a kid, my mother used to grow a garden. We planted corn, peas, butter beans, okra, and tomatoes. She'd go out there and pick whatever we had in the garden, put it on the truck, and go into town. It might not seem like much now, but back in the '60s if she went to Mer Rouge and made $65 or $70 per day selling produce when other people were working in the fields for a whole day and making $2.50 or $3.00, that was a world of difference. You think slavery ended in 1865, but it really didn't end until 1965. Up until then, you were making $3 a day working for a white man. You were in the white women's kitchen and cleaning their houses for $2 a day. That was common. But we were blessed; we had this farm. We worked on it, and we had what we needed."

With that memory of his mother's success in mind, Harper decided to grow produce. He told Ashley, "We own four hundred acres of land. Instead of us farming two thousand of leased land, we'll concentrate on growing produce; we don't have to run all over the parish." They started with watermelons and purple hull peas, gradually expanding their produce to include butter beans, squash, snap beans, cantaloupe, and greens in the fall. The decision has resurrected the Armstrongs' business. Customers come from as far as Arizona to buy their produce.

And this is where having a daughter who is a millennial comes in handy. It was Ashley's idea to use social media to reach customers. "Starting a Facebook page for our farm just seemed like common sense to me," Ashley says. "I stay in Monroe. I tried to participate in some of the local farmers' markets, but it's hard when we're out here trying to harvest and package everything, so I put our produce on Facebook." Each week she posts an announcement on Facebook, letting customers know what produce is available and where her truck will be parked. "I let people know what we were planting and invite other pages and groups to see what we were doing. I show that we were local and that our produce is fresh and affordable. Our customers can either come out here to get it, or they can meet me at a certain place in Monroe. Every evening I get my orders up, load my truck, and my customers meet me. It's worked for the past two years. We move a lot of produce. It's hard to keep up with the demand. If we pick thirty to forty bushels a day and I put it on Facebook, we sell out that day."

Today, the Armstrongs have 880 Facebook followers and sell directly to their customers. Internet sales account for 80 percent of their business. The rest is by word of mouth. As their produce operation has expanded, Ashley has even found some of the equipment they've needed on Facebook.

Watching this father-daughter team, it's clear how much they enjoy working together. "I'm the only child," Ashley says. "I know I'm a big asset out here. Now that I'm thirty, I have finally accepted that farming is in my blood. I used to think I was missing out on other things in life, but over the years, I've realized farming with my family has exposed me to more things than I could ever imagine."

"Right now with our produce, we have a machine to pick it," Harper says. "We shell it and bag it. We're selling our peas for $2.50 per pound and could get more. Eventually, Ashley will build one hell of a business right here, little bit by little bit."

"We're trying to venture out with different varieties," Ashley says. "This year we're growing different types of beans, and they're selling. I like the produce more than the traditional crops. It's more hands on and direct. With corn, soybeans, and cotton, you plant it, spray it, harvest it, and you're done. You don't see where it's going. With produce you see the whole process, and you get to meet the people who are enjoying it. You also get feedback. We get good feedback, so apparently we're doing something right.

"I majored in business administration with a minor in computer information systems at ULM. Some of my friends graduated and got corporate jobs. They go to their jobs, do what they have to do, and go home. I believe I have more entrepreneurial sense by being out here on the farm. Out here, you have to make it for yourself. You have to make a plan. It takes a lot of skills other than going to a job.

"I want us to be more produce-driven. It's exciting. I'd like us to have a facility that allows us to take everything we need from the fields to harvesting to packaging to shipping it right here. That's my vision. We don't have anything like that around here. That would really help this area."

These days Harper is committed to helping others get started. He's given up some of the land he used to lease so that younger Black farmers can farm it. "I think Black people ought to have something. Anything we have these other folks think they should have. The majority of the land I was farming was Black-owned, and I wanted to keep it in the Black community. In this parish during the '60s, we had more Black landowners than white landowners. Whites owned more *land* in terms of acreage, but as far as land*owners*, almost everyone was Black. In the '60s, all my classmates had farms. They had land."

In 2008, Harper and some other farmers formed the National Black Growers Council, an organization devoted to encouraging Black farmers to think strategically about how they might work together. "I keep telling Black farmers, 'We're fighting a losing battle with some of us farming two hundred or five hundred or six hundred acres. We need to join forces and turn this into a business. If we run it as a business, it'll still get done. If we join forces, then everyone would have a job, and we'd be a force that the banks and FSA would work with rather than a force they're trying to destroy.'

"We need to start educating our folks that if you don't have this land, you don't have nothing. That's what other people all over the world are fighting about. If you don't have land, you don't have control.

"I finished high school—that's as far as I went—but I always had a vision. I've lived comfortably. Anything I want, and anywhere I want to go, the Lord has blessed me and I've been able to do it. I looked at my classmates, some in California. Most of them who've worked in corporate America, they haven't done better than me. That's why I've told Ashley, 'Don't let nobody talk down on your profession.' I got to work and I work hard every day, but I'm happy. I'm doing something I *want* to do. I tell people, 'If you're doing a job that you don't like, you ought to quit and do something you like.' I like doing what I do. I might get sweaty and nasty and hot sometimes, but I like what I do. I can enjoy it, and it doesn't worry me.

"We're living. We've got a good-looking crop. I've had a good life. The Lord has blessed me to get to seventy-four. I'm looking to get to one hundred and something before I leave here. Even with all the trials I've been through, I can be thankful, and I'm blessed because I've never suffered for nothing. I tell people all the time, you can't succeed if you don't try. You've got to be open. You've got to get out there and try something."

12.

*T*o the Fig Tree
on 9th and Christian

BY ROSS GAY

Tumbling through the
city in my
mind without once
looking up
the racket in
the lugwork probably
rehearsing some
stupid thing I
said or did
some crime or
other the city they
say is a lonely
place until yes
the sound of sweeping
and a woman
yes with a

broom beneath
which you are now
too the canopy
of a fig its
arms pulling the
September sun to it
and she
has a hose too
and so works hard
rinsing and scrubbing
the walk
lest some poor sod
slip on the
silk of a fig
and break his hip
and not probably
reach over to gobble up
the perpetrator
the light catches
the veins in her hands
when I ask about
the tree they
flutter in the air and
she says take
as much as
you can
help me
so I load my
pockets and mouth
and she points
to the step-ladder against
the wall to
mean more but

I was without a
sack so my meager
plunder would have to
suffice and an old woman
whom gravity
was pulling into
the earth loosed one
from a low slung
branch and its eye
wept like hers
which she dabbed
with a kerchief as she
cleaved the fig with
what remained of her
teeth and soon there were
eight or nine
people gathered beneath
the tree looking into
it like a
constellation pointing
do you see it
and I am tall and so
good for these things
and a bald man even
told me so
when I grabbed three
or four for
him reaching into the
giddy throngs of
yellow-jackets sugar
stoned which he only
pointed to smiling and
rubbing his stomach

I mean he was really rubbing his stomach
like there was a baby
in there
it was hot his
head shone while he
offered recipes to the
group using words which
I couldn't understand and besides
I was a little
tipsy on the dance
of the velvety heart rolling
in my mouth
pulling me down and
down into the
oldest countries of my
body where I ate my first fig
from the hand of a man who escaped his country
by swimming through the night
and maybe
never said more than
five words to me
at once but gave me
figs and a man on his way
to work hops twice
to reach at last his
fig which he smiles at and calls
baby, *c'mere baby*,
he says and blows a kiss
to the tree which everyone knows
cannot grow this far north
being Mediterranean
and favoring the rocky, sunbaked soils
of Jordan and Sicily

but no one told the fig tree
or the immigrants
there is a way
the fig tree grows
in the groves it wants,
it seems, to hold us,
yes I am anthropomorphizing
goddammit I have twice
in the last thirty seconds
rubbed my sweaty
forearm into someone else's
sweaty shoulder
gleefully eating out of each other's hands
on Christian St.
in Philadelphia a city like most
which has murdered its own
people
this is true
we are feeding each other
from a tree
at the corner of Christian and 9th
strangers maybe
never again.

13.

On Top of Moon Mountain

BRENAE ROYAL

Monte Rosso Vineyard
Sonoma, California

It's harvest time in wine country, and all across Sonoma County, which lies an hour north of San Francisco, the leaves on the grape vines have turned from deep emerald to butterscotch, copper, and crimson. For the last three months, workers have fanned out across the valley picking grapes for the harvest commonly referred to as the "Crush." They started back in August, picking aromatic whites (Chardonnay, Sauvignon Blanc, Riesling, and Pinot Grigio) before moving on to the reds—the delicate Pinot Noir first, then the sturdier Merlot, Malbec, Zinfandel, and Syrah, and finally the hearty Cabernet Sauvignon.

Now it's late October, and the harvest has just ended. Up on Moon Mountain, at Monte Rosso Vineyard, thirteen hundred feet above the valley floor, a small crew is buttoning up for the season. In their reflective yellow vests, they move across the terraced hillside. Mariachi music wafts from their radio. The light breeze carries the echo of their friendly chatter as they move along the rows. Otherwise, it's absolutely quiet across the 575-acre vineyard—which is exactly the way vineyard manager Brenae Royal likes it.

For the last six years, Brenae has lived and worked on Moon Mountain. At twenty-nine, she is the youngest vineyard manager that E. & J. Gallo Winery has employed on this famous 133-year-old vineyard. Brenae is comfortable with old things. She lives in a Victorian house that was built in 1903, and her office is in a weather-beaten barn. She farms 79-year-old Cabernet Sauvignon vines, the oldest in California; 126-year-old Zinfandel; and 133-year-old Semillon, which are some of the oldest vines of that type in the world. On a clear day she has a view of the 86-year-old Golden Gate Bridge and the city of San Francisco, whose history dates to the gold rush. She even describes herself as an "old lady" when she tells the story of how she first discovered her passion for wine. But when she rolls up in her newish Ford F-150 pickup, with its chrome wheels and tinted windows, it's clear that while Brenae appreciates the past, she isn't stuck in it. She is dialed in to what's current and has a vision for how she wants her life to unfold.

"I was born in Biloxi, Mississippi, and spent time in Florida and Virginia as a young child," she begins. She glances behind her seat to check on her black Labrador retriever, Violet Mae, who is stretched out on a blanket. "I'll still say I'm a southern belle, even though I can't claim that at all." While Brenae's family roots are southern, she spent most of her childhood in California's Central Valley—450 miles of fertile farmland stretching down the state's spine from Redding to Bakersfield. The Central Valley is California's single most productive agricultural region. Farmers grow everything from tomatoes, almonds, and soybeans to lettuce and berries.

Given Brenae's upbringing in California's bread basket, it's understandable that she'd find her way to agriculture. Her story begins close to home, with her grandmother Phyllis Leggett. "She had an amazing garden. She grew all types of flowers and a few vegetables. I was the only grandchild who actually wanted to pull weeds for her. She would give me tulip bulbs every year. To this day, my twin sister and my brother won't get their hands dirty, but I remember loving being in the dirt. Pulling weeds is the most therapeutic thing I think you can do." Brenae was seven when she realized she wanted a career that kept her closely connected to the soil.

She held on to that dream through high school, where she joined Future Farmers of America (FFA) and started raising pigs. She traveled up and down the state competing and even became an officer in her local Atwater FFA chapter. "I remember a neighbor's pigs from blocks down the road made it into our neighborhood. I got a call at nine in the morning. They were like, "Brenae, there are these pigs in our back-yard. We need you to bring your stuff and catch them."

In high school, Brenae joined clubs and played in the school band. Her extracur-riculars were a way of getting out and seeing the world. She developed an appetite for adventure and enjoyed seeing what lay beyond the limits of her town. But when it came time to apply for college, she knew her family couldn't afford a pricey educa-tion. "My family isn't very affluent. I was trying to figure out how to afford college. I knew I wanted to do agriculture, but all of the schools were forty-five minutes to three hours away." Her hard work in school paid off, and Chico State gave her an academic scholarship. "That kind of sealed the deal for me."

Brenae planned to major in animal science, but three weeks into her first semes-ter she learned that Chico had a meat slab, otherwise known as a meat-processing facility. "I probably should have known going in that I didn't have the emotional capacity for that, but the meat slab was the nail in the coffin—pun intended—so I switched majors to plant science, specifically crops and horticulture science."

But it wasn't until her senior year that Brenae discovered wine. "I was working full-time and going to school full-time. I would come home, have a glass of wine, and watch *Jeopardy*. I was such an old lady." Her favorite wine was E. & J. Gallo's Apothic Red, a special blend of Zinfandel, Merlot, and Syrah with notes of black cherry and rhubarb. "Apothic Red was the signature of my entire senior year."

In 2013, as her senior year wound to a close, Brenae was still unsure what she wanted to do or where she wanted to go. She toyed with the idea of going to UC Davis for a graduate degree in international agricultural development when she hap-pened to attend a career fair where E. & J. Gallo had set up a booth. "They had a magnum of Apothic Red on the table. I went up to the recruiters and I was like, 'Look, I've never seen a grapevine up close in my life, but we can make this work. I have a crops and horticulture degree, I'm graduating, please hire me.' They were like, 'Whoa, slow your roll.' But they gave me an interview two weeks later, and after a two-hour session they asked me when I would like to hear from them with their decision. My birthday was in three days. I told them, 'If you have good news, call me then.' They called me the day before to tell me I got the job."

Brenae's first position with Gallo was as their vineyard operations intern. For six months, she worked at Monte Rosso and five other Gallo vineyards in the Russian

River Valley. When her internship ended, she returned to Gallo full-time as a viticulture technician, which gave her the opportunity to learn the technical side of farming. Eleven months later, she was promoted to vineyard manager for Monte Rosso. Suddenly, she found herself managing ten varieties of grapes spread across sixty-four different blocks and as many as one hundred people during the height of the harvest. They looked to her to make decisions about everything from how far apart to space and train the newly planted vines to how to prune the existing stock to maximize yield. "I remember looking around and being like, 'Okay, you have the basics of farming. You have a green thumb. You know it takes water, fertile soil, and sunlight to get something to grow. It's basic, but that's the foundation if you're getting into any crop. As far as grapevines go, you know whatever you're doing to the vine is going to influence the wine.'" She had to anticipate weather, develop strategies for erosion prevention, and make plans for irrigation—and she had to do it all in Spanish. When she was an intern, Gallo provided a tutor who helped her recall the Spanish she'd learned in high school. "When I first started, I did a lot of pointing and speaking Spanglish. I remember the main tractor operator was like, 'You really need to learn Spanish.' In his broken English he told me that, and I was like, 'Yikes, I know.'" Slowly, the language started coming back. "Now it's a running joke that I'm getting better and better every year. I can talk to my crew all day long. We all speak Spanish. If we're speaking English, that's just an off day. Even though my Spanish isn't perfect, I think my team appreciates that I'm giving it my all."

The key to managing a vineyard, Brenae discovered early on, was being flexible and patient, knowing that any combination of opportunities and setbacks is likely to happen. "I don't ever rely on plan A," she says, explaining the series of unforeseen challenges she faced in 2019. "In 2019, nothing really went the way anybody predicted. We started the season early. Generally, the vineyard likes to start active growth at the end of February or the beginning of March, but for two years in a row now, I've had vines growing at the beginning of February, which is a problem." Even though Monte Rosso is a high elevation, southwest-facing, and temperatures don't drop drastically, she has to anticipate cold spells. "This year, I had vines starting to grow and then it snowed for the first time in fifteen years. We had fifty-five inches of rain, twenty-eight of which fell between the beginning of February and May. It was a very condensed season. We were counting the days we could work when it wasn't drizzling or raining." Typically, Brenae prefers to restrict the amount of water the vines receive. Operating at a deficit allows her to control the size of the fruit. But in 2019, she couldn't control the amount of rainfall, and the vines absorbed excess water. "The vineyard was pretty stagnant at first. Then, once we got into June and had our first hot week, everything took off. We had a jungle. Excess rain meant really big clusters and really big berries. At Monte Rosso, I'm looking for a much more concentrated, small to medium berry.

"We always start with plan A, but in farming, if plan A ever comes to fruition, that's a unicorn week. That means we had it all together. That means there was no human error, there were no tractor errors, and the weather played by the rules. Generally, we like plan B, and sometimes we have to go with plan C. This season made me reach for plan C, D, and E."

Listening to Brenae describe her experience at Monte Rosso, it's clear that part of the trick is not letting the obstacles throw you. "It takes a lot to freak me out these days," she says. "Getting into farming was probably the best thing I could do to learn patience because over half of what we're up against is out of our control. Each year, we've got the same task in front of us. We know what's forecast in terms of weather, but what happens may be totally different. I can't control the weather. I can't control breakdowns, and I can't control human error. What I can control is my response. How I respond and continue to grow is what keeps it interesting and allows me to be successful. I don't freak out unless things that are in my control start going out of control."

One thing that was beyond Brenae's control was the fires that raged through Napa and Sonoma in 2017. Described as the most destructive fires in California history to that date, the Northern California firestorm and the Wine Country fires burned 36,807 acres across half a dozen Northern California counties. "We were harvesting the night the fires broke out. The winds were already up to twenty-seven miles per hour. But then the gusts got up to seventy-five miles per hour, and all of our macro bins that we harvest into and weigh ninety-three pounds each, were flying across the yard. There was dirt everywhere. All the straw we'd laid out for erosion control was gone. There were branches in the air. Trees had fallen. Then, later that night the power got shut off. We were watching the Atlas Peak fire in Napa, and then we were watching little brush fires back here along the ridge. I was on the phone with my managers, and they were telling me to get off the mountain, there was nothing I could do. I was trying to see if I could run the sprinklers or something, but they were telling me no, their priority was safety.

"I remember settling into this state before I'd left Monte Rosso that night, where I thought, 'We're fine. The fire isn't going to get here.' I was in such a state of denial that my neighbors called and told me, 'You have to go. There are trees down on Moon Mountain. We have a chain saw and can hop out and cut branches, but you need to go.' Her team evacuated to Petaluma, but Brenae stayed nearby. "I went into the town of Boyes Hot Springs just below us. I came back to the vineyard when the sun came up, and that's when it was apparent I needed to start taking pictures and closing the ranch. The fire was on the ridge a couple of miles north of us. I started thinking we may not come back to the vineyard. I didn't know how long I was going to be gone." She packed up her clothes and her pets and left. Weather maps showed the fire had reached Monte Rosso. "The next day I got a call from a friend who was nearby saying they couldn't see my house anymore." Nine days after Brenae evacuated, the fire department lifted the evacuation order. When she returned, she was surprised to see the randomness with which the fire had burned some rows but not others. "They had bulldozed up Moon Mountain. I was driving around with my jaw dropped." In the end, most of the vineyard was spared. But the ranch had lost power. Fires were still burning nearby, and the smoke made it difficult to breathe. Brenae went to stay with her brother in Sacramento. Eventually, she and her team reassembled and finished the harvest. "We were all traumatized, so it was nice to know we were all safe and had the harvest to focus on."

Like farmers across the country, Brenae uses technology to make her job easier. "Common misperceptions about farmers are that we're out here with a pitchfork, testing the wind with our fingers in the air. I would say farmers are scientists. You're taking so many different variables into consideration, from Mother Nature to grape physiology to wine and phenolics. We work with technology in the fields—tensiometers, which measure the soil's moisture, water mark readers, weather stations. Before 2017, the irrigators and I would be out here turning on different keys, opening and closing valves, and doing night irrigation to avoid water loss during the heat of the day. I haven't woken up at midnight to do irrigation in a while. Now, I control our new water tank and set irrigation schedules with my phone. Before, we'd be out here with an auger looking at soil pits. Now you stick a probe in the ground and call it good."

You don't see many pickup trucks in Sonoma, despite it being an agricultural community, and of those you do, it's rare to see a young Black woman behind the wheel. Brenae is used to standing out. "I grew up in the Central Valley, so I became accustomed to that. I was one of two Black girls in FFA. In band, I was one of three. In softball, in tennis—all that." Still, she looks forward to the day when the wine industry will be more diverse and inclusive. "Back in 2013, when I started, I didn't see many other Black people in my immediate vicinity in the industry. This is such a cliché thing to say and I'm tired of it, but I felt like a unicorn. There was a moment in 2015 when I realized that even though me and my male counterparts had the same experiences and the same interactions, we didn't have the same actual lived experiences. I could be the same level or higher with everyone else in the room, but I got approached as the secretary or a marketer. I never got that from my peers here at Gallo; it was always vendors or people who didn't expect to see me there. And even when it came as a compliment, it was always like, 'Wow, you're Black, you're a woman, you're attractive, you're young,' and I'd think, 'Cool. But none of those things got me my job.' Then, fast-forward to today. I get recognized because I'm a Black woman, and I'm in vineyard management. I think I'm one of five Black women in the United States farming vineyards. There's a lot of power in that, and I'm very proud of it.

"I've always been outspoken. I've always put my opinion out there. I knew that I was already standing out and I needed to use that to my advantage, especially when it comes to leading the way for Black women in agriculture. I want to say to any Black person thinking of joining the industry to recognize that they are going to stand out, but don't look at that as a negative thing. Use that to your advantage because you've got the same qualifications to do your job well. You've worked just as hard to be where you are. There's going to be a day when you look around and realize half the room looks like you or relates to you in some way. We don't have a whole lot of that right now. But I will say that with the power of social media and more people shining a light on people of color in the industry, it's going to be hard to say you're a unicorn in the future."

Eventually, Brenae would like to lead other vineyard managers like herself, but for now, she is content to continue managing Monte Rosso, visit different vineyards, and encourage the next generation of people. "It's a lot of fun. I have to pinch myself from time to time."

Brenae is wrapping up 2019, and in a few weeks she'll start planning 2020. The holidays are around the corner. "There's nothing going on in January," she says. "Everything is pretty quiet. But February is when we'll start to see the sap start to push through the vines. That's your first signal that the vines are waking up and coming out of dormancy." But for now, she'll take time to decompress. "This is my favorite time of the season, when the vines are dormant. You can truly see the architecture of the vines and gauge how the season went. The thing that gets me up in the morning is knowing that I'm farming a grapevine that's going to go to wine and that wine is most likely going to live longer than me. I want the wine to be the best because people are going to be drinking it for years to come. I know for me, whenever I drink wine, I'm thinking about the decisions people made to get there.

"Monte Rosso is a vineyard whose wine speaks to the vineyard site. You can taste all the differences throughout the vineyard regardless if they get blended together or stay single. Growing grapes is a craft. It's an art. You get one shot each year to do it right. Now that the harvest is over, we're all wondering, 'How's next year tasting?' I'll go to Louis M. Martini in January to taste the wines once they've completed fermentation. I'll get to taste all the labor and decisions that went into such a strenuous year. For me, that's a lot. I love that wine is a product that my children might be tasting one day.

"I'm trying to farm for the best wine. You can't do any of that without taking care of the soil first. You can't do any of that without managing how you cultivate the earth. If you're not doing that well, everything else you do is going to be reflective of that. So, to say that I'm managing land to the best of my ability, remaining sustainable, and still providing a commodity fills me with a lot of pride. You can still go back and find wines from the '50s and '60s that are holding up really well. Wine is a living thing. I hope that when people look at the vintages I oversaw, they'll say, 'Okay. She got it. She did it right.'"

By far, the most pressing of . . . [the freedman's] problem as a worker was that of land. This land hunger—this absolutely fundamental and essential thing to any real emancipation of the slaves—was continually pushed by all emancipated Negroes and their representatives in every Southern state.

—W. E. B. DUBOIS, *BLACK RECONSTRUCTION*, 1935

14.

Money Talk

CLIF SUTTON AND DEXTER FAISON

Straw Hat Farms
Turkey, North Carolina

Watching Clif Sutton move around the Straw Hat Farms office, the word that comes to mind is "energy." You can almost see it surging through his limbs as he flips the light switch, adjusts the blinds, hauls extra folding chairs from the back room, and clears the desk. You can feel it in the way he looks directly at you. You can hear it in the rapid-fire way he speaks. He never stops moving. His mind is always going. Just off work, his attire—a crisp dress shirt and slacks—suggests a career in law, banking, or advertising. He drives a Toyota Prius. But spend two minutes with Clif and you quickly discover what's on his mind and in his heart. Agriculture. Business. The future of farming. He named his farm in honor of his grandfather Johnnie Lee Faison, who always wore a straw hat while he worked.

We're still settling in and getting acquainted when the office door swings open and Dexter Faison, Clif's father, steps in. He has a commanding presence and carries himself like a man who is comfortable being in charge, but dressed in shorts, a T-shirt, and a baseball cap, he projects a casual vibe. He takes a seat in the big office chair, which suddenly looks more like a throne.

Watching these men, you can't help but wonder how this father-and-son team manage to work together, how two men who seem to be exact opposites run a successful farming operation. But look closer and you can see the same glint of determination in their eyes, the same hint of amusement in their expressions. When you hear them talk about their lives as farmers, you quickly understand how well they complement each other. For these two, farming is as much about what you learn in the process as what you reap in the end. Passing down expertise and wisdom, and keeping your eyes trained on the future, is as important as what you plant in the ground.

DEXTER FAISON

My dad, Johnnie Faison, was a farmer. He mainly farmed peppers, squash, and cucumbers on about 110 acres, with a two-row tractor and a one-row tractor, and no air-conditioning. We always did our own farming. We never sharecropped. My dad used to say, "We never worked on other people's farms." We never stayed in somebody else's house. My dad was able to do that because he farmed and he had a public job. That's what kept us going. There wasn't a lot of money left, but we ate. I'm the youngest of seven siblings. My father didn't give us an allowance at the end of the week or at the end of the year; we got school clothes.

My daddy showed us there was profit in farming. With my dad, part of our job was to go to the market. When I was a kid, we picked up red peppers and carried them to market on the back of the tractor. You'd get your box of peppers in five minutes and make yourself five dollars—that was money to you. We got a chance to present our produce and see what the product cost. We got a chance to see the real money. That experience gave us a different view. Most farmers never got a chance to go to the market to see the prices and what things sold for. They went to the fields, then they went home. We got to see the money side. My daddy brought his own check home, not Mr. Charlie's check. We saw the whole picture. That made a big difference.

More than owning land, one of my father's and grandfather's main goals was owning their own home. When you get to where you can't work or you're not able to work, you always had to move. If you didn't have anything else of your own, at least once you had your own farm you had a shack of your own. That was the main thing—knowing where you could lay your head. That's what made them more determined to get their own. That's why he told us, 'There's nothing like having your own.' It's not about how many acres you tend, but how many acres you tend right. Don't take a one-thousand-acre farm if you can't handle it. Get one hundred acres and do it right; tend them right, and you're way ahead of the game.

There's a Cost to Everything

When you don't have money, people will charge what they want to charge. You're at the mercy of the court. My sons got a chance to go with me to the farm office. Now they know how to read the maps. They know how to break the money down. A lot of kids haven't gotten that kind of exposure.

My sons got a chance to go to the grain and tobacco market. I told them there's a cost to everything. The main thing is to have something to offer. Get some money in your pocket. Truth be told, if you have money in your pocket, people will treat you different. If you have money in your pocket, people just look at you different. I don't care what color you are—all they'll see is green. That's the way life goes.

Another thing I taught my kids about was their credit. It's as important as making money. Once you've got a bad name, you never erase it. You can get just as much bad credit with a stereo as you can have with a million dollars. A red dot is a red dot. Bad credit is bad credit. These are some of the things I helped my kids realize at a young age. When they went off to college, I told them, do not bother with those credit cards. Start with a Walmart card. Don't borrow that money because it has to be paid back.

It's the same thing with farming. If you use your own money, you can maneuver more. If you borrow money, you've got to show where and how it was spent. If you use your own money, you can cut a deal. The more people who handle your money, the more people who will get a piece of it.

Work Will Never Kill You

I tell the young guys, "Y'all should be working sixteen and resting eight." Most people want to work eight and rest sixteen. If you do the same thing everybody else is doing, you're going to have the same results—and working never hurts nobody. Work will never kill you. Sometimes you've got to push the extra mile. You've got to talk to your body; it'll do what you need it to do because you have a goal on the other end. You're only allotted so much time to get it. When that time is gone, you can't get it back.

Passing the Torch

I've turned everything over to my son. I feel like, at a certain time, I've done all I can do. If I don't use him, use his mind, while he's young, I'm going to carry all my knowledge into the ground with me. Then what have I got? Plus, if I know it all, I have to do it all.

You never see two or three farmers together—that never lasts long. Farming is something that goes according to how you feel—when you're going to get up and when you're going to get through the day; whether you're going to work in the rain or not. It's more like a self thing versus a group thing. You both can't control the situation. It'll bring tension and disagreement. If we're both trying to run the show, we won't last no time because we're both bull-headed. Not everybody can be in the driver's seat. That's why I'm getting in the back seat and letting it ride.

A lot of people are in school for their mama and them. Their parents tell them, "If you don't go to school, you're not going to get this car," but it's not really where they want to be. I never told my kids to go to school. I told my kids to do whatever their hearts desired. You have to find your way. At some point, college is about knowing you're teachable. Once you graduate and get out of there, that's when you get your master's degree—in the real world—that's when you're going to learn something.

When my kids went to school, people said, "Those guys should be helping you work." I said, "No, they shouldn't be helping me work. That's my dream. Let them live out their own dream." When they came to me and said, "Daddy, I think I want to farm," I said, "Are you sure?" They said yes. So I said, "Okay, now's your time."

You have to want to farm. Someone can't make you do it. You can't buy your way into it. If you don't want it, it's over. You have to want this kind of life.

The Long View

You don't have to rush life. You've got to take your time; it'll come to you. You never have to argue over land. Just take what you've got, work with that. I guarantee next year, some more will come up. Farming isn't an overnight process; you do a little bit at a time. Farming is a year-round, twenty-four-hour thing. There aren't certain times. If you want it bad enough, you'll find a way. That's the way it works. You have to walk your way up through life. You do it right, you'll draw people's attention.

CLIF SUTTON

My dad paid us to work. We didn't get adult pay, but we got paid. I'm good with money, and I always liked numbers. When I was in elementary school, I had a $100 bill. My friends thought it was Monopoly money.

I went to North Carolina A&T and majored in agriculture education. After graduation, I was an extension agent for two years. I worked in three counties. My job was [as] a small farms management agent. We realized that people were out of the system—they were great farmers, but there were certain things they weren't privy to. We helped them innovate, transition, and find new crops. We helped them with production and management practices. For the last ten years, I've worked as an agriculture marketing specialist.

Financial Literacy

Most farmers don't have full financial literacy of the agriculture industry. They only know the check they received from the crops sold as the grower. They didn't follow the food chain. If you don't know all the steps in the food chain, you're missing the money.

We've still got farmers now who don't have crop insurance. They don't enroll in government programs, file business taxes or a Schedule F. As much as you say the information is there, if you're not in that circle or you haven't been invited in, what good does that do you? That's the advantage of financial literacy of agriculture. People think about farming, but they don't think about it from a business perspective. You have to know about credit and interest rates, what drives the markets, and other things that affect what you get paid.

There's a system that has kept Black farmers a certain way. A lot of people farmed full-time. They didn't have something to fall back on. They didn't have the extra revenue that relieved some of the financial burden. My family has always worked for ourselves and had other income. That's what has helped us have a different mindset about the industry around us.

Smart Money

I bought a tractor that lights up the fields, so if I have to run it, I can run it all night. I can run it until 2:00 a.m. if I have to. It doesn't take long now with the equipment we have. You have all the amenities and comforts you want. It's like you're driving a Cadillac through the fields.

When you go to an equipment sale and you have money, you can buy something cheaper. When you have to have a loan, the bank will only approve you for so much. A little bit of cash will go longer. But you have to know the cost. Let's say I was going to finance something. I know how much the payment is going to be. I know how many acres I'm going to farm. I divide that by the cost, and that's my price per acre. If you don't have that calculation in your cash flow, you don't buy it. Even if it is a good deal. You can't afford it.

Equipment is subjective to who needs it. It may be worth $500 to me, but it might be worth $5,000 to you. You have to know the sale environment—when to buy. Everybody has a smartphone now. If you see a tractor you want, you can pull up the price while you're bidding. You can see the average price in your area, so you know when to get out of bidding. It's all about doing the research and having the financial freedom to wait and seek the deal. Keeping your equipment cost low is a major key to staying out of the red.

The Future of Farming

Some people just want to grow their own food. Some people have found their family history in agriculture. They've researched their family history and discovered that their great-grandfather owned a ten-acre farm. A lot of people have seen documentaries or shows like *Queen Sugar*, so exposure has brought people back to farming. Some of these young folks are making a lot of money in other industries in other parts of the country. Once you have made a lot of money, you can do what you really have an interest in. Those folks can come back down south and buy some farmland and afford to start a farm.

But farming isn't built to start from scratch—to buy land, to buy a tractor, and pay for labor—it's designed to start generationally. The system is designed and priced for certain folks to thrive. The farmer who didn't have to purchase or rent land, buy new equipment, or hire outside labor will have a financial advantage over anyone else. Think about the advantage the Homestead Act gave those recipients over people who had to pay full price for land.

There is a difference between the young people who make it and the young people who don't. Farming is a culture—Black or white, it's a culture. You have to know the culture and the lingo and the lifestyle. The young people who come and seek the culture, who understand the culture, they'll survive. It'll be slow: they might start with a backyard garden, then they'll go to a half-acre, then an acre. Before you know it, they have a booming roadside stand or a whole business. Once they understand that, those are the young people who stay.

Some people figure out they just want to be landowners and rent their land. If you look up small farming on YouTube, you'll see ten to fifteen videos that say you can make $100,000 off an acre. You can, but what they're not telling you is that's a specific market and there's no more room for you in it. They've made it because they understand that market, but how many more heads of romaine lettuce can that market hold that pays that premium? You might make $30,000—which is a very great profit from an acre or two—but you're not going to make $100,000. I see young people who come to farming, but whether they stay is yet to be determined.

Let's say you have two scenarios. You have a young person who has worked for Facebook. They have a pocket full of money. They come and they want to be farmers. Then you have someone who doesn't have a lot of money. What advice would you give each of them?

My advice is the same. My first question is, How much work do you really want to do? What you see on YouTube or on a documentary is only a small glimpse. My second question is, When do you normally take vacation? If you're a person who says, "I've got to go to the beach on this holiday," I'm telling you right now, your crops and profits don't wait on you. A summer crop is not for you. If you're a person who likes to vacation all summer, maybe you need an indoor operation where you can grow in greenhouses in the wintertime. That may be your fit. There are a lot of personal questions you have to answer. You have to understand the lifestyle. The person without the money is easier to work with—I can teach you how to get money—but a fool with money is a harder conversation.

If you want to farm, there's a way you can do it. But it's a question of how many hours do you want to work? What social events are you willing to miss? You're not going to the club tonight. It's a lifestyle question. If you're a person who likes to socialize and party, you need to find a way to do that, and it means you might not be growing crops. You might be an organizer or a community person in agriculture. Or you might want to work for a nonprofit. Or you might want to work on a farm or be a wholesaler or marketer. Most likely, that person just wants to be in agri*culture*. They want to be in *the culture*. They've seen the money in farming first, but they haven't seen the other part—the marketing, the advertising, the irrigation, the distribution, the failed crops, the hurricanes, the equipment failures, etc. Nobody talks to them about the lifestyle. You most definitely need vacation time, otherwise you'll burn out.

Legacy

I have siblings, but I'm the only one who is farming. This was my dream. This is a generational thing. My thing is to own land. If you own land, you have the ability to go out of the industry and assess when to come back in. You can always sell a tractor and buy another one; they make tractors every day. But you can never get land back. If I have kids, they can go out and do whatever they want to, and if they decided to come back to farming, they won't have the land argument. The land will be there. Owning land gives you an exit and a reentry. We'll accumulate more; we'll add more land, buy more land. Whoever comes behind me will take the land my dad has and the land I bought and the land my brother bought. That's the other advantage of it being generational. We'll keep adding. One day, my kids will say, "My granddaddy had this much land, my dad has more than my granddaddy has, I have more than my dad." The land will be there.

15.

Barking

BY LENARD D. MOORE

Now it's twilight, I walk
the boundaries of the farmstead,
caught in snowflakes.
A sudden bark echoes and echoes again
In the distance. And still,
groping toward that voice,

I come to a splintered barn
that leans beside a dried pond.
This is where the hacked-down trees
lie in ferns, leafless
and slender like beanpoles.
So I stop here, then see the ruins
of the stables. I close my eyes.
This reminds me of my grandfather
who worked the farm from dawn to dusk;
and it was always summer.
At the edge of the starlit woods
and standing still like a statue,
I think: even now, I cannot walk
from this farm of my dream.

16.

*D*ispossessed: Their Family Bought Land One Generation After Slavery. The Reels Brothers Spent Eight Years in Jail for Refusing to Leave It

BY LIZZIE PRESSER

In the spring of 2011, the brothers Melvin Davis and Licurtis Reels were the talk of Carteret County, on the central coast of North Carolina. Some people said that the brothers were righteous; others thought that they had lost their minds. That March, Melvin and Licurtis stood in court and refused to leave the land that they had lived on all their lives, a portion of which had, without their knowledge or consent, been

sold to developers years before. The brothers were among dozens of Reels family members who considered the land theirs, but Melvin and Licurtis had a particular stake in it. Melvin, who was 64, with loose black curls combed into a ponytail, ran a club there and lived in an apartment above it. He'd established a career shrimping in the river that bordered the land, and his sense of self was tied to the water. Licurtis, who was 53, had spent years building a house near the river's edge, just steps from his mother's.

Their great-grandfather had bought the land a hundred years earlier, when he was a generation removed from slavery. The property—65 marshy acres that ran along Silver Dollar Road, from the woods to the river's sandy shore—was racked by storms. Some called it the bottom, or the end of the world. Melvin and Licurtis's grandfather Mitchell Reels was a deacon; he farmed watermelons, beets and peas, and raised chickens and hogs. Churches held tent revivals on the waterfront, and kids played in the river, a prime spot for catching red-tailed shrimp and crabs bigger than shoes. During the later years of racial-segregation laws, the land was home to the only beach in the county that welcomed Black families. "It's our own little Black country club," Melvin and Licurtis' sister Mamie liked to say. In 1970, when Mitchell died, he had one final wish. "Whatever you do," he told his family on the night that he passed away, "don't let the white man have the land."

Mitchell didn't trust the courts, so he didn't leave a will. Instead, he let the land become heirs' property, a form of ownership in which descendants inherit an interest, like holding stock in a company. The practice began during Reconstruction, when many African Americans didn't have access to the legal system, and it continued through the Jim Crow era, when Black communities were suspicious of white Southern courts. In the United States today, 76% of African Americans do not have a will, more than twice the percentage of white Americans.

Many assume that not having a will keeps land in the family. In reality, it jeopardizes ownership. David Dietrich, a former co-chair of the American Bar Association's Property Preservation Task Force, has called heirs' property "the worst problem you never heard of." The US Department of Agriculture has recognized it as "the leading cause of Black involuntary land loss." Heirs' property is estimated to make up more than a third of Southern Black-owned land—3.5 million acres, worth more than $28 billion. These landowners are vulnerable to laws and loopholes that allow speculators and developers to acquire their property. Black families watch as their land is auctioned on courthouse steps or forced into a sale against their will.

Between 1910 and 1997, African Americans lost about 90% of their farmland. This problem is a major contributor to America's racial wealth gap; the median wealth among Black families is about a tenth that of white families. Now, as reparations have become a subject of national debate, the issue of Black land loss is receiving renewed attention. A group of economists and statisticians recently calculated that, since 1910, Black families have been stripped of hundreds of billions of dollars because of lost land. Nathan Rosenberg, a lawyer and a researcher in the group, told me, "If you want to understand wealth and inequality in this country, you have to understand Black land loss."

By the time of Melvin and Licurtis' hearing in 2011, they had spent decades fighting to keep the waterfront on Silver Dollar Road. They'd been warned that they would go to jail if they didn't comply with a court order to stay off the land, and they felt betrayed by the laws that had allowed it to be taken from them. They had been baptized in that water. "You going to go there, take my dreams from me like that?" Licurtis asked on the stand. "How about it was you?"

They expected to argue their case in court that day. Instead, the judge ordered them sent to jail, for civil contempt. Hearing the ruling, Melvin handed his 83-year-old mother, Gertrude, his flip phone and his gold watch. As the eldest son, he had promised relatives that he would assume responsibility for the family. "I can take it," he said. Licurtis looked at the floor and shook his head. He had thought he'd be home by the afternoon; he'd even left his house unlocked. The bailiff, who had never booked anyone in civil superior court, had only one set of handcuffs. She put a cuff on each brother's wrist, and led them out the back door. The brothers hadn't been charged with a crime or given a jury trial. Still, they believed so strongly in their right to the property that they spent the next eight years fighting the case from jail, becoming two of the longest-serving inmates for civil contempt in US history.

Land was an ideological priority for Black families after the Civil War, when nearly 4 million people were freed from slavery. On Jan. 12, 1865, just before emancipation, the Union Army Gen. William Tecumseh Sherman met with 20 Black ministers in Savannah, Georgia, and asked them what they needed. "The way we can best take care of ourselves is to have land," their spokesperson, the Rev. Garrison Frazier, told Sherman. Freedom, he said, was "placing us where we could reap the fruit of our own labor." Sherman issued a special field order declaring that 400,000 acres formerly held by Confederates be given to African Americans—what came to be known as the promise of "40 acres and a mule." The following year, Congress passed the Southern Homestead Act, opening up an additional 46 million acres of public land for Union supporters and freed people.

The promises never materialized. In 1876, near the end of Reconstruction, only about 5% of Black families in the Deep South owned land. But a new group of Black landowners soon established themselves. Many had experience in the fields, and they began buying farms, often in places with arid or swampy soil, especially along the coast. By 1920, African Americans, who made up 10% of the population, represented 14% of Southern farm owners.

A white-supremacist backlash spread across the South. At the end of the 19th century, members of a movement who called themselves Whitecaps, led by poor white farmers, accosted Black landowners at night, beating them or threatening murder if they didn't abandon their homes. In Lincoln County, Mississippi, Whitecaps killed a man named Henry List, and more than 50 African Americans fled the town in a single day. Over two months in 1912, violent white mobs in Forsyth County, Georgia, drove out almost the entire Black population—more than a thousand people. Ray Winbush, the director of the Institute for Urban Research, at Morgan State University, told me, "There is this idea that most Blacks were lynched because they did something untoward to a young woman. That's not true. Most Black men were lynched between 1890 and 1920 because whites wanted their land."

By the second half of the 20th century, a new form of dispossession had emerged, officially sanctioned by the courts and targeting heirs' property owners without clear titles. These landowners are exposed in a variety of ways. They don't qualify for certain Department of Agriculture loans to purchase livestock or cover the cost of planting. Individual heirs can't use their land as collateral with banks and other institutions, and so are denied private financing and federal home-improvement loans. They generally aren't eligible for disaster relief. In 2005, Hurricane Katrina laid bare the extent of the problem in New Orleans, where 25,000 families who applied for rebuilding grants had heirs' property. One Louisiana real-estate attorney estimated that up to $165 million of recovery funds were never claimed because of title issues.

Heirs are rarely aware of the tenuous nature of their ownership. Even when they are, clearing a title is often an unaffordable and complex process, which requires tracking down every living heir, and there are few lawyers who specialize in the field. Nonprofits often pick up the slack. The Center for Heirs' Property Preservation, in South Carolina, has cleared more than two hundred titles in the past decade, almost all of them for African-American families, protecting land valued at nearly $14 million. Josh Walden, the center's chief operating officer, told me that it had mapped out a hundred thousand acres of heirs' property in South Carolina. He said that investors hoping to build golf courses or hotels can target these plots. "We had to be really mindful that we didn't share those maps with anyone, because otherwise they'd be a shopping catalogue," he told me. "And it's not as if it dries up. New heirs' property is being created every day."

Through interviews and courthouse records, I analyzed more than three dozen cases from recent years in which heirs' property owners lost land—land that, for many of them, was not only their sole asset but also a critical part of their heritage and their sense of home. The problem has been especially acute in Carteret County. Beaufort, the county seat, was once the site of a major refugee camp for freed people. Black families eventually built homes near where the tents had stood. But in the 1970s the town became a tourist destination, with upscale restaurants, boutiques, and docks for yachts. Real-estate values surged, and out-of-town speculators flooded the county. David Cecelski, a historian of the North Carolina coast, told me, "You can't talk to an African-American family who owned land in those counties and *not* find a story where they feel like land was taken from them against their will, through legal trickery."

Beaufort is a quaint town, lined with coastal cottages and Colonial homes. When I arrived, last fall, I drove 20 miles to Silver Dollar Road, where Melvin and Licurtis' family lives in dozens of trailers and wood-panelled houses, scattered under pine and gum trees.

Melvin and Licurtis' mother, Gertrude, greeted me at her house and led me into her living room, where porcelain angels lined one wall. Gertrude is tough and quiet, her high voice muffled by tobacco that she packs into her cheek. People call her Mrs. Big Shit. "It's because I didn't pay them no mind," she told me. The last of Mitchell Reels's children to remain on the property, she is the family matriarch. Grandchildren, nieces, and nephews let themselves into her house to pick up mail or take out her trash. Around dinnertime on the day I was there, the trickle of visitors turned into a crowd. Gertrude went into the kitchen, coated fish fillets with cornmeal, and fried them for everyone.

Her daughter Mamie told me that Melvin and Licurtis had revelled in the land as kids, playing among the inky eels and conch shells. In the evenings, the brothers would sit on the porch with their cousins, a rag burning to keep the mosquitoes away. On weekends, a pastor strode down the dirt street, robed in white, his congregants singing "Wade in the Water." Licurtis was a shy, humble kid who liked working in the cornfields. Melvin was his opposite. "When the school bus showed up, when he come home, the crowd would come with him and stay all night," Gertrude said. When Melvin was 9, he built a boat from pine planks and began tugging it along the shore. A neighbor offered to teach him how to shrimp, and, in the summer, Melvin dropped nets off the man's trawler. He left school in the 10th grade; his catch was bringing in around a thousand dollars a week. He developed a taste for sleek cars, big jewelry and women, and started buying his siblings Chuck Taylors and Timberlands.

Gertrude was the administrator of the estate. She'd left school in the eighth grade and wasn't accustomed to navigating the judicial system, but after Mitchell's death she secured a court ruling declaring that the land belonged to his heirs. The judgment read, "The surviving eleven (11) children or descendants of children of Mitchell Reels are the owners of the lands exclusive of any other claim of any one."

In 1978, Gertrude's uncle Shedrick Reels tried to carve out for himself the most valuable slice of land, on the river. He used a legal doctrine called adverse possession, which required him to prove that he had occupied the waterfront for years, continuously and publicly, against the owners' wishes. Shedrick, who went by Shade and worked as a tire salesman in New Jersey, hadn't lived on Silver Dollar Road in 27 years. But he claimed that "tenants" had stood in for him—he had built a house on the waterfront in 1950, and relatives had rented it or run it as a club at various times since. Some figured that it was Shade's land. He also produced a deed that his father,

Elijah, had given him in 1950, even though Mitchell, another of Elijah's sons, had owned the land at the time.

Shade made his argument through an obscure law called the Torrens Act. Under Torrens, Shade didn't have to abide by the formal rules of a court. Instead, he could simply prove adverse possession to a lawyer, whom the court appointed, and whom he paid. The Torrens Act has long had a bad reputation, especially in Carteret. "It's a legal way to steal land," Theodore Barnes, a land broker there, told me. The law was intended to help clear up muddled titles, but, in 1932, a law professor at the University of North Carolina found that it had been co-opted by big business. One lawyer said that people saw it as a scheme "whereby rich men could seize the lands of the poor." Even Shade's lawyer, Nelson Taylor, acknowledged that it was abused; he told me that his own grandfather had lost a 50-acre plot to Torrens. "First time he knew anything about it was when somebody told him that he didn't own it anymore," Taylor said. "That was happening more often than it ever should have."

Mitchell's kids and grandkids were puzzled that Shade's maneuver was legal—they had Mitchell's deed and a court order declaring that the land was theirs. And they had all grown up on that waterfront. "How can they take this land from us and we on it?" Melvin said. "We been there all our days." Gertrude's brother Calvin, who handled legal matters for the family, hired Claud Wheatly III, the son of one of the most powerful lawyers in town, to represent the siblings at a Torrens hearing about the claim. Gertrude, Melvin and his cousin Ralphele Reels, the only surviving heirs who attended the hearing, said that they left confident that the waterfront hadn't gone to Shade. "No one in the family thought at the end of the day that it was his land and we were going to walk away from it forever," Ralphele told me.

Wheatly told me a different story. In his memory, the Torrens hearing was chaotic, but the heirs agreed to give Shade, who has since died, the waterfront. When I pressed Wheatly, he conceded that not all the heirs liked the outcome, but he said that Calvin had consented. "I would have been upset if Calvin had not notified them, because I generally don't get involved in those things without having a family representative in charge," he told me. He said that he never had a written agreement with Calvin—just a conversation. (Calvin died shortly after the hearing.) The lawyer examining Shade's case granted him the waterfront, and Wheatly signed off on the decision. The Reels family, though it didn't yet know it, had lost the rights to the land on the shoreline.

Licurtis had set up a trailer near the river a couple of years earlier, in 1977. He was working as a brick mason and often hosted men from the neighborhood for Budweiser and beans in the evenings. Melvin had become the center of a local economy on the shore. He taught the men how to work the water, and he paid the women to prepare his catch, pressing the soft crevice above the shrimps' eyes and popping off their heads. He had a son, Little Melvin, and in the summers his nephews and cousins came to the beach, too. One morning, he took eight of them out on the water and then announced that he'd made a mistake: only four were allowed on the boat. He threw them overboard one by one. "We're thinking, We're gonna drown," one cousin told me. "And he jumps off the boat with us and teaches us how to swim."

In 1982, Melvin and Gertrude received a trespassing notice from Shade. They took it to a lawyer, who informed them that Shade now legally owned a little more than 13 acres of the 65-acre plot. The family was stunned, and suspicious of the claim's validity. Many of the tenants listed to prove Shade's continuous possession were vague or unrecognizable, like "Mitchell Reels's boy," or "Julian Leonard," whom Gertrude had never heard of. (She had a sister named Julia and a brother named Leonard but no memory of either one living on the waterfront.) The lawyer who granted the land to Shade had also never reported the original court ruling that Gertrude had won, as he should have done.

Shade's ownership would be almost impossible to overturn. There's a one-year window to appeal a Torrens decision in North Carolina, and the family had missed it by two years. Soon afterward, Shade sold the land to developers.

The Reelses knew that if condos or a marina were built on the waterfront the remaining 50 acres of Silver Dollar Road could be taxed not as small homes on swampy fields but as a high-end resort. If they fell behind on the higher taxes, the county could auction off their property. "It would break our family right up," Melvin told me. "You leave here, you got no more freedom."

This kind of tax sale has a long history in the dispossession of heirs' property owners. In 1992, the NAACP accused local officials of intentionally inflating taxes to push out Black families on Daufuskie, a South Carolina sea island that has become one of the hottest real-estate markets on the Atlantic coast. Property taxes had gone up as much as 700% in a single decade. "It is clear that the county has pursued a pattern of conduct that disproportionately displaces or evicts African-Americans from Daufuskie, thereby segregating the island and the county as a whole," the NAACP wrote to county officials. Nearby Hilton Head, which as recently as two decades ago comprised several thousand acres of heirs' property, now, by one esti-mate, has a mere 200 such acres left. Investors fly into the county each October to bid on tax-delinquent properties in a local gymnasium.

In the upscale town of Summerville, South Carolina, I met Wendy Reed, who, in 2012, was late paying $83.81 in taxes on the lot she had lived on for nearly four decades. A former state politician named Thomas Limehouse, who owned a luxury hotel nearby, bought Reed's property at a tax sale for $2,000, about an eighth of its value. Reed had a year to redeem her property, but, when she tried to pay her debt, officials told her that she couldn't get the land back, because she wasn't officially listed as her grandmother's heir; she'd have to go through probate court. Here she faced another obstacle: heirs in South Carolina have 10 years to probate an estate after the death of the owner, and Reed's grandmother had died 30 years before. Tax clerks in the county estimate that each year they send about a quarter of the people who try to redeem delinquent property to probate court because they aren't listed on the deed or named by the court as an heir. Limehouse told me, "To not probate the estate and not pay the taxes shouldn't be a reason for special dispensation. When you let things go, you can't blame the county." Reed has been fighting the case in court since 2014. "I'm still not leaving," she told me. "You'll have to pack my stuff and put me off."

For years, the conflict on Silver Dollar Road was dormant, and Melvin continued expanding his businesses. Each week, Gertrude packed two-pound bags of shrimp to sell at the farmers' market, along with petunias and gardenias from her yard. Melvin was also remodeling a night club, Fantasy Island, on the shore. He'd decked it out with disco lights and painted it white, he said, so that "on the water it would shine like gold."

The majority of the property remained in the family, including the land on which Gertrude's house stood. But Licurtis had been building a home in place of his trailer on the contested waterfront. "It was the most pretty spot," he told me. "I'd walk to the water, and look at my yard, and see how beautiful it was." He'd collected the signatures of other heirs to prove that he had permission, and registered a deed.

When real-estate agents or speculators came to the shore, Melvin tried to scare them away. A developer told me that once, when he showed the property to potential buyers, "Melvin had a roof rack behind his pickup, jumped out, snatched a gun out." It wasn't the only time that Melvin took out his rifle. "You show people that you got to protect yourself," he told me. "Any fool who wouldn't do that would be crazy." His instinct had always been to confront a crisis head on. When hurricanes came through and most people sought higher ground, he'd go out to his trawler and steer it into the storm.

The Reels family began to believe that there was a conspiracy against them. They watched Jet Skis crawl slowly past in the river and shiny SUVs drive down Silver Dollar Road; they suspected that people were scouting the property. Melvin said that he received phone calls from mysterious men issuing threats. "I thought people were out to get me," he said. Gertrude remembers that, one day at the farmers' market, a white customer sneered that she was the only thing standing in the way of development.

In 1986, Billie Dean Brown, a partner at a real-estate investment company called Adams Creek Associates, had bought Shade's waterfront plot sight unseen to divide and sell. Brown was attracted to the strength of the Torrens title, which he knew was effectively incontrovertible. When he discovered that Melvin and Licurtis lived on the property, he wasn't troubled. Brown was known among colleagues as Little Caesar—a small man who finished any job he started. In the early 2000s, he hired a lawyer: Claud Wheatly III. The man once tasked with protecting the Reels family's land was now being paid to evict them from it. Melvin and Licurtis saw Wheatly's involvement as a clear conflict of interest. Their lawyers tried to disqualify Wheatly, arguing that he was breaching confidentiality and switching sides, but the judge denied the motions.

Earlier this year, I met Wheatly in his office, a few blocks from the county courthouse. Tall and imposing, he has a ruddy face and a teal-blue stare. We sat under the head of a stuffed warthog, and he chewed tobacco as we spoke. He told me that he had no confidential information about the Reelses, and that he'd never represented Melvin and Licurtis; he'd represented their mother and her siblings. "Melvin won't own one square inch until his mother dies," he said.

In 2004, Wheatly got a court order prohibiting the brothers from going on the waterfront property. The Reels family began a series of appeals and filings asking for the decree to be set aside, but judge after judge ruled that the family had waited too long to contest the Torrens decision.

Licurtis didn't talk about the case, and tried to hide his stress. But, Mamie told me, "you could see him wearing it." Occasionally, she would catch a glimpse of him pacing the road early in the morning. When he first understood that he could face time in jail for remaining in his house, he tried removing the supports underneath it, thinking that he could hire someone to wrench the foundation from the mud and move it elsewhere. Gertrude wouldn't allow him to go through with it. "You're not going with the house nowhere," she told him. "That's yours."

At 4 a.m. on a spring day in 2007, Melvin was asleep in his apartment above the club when he heard a boom, like a crash of thunder. He went to the shore and found that his trawler, named Nancy J., was sinking. Yellow plastic gloves, canned beans and wooden crab boxes floated in the water. There was a large hole in the hull, and Melvin realized that the boom had been an explosion. He filed a report with the sheriff's office, but it never confirmed whether an explosive was used or whether it was an accident, and no charges were filed. Melvin began to wake with a start at night, pull out his flashlight, and scan the fields for intruders.

By the time of the brothers' hearing in 2011, Melvin had lost so much weight that Licurtis joked that he could store water in the caverns by his collarbones. The family had come to accept that the dispute wasn't going away. If the brothers had to go to jail, they would. Even after the judge in the hearing found them guilty of civil contempt, Melvin said, "I ain't backing down." Licurtis called home later that day. "It'll be all right," he told Gertrude. "We'll be home soon."

One of the most pernicious legal mechanisms used to dispossess heirs' property owners is called a partition action. In the course of generations, heirs tend to disperse and lose any connection to the land. Speculators can buy off the interest of a single heir, and just one heir or speculator, no matter how minute his share, can force the sale of an entire plot through the courts. Andrew Kahrl, an associate professor of history and African-American studies at the University of Virginia, told me that even small financial incentives can have the effect of turning relatives against one another, and developers exploit these divisions. "You need to have some willing participation from Black families—driven by the desire to profit off their land holdings," Kahrl said. "But it does boil down to greed and abuse of power and the way in which Americans' history of racial inequality can be used to the advantage of developers." As the Reels family grew over time, the threat of a partition sale mounted; if one heir decided to sell, the whole property would likely go to auction at a price that none of them could pay.

When courts originally gained the authority to order a partition sale, around the time of the Civil War, the Wisconsin Supreme Court called it "an extraordinary and dangerous power" that should be used sparingly. In the past several decades, many courts have favored such sales, arguing that the value of a property in its entirety is greater than the value of it in pieces. But the sales are often speedy and poorly advertised, and tend to fetch below-market prices.

On the coast of North Carolina, I met Billy Freeman, who grew up working in the parking lot of his uncle's beachside dance hall, Monte Carlo by the Sea. His family, which once owned thousands of acres, ran the largest Black beach in the state, with juke joints and crab shacks, an amusement park and a three-story hotel. But, over the decades, developers acquired interests from other heirs, and, in 2008, one firm petitioned the court for a sale of the whole property. Freeman attempted to fight the partition for years. "I didn't want to lose the land, but I felt like everybody else had sold," he told me. In 2016, the beach, which covered 170 acres, was sold to the development firm for $1.4 million. On neighboring beaches, that sum could buy a tiny fraction of a parcel so large. Freeman got only $30,000.

The lost property isn't just money; it's also identity. In one case that I examined, the mining company PCS Phosphate forced the sale of a 40-acre plot, which contained a family cemetery, against the wishes of several heirs, whose ancestors had been enslaved on the property. (A spokesperson for the company told me that it is a "law-abiding corporate citizen.")

Some speculators use questionable tactics to acquire property. When Jessica Wiggins's uncle called her to say that a man was trying to buy his interest in their family's land, she didn't believe him; he had dementia. Then, in 2015, she learned that a company called Aldonia Farms had purchased the interests of four heirs, including her uncle, and had filed a partition action. "What got me was we had no knowledge of this person," Wiggins told me, of the man who ran Aldonia. (Jonathan S. Phillips, who now runs Aldonia Farms, told me that he wasn't there at the time of the purchase, and that he's confident no one would have taken advantage of the uncle's dementia.) Wiggins was devastated; the 18 acres of woods and farmland that held her great-grandmother's house was the place that she had felt safest as a child. The remaining heirs still owned 61% of the property, but there was little that they could do to prevent a sale. When I visited the land with Wiggins, her great-grandmother's house had been cleared, and Aldonia Farms had erected a gate. Phillips told me, "Our intention was not to keep them out but to be good stewards of the property and keep it from being littered on and vandalized."

Last fall, Wiggins and her relatives gathered for the auction of the property on the courthouse steps in the town of Windsor. A bronze statue of a Confederate soldier stood behind them. Wiggins' cousin Danita Pugh walked up to Aldonia Farms' lawyer and pulled her deed out of an envelope. "You're telling me that they're going to auction it off after showing you a deed?" she said. "I'm going to come out and say it. The white man takes the land from the Black."

Hundreds of partition actions are filed in North Carolina every year. Carteret County, which has a population of 70,000, has one of the highest per-capita rates in the state. I read through every Carteret partition case concerning heirs' property from the past decade, and found that 42% of the cases involved Black families, despite the fact that only 6% of Carteret's population is Black. Heirs not only regularly lose their land; they are also required to pay the legal fees of those who bring the partition cases. In 2008, Janice Dyer, a research associate at Auburn University, published a study of these actions in Macon County, Alabama. She told me that the lack of secure ownership locks Black families out of the wealth in their property. "The Southeast has these amazing natural resources: timber, land, great fishing," she said. "If somebody could snap their fingers and clear up all these titles, how much richer would the region be?"

Thomas W. Mitchell, a property-law professor at Texas A&M University School of Law, has drafted legislation aimed at reforming this system, which has now passed in 14 states. He told me that heirs' property owners, particularly those who are African-American, tend to be "land rich and cash poor," making it difficult for them to keep the land in a sale. "They don't have the resources to make competitive bids, and they can't even use their heirs' property as collateral to get a loan to participate in the bidding more effectively," he said. His law, the Uniform Partition of Heirs Property Act, gives family members the first option to buy, sends most sales to the open market, and mandates that courts, in their decisions to order sales, weigh non-economic factors, such as the consequences of eviction and whether the property has historic value. North Carolina is one of eight states in the South that has held out against these reforms. The state also hasn't repealed the Torrens Act. It is one of fewer than a dozen states where the law is still on the books.

Last year, Congress passed the Agricultural Improvement Act, which, among other things, allows heirs' property owners to apply for Department of Agriculture programs using nontraditional paperwork, such as a written agreement between heirs. "The alternative documentation is really, really important as a precedent," Lorette Picciano, the executive director of Rural Coalition, a group that advocated for the reform, told me. "The next thing we need to do is make sure this happens with FEMA, and flood insurance, and housing programs." The bill also includes a lending program for heirs' property owners, which will make it easier for them to clear titles and develop succession plans. But no federal funding has been allocated for these loans.

The first time I met Melvin and Licurtis in the Carteret jail, Melvin filled the entire frame of the visiting-room window. He is a forceful presence, and prone to exaggeration. His hair, neatly combed, was streaked with silver. He didn't blink as he spoke. Licurtis had been given a diagnosis of diabetes, and leaned against a stool for support. He still acted like a younger brother, never interrupting Melvin or challenging his memory. He told me that, at night, he dreamed of the shore, of storms blowing through his house. "The water rising," Licurtis said. "And I couldn't do nothing about it." He was worried about his mother. "If they took this land from my mama at her age, and she'd been farming it all her life, you know that would kill her," he told me.

The brothers were seen as local heroes for resisting the court order. "They want to break your spirits," their niece Kim Duhon wrote to them. "God had you both picked out for this." Even strangers wrote. "When I was a kid, it used to sadden me that white folks had Radio Island, Atlantic Beach, Sea Gate and other places to swim, but we didn't!" one letter from a local woman read. She wrote that, when she was finally taken to Silver Dollar Road, "I remember seeing nothing but my own kind (Blk Folks!)."

In North Carolina, civil contempt is most commonly used to force defendants to pay child support. When the ruling requires a defendant to pay money other than child support, a new hearing is held every 90 days. After the first 90 days had passed, Melvin asked a friend in jail to write a letter on his behalf. (Melvin couldn't read well, and he needed help writing.) "I've spent 91 days on a 90 day sentence and I don't understand why," the letter read. "Please explain this to me! So I can go home, back to work. Sincerely, Melvin Davis." The brothers learned that although Billie Dean Brown's lawyer had asked for 90 days, the court had decided that there would be no time restriction on their case, and that they could be jailed until they presented evidence that they had removed their homes. They continued to hold out. Brown wasn't demolishing their buildings while they were incarcerated, and so they believed that they still had a shot at convincing the courts that the land was theirs. That fall, Brown told the Charlotte *Observer*, "I made up my mind, I will die and burn in hell before I walk away from this thing." When I reached Brown recently, he told me that he was in an impossible position. "We've had several offers from buyers, but once they learned of the situation they withdrew," he said.

Three months turned into six, and a year turned into several. Jail began to take a toll on the brothers. The facility was designed for short stays, with no time outside, and nowhere to exercise. They couldn't be transferred to a prison, because they hadn't been convicted of a crime. Early on, Melvin mediated fights between inmates and persuaded them to sneak in hair ties for him. But over time he stopped taking care of his appearance and became withdrawn. He ranted about the stolen land, though he couldn't quite nail down who the enemy was: Shade or Wheatly or Brown, the sheriffs or the courts or the county. The brothers slept head to head in neighboring beds. "Melvin would say crazy things," Licurtis told me. "Lay on down and go to sleep, wake up, and say the same thing again. It wore me down." Melvin is proud and guarded, but he told me that the case had broken him. "I'm not ashamed to own it," he said. "This has messed my mind up."

Without the brothers, Silver Dollar Road lost its pulse. Mamie kept her blinds down; she couldn't stand to see the deserted waterfront. At night, she studied her brothers' case, thumbing through the court files and printing out the definitions of words that she didn't understand, like "rescind" and "contempt." She filled a binder with relatives' obituaries, so that once her brothers got out they would have a record of who had passed away. When Claud Wheatly's father died, she added his obituary. "I kept him for history," she told me.

Gertrude didn't have the spirit to farm. Most days, she sat in a tangerine armchair by her window, cracking peanuts or watching the shore like a guard. This winter, we looked out in silence as Brown's caretaker drove through the property. Melvin and Licurtis wouldn't allow Gertrude to visit them in jail. Licurtis said that "it hurt so bad" to see her leave.

Other members of the family—Melvin and Licurtis' brother Billy, their nephew Roderick, and their cousin Shawn—kept trying to shrimp, but the river suddenly seemed barren. "It might sound crazy, but it was like the good Lord put a curse on this little creek, where ain't nobody gonna catch no shrimp until they're released," Roderick told me. Billy added, "It didn't feel right no more with Melvin and them not there, because we all looked out for one another. Some mornings, you didn't even want to go."

Sheriff's deputies came to the property a few times a week, and they wouldn't allow the men to dock their boats on the pier. One by one, the men lost hope and sold their trawlers. Shawn took a job at Best Buy, cleaning the store for $11.50 an hour, and eventually moved to Newport, 30 miles southwest, where it was easier to make rent. Billy got paid to fix roofs but soon defaulted on the mortgage for his house on Silver Dollar Road. "One day you good, and the next day you can't believe it," he told me.

Roderick kept being charged with trespassing, for walking on the waterfront, and he was racking up thousands of dollars in legal fees. He'd recently renovated his boat—putting in an aluminum gas tank, large spotlights and West Marine speakers—but, without a place to dock, he saw no way to hold on to it. He found work cutting grass and posted his boat on Craigslist. A white man responded. They met at the shore, and, as the man paid, Roderick began to cry. He walked up Silver Dollar Road with his back to the river. He told me, "I just didn't want to see my boat leave."

The Reels brothers were locked in a hopeless clash with the law. One judge who heard their case likened them to the Black Knight in "Monty Python and the Holy Grail," who attempts to guard his forest against King Arthur. "Even after King Arthur has cut off both of the Black Knight's arms and legs, he still insists that he will continue to fight and that no one may pass—although he cannot do anything," the judge wrote, in an appeals-court dissent.

In February, nearly eight years after Melvin and Licurtis went to jail, they stood before a judge in Carteret to request their release. They were now 72 and 61, but they remained defiant. Licurtis said that he would go back on the property "just as soon as I walk out of here." Melvin said, "I believe that land is mine." They had hired a new lawyer, who argued that it would cost almost $50,000 to tear down the brothers' homes. Melvin had less than $4,000 in the bank; Licurtis had nothing. The judge announced that he was releasing them. He warned them, however, that if they returned to their homes they'd "be right back in jail." He told them, "The jailhouse keys are in your pockets."

An hour later, the brothers emerged from the sheriff's department. Melvin surveyed the parking lot, which was crowded with friends and relatives. "About time!" he said, laughing and exchanging hugs. "You stuck with me." When he spotted Little Melvin, who was now 39, he extended his arm for a handshake. Little Melvin pulled it closer and buried his face in his father's shoulder, sobbing.

When Licurtis came out, he folded over, as if his breath had been pulled out of him. Mamie wrapped her arms around his neck, led him to her car, and drove him home. When they reached Silver Dollar Road, she honked the horn all the way down the street. "Back on Silver Dollar Road," Licurtis said, pines flickering by his window. "Mm-mm-mm-mm-mm."

Melvin spent his first afternoon shopping for silk shirts and brown leather shoes and a cell phone that talked to him. Old acquaintances stopped him—a man who thanked him for his advice about hauling dirt, a DJ who used to spin at Fantasy

Island. While in jail, Melvin had been keeping up with his girlfriends, and 11 women called looking for him.

Melvin told me that he'd held on for his family, and for himself, too. But away from the others his weariness showed. He acknowledged that he was worried about what would happen, his voice almost a whisper. "They can't keep on doing this. There's got to be an ending somewhere," he said.

A few days later, Gertrude threw her sons a party, and generations of relatives came. The family squeezed together on her armchairs, eating chili and biscuits and lemon pie. Mamie gave a speech. "We gotta get this water back," she said, stretching her arms wide. "We gotta unite. A chain's only as strong as the links in it." The room answered, "That's right." The brothers, who were staying with their mother, kept saying, "Once we get this land stuff sorted out . . ." Relatives who had left talked about coming back, buying boats and go-karts for their kids. It was less a plan than a fantasy—an illusion that their sense of justice could overturn the decision of the law.

The brothers hadn't stepped onto the waterfront since they'd been back. The tract was 100 feet away but out of reach. Fantasy Island was a shell, the plot around it overgrown. Still, Melvin seemed convinced that he would restore it. "Put me some palm trees in the sand and build some picnic tables," he said.

After the party wound down, I sat with Licurtis on his mother's porch as he gazed at his house, which was moldy and gutted, its frame just visible in the purple dusk. He reminisced about the house's wood-burning heater, the radio that he'd always left playing. He said that he planned to build a second story and raise the house to protect it from floods. He wanted a wraparound deck and big windows. "I'll pour them walls solid all the way around," he said. "We'll bloom again. Ain't going to be long."

This essay was originally published by ProPublica on July 15, 2019.

IN THE FIELD, SAVANNAH, GEORGIA, JANUARY 16TH, 1865. SPECIAL FIELD ORDERS, NO. 15.

III. Whenever three respectable negroes, heads of families, shall desire to settle on land, and shall have selected for that purpose an island or a locality clearly defined, within the limits above designated, the Inspector of Settlements and Plantations will himself, or by such subordinate officer as he may appoint, give them a license to settle such island or district, and afford them such assistance as he can to enable them to establish a peaceable agricultural settlement. The three parties named will subdivide the land, under the supervision of the Inspector, among themselves and such others as may choose to settle near them, so that each family shall have a plot of not more than (40) forty acres of tillable ground, and when it borders on some water channel, with not more than 800 feet water front, in the possession of which land the military authorities will afford them protection, until such time as they can protect themselves, or until Congress shall regulate their title. The Quartermaster may, on the requisition of the Inspector of Settlements and Plantations, place at the disposal of the Inspector, one or more of the captured steamers, to ply between the settlements and one or more of the commercial points heretofore named in orders, to afford the settlers the opportunity to supply their necessary wants, and to sell the products of their land and labor.

—GENERAL WILLIAM TECUMSEH SHERMAN

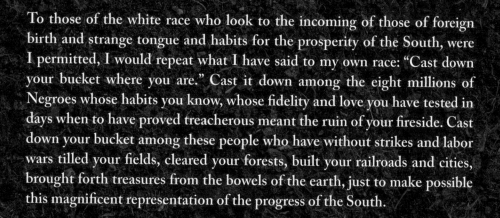

To those of the white race who look to the incoming of those of foreign birth and strange tongue and habits for the prosperity of the South, were I permitted, I would repeat what I have said to my own race: "Cast down your bucket where you are." Cast it down among the eight millions of Negroes whose habits you know, whose fidelity and love you have tested in days when to have proved treacherous meant the ruin of your fireside. Cast down your bucket among these people who have without strikes and labor wars tilled your fields, cleared your forests, built your railroads and cities, brought forth treasures from the bowels of the earth, just to make possible this magnificent representation of the progress of the South.

—BOOKER T. WASHINGTON, 1895, SPEECH BEFORE
THE COTTON STATES AND INTERNATIONAL
EXPOSITION IN ATLANTA, GEORGIA

17.

*L*ouisiana Daughters: A Conversation

LALITA TADEMY AND MARGARET WILKERSON SEXTON
Oakland, California

On a cool fall morning, authors Lalita Tademy and Margaret Wilkerson Sexton sat down with me for an honest conversation about being Black women, the writing life, and our relationship to the South. We were three novelists, all Bay Area residents with a connection to Louisiana. Lalita Tademy is the author of the bestselling historical novel and Oprah Book Club selection *Cane River*, which she followed with *Red River* and *Citizens Creek*. Margaret Wilkerson Sexton's debut novel, *A Kind of Freedom*, was nominated for a National Book Award. She has published essays in Oprah.com, *Lenny Letter*, *The Massachusetts Review*, and elsewhere. Her recent novel *The Revisioners* was released in October 2019.

NB: Let's start with you telling me about your connection to Louisiana and how you became a writer.

MWS: I grew up in New Orleans, but I moved to Connecticut with my mother when I was twelve. My father stayed in New Orleans. I went back to New Orleans for every holiday, and I spent every summer there. I never lost that affiliation with the city.

I was a day student at a boarding school in Connecticut for high school. My teachers were very supportive. For instance, my junior year I didn't want to take a science class, and they said, "Do an independent study project," and I ended up writing a book which my mom still has. I think the empowerment of writing a book at that age and having people support me made a big difference. I wrote in college, then I took two years and traveled and worked at Google. I didn't write at all.

But really, it was my mom. She is amazing at picking out people's gifts and nurturing them. She believed it was totally legitimate to dream of becoming writer. My mom cried when I decided to go to law school. I went because I thought being a writer wasn't realistic. I thought, "My dad was a lawyer, I'll be a lawyer. It's basically the same thing [as being a writer]."

But my mom was devastated. She said, "That's not your thing. Why would you do that?" She actually believed I would be more successful as a writer—she meant financially, too. She really believed that, and she still does.

NB: *Who is your mother?*

LT: Get her in here!

NB: Honestly! I'm shocked. I can't tell you how unusual that is—especially from a Black parent. So many Black families, understandably, would say, "Oh, no. Law school is a great decision."

MWS: It's crazy. I know. And she's not a privileged person. That's how she's always been. I needed her as a mother or I wouldn't have been able to do this. My father's side of the family is completely different. They're totally risk averse. If I'd grown up with just my father, I never would have had the courage to leave my job.

NB: I often feel this ambivalence when I speak to young writers and encourage them to pursue their passion, especially when the economy is uncertain. It's hard to tell people, "Take that leap! Do that thing that wakes you up in the morning," when I know many are getting pressure from their families to make the safer choice.

MWS: I don't know that before today I've ever shared just how influential my mother has been.

NB: When you were practicing law, were you writing on the side?

MWS: I was really into the fact that I worked at a firm. I got a lot of empowerment from that. I'd started a book in 2005, and my mom would call me all the time and ask, "How's your book coming?" I'd get so irritated.

I practiced law for two years, but then it became clear that my firm didn't have enough work. They didn't want people to know they were going through hard times, so they started offering severance packages. I took the package before they went bankrupt. I didn't know what I wanted to do. I thought about trying out psychology, but I didn't want to get another degree. So, I thought, let's just try this writing thing. I finished the book I'd started in 2005, but I couldn't get it published. I had hundreds of rejections from agents. No joke. *Hundreds.* Then I met a woman who ended up being my editor. She encouraged me to write a different book. That's when I wrote *A Kind of Freedom*, which was set in New Orleans. I wrote it in six months. It just flowed. I couldn't believe it.

NB AND LT: [*laugh*] Six months!

NB: Lita, what made you decide to take the leap?

LT: I didn't grow up thinking I was going to be a writer. All along, teachers said I needed to be a writer, but to me that was total and complete foolishness because there was no money in it. I had no interest in anything that wasn't going to further my objective of being independent and taking care of my family. I had a twenty-year career in high tech, ending up as an executive in Silicon Valley.

I was piddling around with genealogy on the side, following people and people's stories, going back to where both of my parents were born in the little town of Colfax, Louisiana, which is very close to Cane River. That's where we spent the summers when I was a kid. We would drive from Berkeley, California, to Colfax. It's not that I loved Colfax, because I didn't. It was very clearly the mood of the town, the people, and a way of being that was so very different from anything I'd encountered in California. My life there was mostly among white folks in Castro Valley—that was one way of being, and then there was another way of being in Louisiana, in a community on the "wrong side of the tracks." It was fascinating to me. I didn't want to live there, or even go back a lot, but it was still fascinating and unique.

I tucked all that away, and I had an entire career in business—from getting my MBA to climbing the corporate ladder. My parents, especially my mother, were so proud because climbing the corporate ladder, which they didn't even understand, was their fantasy. They said, "We got her educated, and look what she's done." So, my experience was exactly the opposite of Margaret's.

My first book was about our family and included stories that went back to slavery that my mother didn't know. She was so appalled by the whole concept of writing about slavery because she'd done everything in her power to move us beyond that.

NB: Do you think it was because she felt those stories were in the past? Did she feel shame around your family history?

LT: Definitely. Some of it was about being a striver. Neither of my parents came from privilege.

NB: Whose parents did?

LT: Well, there are some people who came from a modicum of money. Their parents were doctors or undertakers. My family were land-based people from a very small, rural Black community. For my mother, everything was about taking a step up. Anything involving slavery was taking a step back. So she wasn't having it. But she couldn't convince me to stop writing. I was grown. She was incredibly supportive of me as a person; she just hated my subject matter, and she couldn't understand why I was putting family business in the street. It just wasn't acceptable. Eventually she came around, but it wasn't like I was encouraged to write.

When I sat down to write *Cane River*, I hadn't written anything except business plans and papers in college. I didn't know what I was doing. It took me nine months to get a first draft—and that was writing every single day for at least three hours, never taking a day off in those nine months—because I was trying to teach myself how to write.

MWS: My mom was fine with me leaving my job. I don't think I would have had the courage to write so early in life without that support. Maybe I would have come to it later, but without my mother, I know I wouldn't have.

NB: I think a lot of people have a fantasy about what the writing life is like. Talk to me about what it was like to come to the desk every day and have a sense of the story you were trying to tell. What was that creative process like? Margaret, your story is closer to that fantasy of sitting down and having the story flow out of you. Maybe that's because you were writing something you knew instead of writing something you had to research.

LT: For me, it was very tough. In addition to everything you're saying, I'd left a really good job, so I wasn't getting any validation because everyone thought I was an idiot. I mean, *everybody* thought I was an idiot.

NB: Because you'd walked away from your job?

LT: I walked, yes, but I'd planned it. When I talk to people, I always say, "Yes, I decided to quit my job, but I plotted and planned until I could get a package." I knew when the next reorganization was coming. I got enough so that in my head I could say, "I've got a couple of years to get myself together and figure out what I'm going to do." Remember, I had been doing genealogy for years; I had interesting stories. I traveled a lot. I went to Africa. I painted some horrible paintings which I later burned. I was just trying to figure it out. I did not leave my job "to write," but I kept doing this genealogy going further and further back, wanting to reconstruct the characters' lives. Since I'd gone back to Louisiana every summer [as a kid], I had a real sense of that life. I couldn't envision the slavery, but I knew instinctively what the community, the pull of family, the tracks that run down the middle of the town were like. Writing became what filled up my day.

Sitting down to write, and teaching myself in the process, was hard. All of it was hard, especially since I didn't feel anyone cared. If even my mother had said, "You need to do this, girl," that would have been great. But for me it was dogged stubbornness, pure and simple. I envy writers who experience tremendous joy when they sit down to write because for me it was horrible every day. But that's what you have to do to get the words out. I had a deal with myself that I was going to write [for a] three-hour minimum every day, until I could get whatever the story was out. It turned out to be the story of four generations of women.

Once I got to the editing, it was a different thing. That was fun. It was a puzzle. But the blank page staring at me every morning—not only was that enforced therapy, it was just hard, hard work. I often say, "I don't like writing, but I love having written."

NB: That's so true about writing. I often think writing is like laying tiny mosaic tiles.

LT: You're not totally sure how it will come together. You're not totally sure *if* it will come together. I was never sure.

MWS: The process you describe really resonates with me. For the first book, I left my job. I was at a firm where I was working fourteen hours a day. I thought, "Okay, I'll treat writing as a job." I started writing as if I were at work. It was every day. I still treat writing that way. My mother was encouraging, but I still had a lot of demons. When I'd call her, she'd say, "You just have to keep going." She'd say, "Give yourself five years." My father was pretty supportive, too. When I was a lawyer, I loved the feeling of telling people what I did for a living and where I worked. You get on a track with a corporate career, and it's very predictable: if you do this, you're going to get that. My friends were continuing down that track; everyone I knew was continuing down that track. It was very difficult not getting any validation, to really only get rejection. I had no idea when the rejection would stop and whether the writing would ever go anywhere. I think I wrote for five years before I got my agent. I stopped counting the number of rejections at one hundred. What I learned from that process was that I had based my personal value on being productive in a way I could monetize and quantify.

NB: Talk to me about being southern writers and your relationship with the South, particularly Louisiana.

MWS: *A Kind of Freedom* starts in the Jim Crow South. It's a story that can be told in only a few places in the country—New Orleans being one—because, yes, it was the Jim Crow South with its terrible history and a terrible racial environment. But there's a degree to which someone could be insulated in New Orleans that makes that place very special.

LT: One of the things that propelled me to write *Cane River* was stumbling upon a concept I'd never given much thought to: Free People of Color. In Cane River, the Free People of Color occupy a space before the Civil War that's totally unique. They often had more money than their white neighbors. They often had slaves. But they didn't consider themselves white; they weren't trying to be white. They didn't consider themselves Black, and they weren't trying to be Black. Where else would you find that sort of striation other than in Louisiana and have it be so baked into the culture and the nature of the place? There's a lot that's very special about Louisiana.

NB: What was the biggest surprise about this whole process or about yourselves?

LT: It surprised me that telling the story was so hard. For me, working out the story was like going into therapy every day. I was so emotional about the time period I was writing about. For instance, I found a bill of sale that had a slave's first name and how much they were sold for and to whom they were sold, and I was related to both the slave and the person who bought them. I had so many swirling emotional landscapes to navigate and tame. I didn't expect to be on such shifting sand all the time. Plus, I was trying to master the craft. I expected [the writing] to be hard because I didn't know what I was doing. What surprised me was the emotional highs and lows of the process and having to confront so much of my own stuff. Projecting myself into my ancestors on the slave side—that was what people think would be really tough—but that was not nearly as tough as having to project myself onto the slave owner's side. Having a man, my great-great-grandfather, whom I despised, whose picture I had—having to come to terms with the times and understand the rules of the day, the interpersonal interactions—I just felt like I needed therapy all the time.

MWS: Sometimes when I look back, I'll see the many, many emails I sent to agents, and it surprises me that I kept at it. I don't understand why I kept going.

[*all laugh*]

NB: We must be gluttons for punishment.

MWS: I think there was some odd compulsion. I don't know what it was, but I had the audacity to think this story was so important, that my voice is so important, that I was going to keep doing this even though so many [agents] were telling me I wasn't doing a great job.

It surprises me now how the book takes shape on its own. I look back on what I've written and I think, "Where did that come from? How did that come together?" I hear people say that, but it's surprising when you see that in your own work, how you start out with one idea and it totally shifts into something different that you don't feel came from yourself. That's been a surprise to see that in action.

LT: I remember sitting in a chair where I could prop up the footrest. I was struggling to write a scene, and suddenly, I had a revelation about one character, a woman, that informed the entire book. Those moments were absolutely shocking. I worked from six outlines, and that moment wasn't on any of them. As soon as I wrote that scene, I knew it was right; it wasn't open to question. Those moments when things feel right can sustain you for a really long time. It's so interesting the way the universe intrudes.

NB: How much, or not, does faith in any form play a role in your work or in your creative life or, more specifically, in your experience of writing these books? By faith, it could be religious faith or it can be the universe intervening. Maybe it's just faith in yourself.

LT: When I write about Black folks, usually religious faith plays a part because it's such an integral part of the community, but personally, I have to back off the religious faith part. What I will say is that I came to writing after many years of doggedly doing something else in the world that was black and white. But when I started writing, things turned gray. I don't know how to describe this without sounding totally woo-woo, but when I wrote my first book, one of my four characters came to me and told me I'd gotten [the story] wrong. For three days, I felt like I was getting beaten up by this force saying, "Nope, you've got to go back. You have to revisit. This isn't it, this isn't it." That was terrifying, because I didn't believe in it.

NB: Terrifying because you couldn't believe you were having this experience?

LT: Yes. She took huge agency. I was afraid to go to sleep. It was just horrific. I had to figure out a different way to make the plot happen. I went back to the documents and started writing a scene. I really felt her at my back and that she was going to slap the crap out of me if I didn't get it right. It turned out that when I changed the story, the character left. I now believe in those forces more than I did before. I believe in having to have faith in all the tools around you, in whatever is around you that gets you to where you need to go. That's not something I would have said before I started writing because I felt I could do all the shaping. I think there are stories that flow through. And when they feel wrong, they are wrong.

MWS: I read somewhere that someone said that the story is there, you just have to excavate it. Sometimes there are missing pieces or I'm adding pieces that aren't supposed to be there, and I can feel that it's not working. When it's the story that's meant to be told, there is a feeling tone. And I believe that ancestors are telling stories through me, maybe not *my* ancestors but spirits who want stories told. I believe the story is being channeled, and the more open I am, the more accurately I can reflect that story. I wasn't going to mention it before you brought it up, but the reason I kept sending those emails to agents over and over was because I believed writing was a calling. It was a faith thing, almost like I was being called down this road.

NB: I do think you do have to be open. You talked about a flow earlier, and I think there's something about tapping into that energy. I don't know whether it's because you feel like writing is something you have to do or whether someone is appearing saying, "You're not on the right track." It's all part of the creative process.

MWS: Lita, could you see the person who was speaking to you?

LT: No. She was always behind me. She wasn't going away.

NB: I know you, Lita, and I know you're all business, so I can only imagine what that must have been like.

How do you see yourselves as women authors, as Black women authors? Do you feel any kind of sense of obligation? A sense of celebration? What are you trying to convey in your work? I understand it's a big, open-ended question.

MWS: My new book is about a former slave and a former sharecropper who live next door to a white woman. They form an uncertain relationship. The white woman ends up being a member of the women's branch of the Ku Klux Klan. Many generations later, her great-great-great-granddaughter, who is biracial, moves in with her grandmother, and the white grandmother starts behaving erratically. The story lines converge at the end. I'm trying to reflect on the degree to which white women are used as tools of oppression by the greater society. I'm interested in the relationships between white women and Black women and identifying connections between us and being alert to the ways we're both being oppressed.

My husband's white, and through him I have a lot of family members who are white. We have great relationships on the surface, but there's never a moment when I'm in their presence when I don't feel like I'm a Black person. I've never gotten beyond that. I think it's lurking in society. With this second book, I want to excavate that. In my first book, I wanted to show that we have systems—mass incarceration, the war on drugs—that have come in to do the work of Jim Crow. I'm always interested in sociological issues that I feel personally called to discuss. I have cousins who are in and out of jail, and I always wonder, "How did that happen? Our grandfather went to college." It's always personal entry into sociological issues. With the new book, I'm actually saying I want to offer healing for society—whether it's in the way people receive it or the way I'm talking about it. That's the direction I want to move in.

NB: Lita, I wonder how writing historical novels addresses these issues.

LT: I wrote my novels because I wanted to reclaim our history. It was very, very clear to me that what I wanted was to retell our history, and I didn't want it to be *Gone with the Wind*. I wanted my marginalized ancestors to tell a story in their own voices, from their own perspective, and not colored by the old notion that the victor gets to tell the story. The structure of how I told the story was always around real events. You can go to the newspaper. You can find records of all these events. I felt a tremendous obligation to vocalize voices from the past.

NB: Were there ever moments where you were anxious about the characters you were portraying? Margaret, I know that in *A Kind of Freedom*, the story you tell is at times pretty raw. It's contemporary. You have young Black men in that book. Their characters were having sex—and I wondered if in that moment you felt an instinct to protect the portrayal of Black people.

MWS: Absolutely. I only stopped worrying about that when I gave the novel to another Black women whose opinion I respect. I thought, "If she's okay with this, I'll be okay with it." Sometimes I still worry. I know that it's authentic because I have lots of cousins in similar situations, and much of my research was talking to them, following them around, talking to their friends. The worst thing I could have done was to have been pejorative or to have sensationalized the situation. It's a hard balance. I actually feel like it was luck, or divine intervention, or whatever you want to call it, that the story didn't go in either of those directions because it could have. You see that happen all the time. I really love the people in my life that my novel was based on, and I really feel like it's not my life, but I did grow up in similar circumstances. You definitely see it happen with more privileged writers, with white writers, who are trying to portray a situation. I'm not white, but I am privileged in many ways, and I was definitely very concerned.

NB: How much does authority—the authority you feel to, for instance, write a certain kind of character—play into your creative decisions? This conversation about who has the authority to write what, has been occurring in literary circles for a while. I know a lot of white authors feel that they're not welcome to tell a certain kind of story. I wonder if that plays into your thinking about your characters. It could be feeling the authority to write a man. Lita, you had a Native American character, Cow Tom, in your last novel.

LT: I worry about it all the time. I worry about it even though I write historical fiction. I worry about writing from a man's point of view. I try to have male readers. But I do think there's always in every character something that I draw upon as being human. What I'm going for isn't to characterize a Black woman; it's to characterize the humanity in that Black woman and strike some common chords that readers will recognize and project onto others. It's risky business putting anything in the public sphere because someone will come back and tell you that's not how it happened. I know, going in, that my story will be challenged. When I gave a talk on *Cane River* in Cane River there were people in the back of the room from the Cane River Linguistic Society, who were there to monitor the phraseology.

My third book that has a Native American character made me far more nervous, especially with some of the rituals and the food. I did a lot of research, but even so, if it's not your lane you really have to be careful. I don't write about something that's totally and completely out of my lane. I write about a slave of African origin who is growing up in a Native American tribe, so I think there are things I can imply there and hopefully get through with some level of credibility.

At the end of the day, with historical fiction, I make sure the surrounding events are always very accurate. Then it's about character motivation, which frees you from the stereotypes. I have to strive for agency. After that, I just have to hope for the best.

MWS: I worry less so with this third book. But I also do a lot of research. It makes me feel padded. I make sure everything I talk about is logistically possible. Except for the issue with TC, the male character, I felt I was okay.

NB: Can we talk about how you, as two Black women writers, deal with race in your lives and in your work? I think because I grew up in California I've felt that I can go where I want to go, do what I want to do, with relative ease and safety. I can exist here with a certain amount of freedom. When I was spending a lot of time in Louisiana researching for *Queen Sugar* I always wondered what it would be like to live there. Where is the third rail? Most everyone I met was warm and welcoming, but I'd think to myself, "I know there's shit going on here—experiences and conversations that I am not privy to." I always wondered when I was going to come up against that third rail. And in fact, I met some folks there who turned out to be openly racist. They trotted out all the predictable old tropes—like the sheriff who followed me in his car along a country road to make sure I drove through his town and past it without stopping. That was frightening. And there were other things that happened socially. Once, I was at dinner with a group of people and this guy told a joke about a Cajun character named Boudreaux. The joke had something to do with Boudreaux and a Black woman and her breasts—I don't remember—but people around the table cracked up and I was like, "Oh man, are you really going to go there?"

MWS: My grandfather lived in New Orleans, but his sister moved to San Francisco in the '40s. She had all her children here, and her children had their children here. I hang out with my cousins, my contemporaries, all the time. Their conception of race couldn't be more different from mine. They just don't think about race as much as I do. I think I'm obsessed with it. They always say it's because I grew up in the South, in New Orleans. Everywhere I go, I think about it. Lalita, do you think about it?

LT: I absolutely do, and I was born in Berkeley. I'm a generation beyond you two, so I'm surprised to hear you two think about it all the time. I think about race all the time, but it's not about the South. Well, it's a little about the South. But I grew up where we integrated a town. We were getting death threats all the time. It was a very tough place to be. Every face I saw was white—all the time except when we'd go to church back in Berkeley. I'd need to look every single white person in the eye to see if they were a threat. I've carried that with me, and I can't let it go—which is crazy because that's not the world I live in. It's not the people I've surrounded myself with. But I still think of almost everything in terms of race and whether something is dangerous and a threat.

MWS: Just this morning I thought, "I've got to stop thinking about everything in terms of race." And not because race is not a predominant factor in our world, but because carrying the fear of potential racism, the anger at the racism that has already taken place, weighs me down in a way that's not productive or healthy. It hinders relationships with people; I'm very guarded with white people, some of whom don't deserve it. I'm never going to stop writing about race and advocating for Black people, but it's my goal to mitigate the emotional impact it has on me personally, because it's not helping anybody. It's certainly not helping me. You have people who think you need to be angry to make changes in the world, but I don't believe that. I think I would actually be more powerful if I could let some of this go. But it's constant. And I know it's out of a fear of a threat.

LT: It's ever-present.

MWS: Natalie, you feel the same?

NB: Absolutely. I don't necessarily feel fear, and I've never felt restricted by my Blackness—I actually draw strength from it—but I definitely feel a smoldering rage. I'm always aware of how race is playing out.

LT: We've had to.

MWS: But I have Black friends who don't think about race all the time. They're conscious and progressive, but they're not emotionally consumed by fear and anger. I'm thinking of one friend who grew up in Lexington, Kentucky. She went to predominantly white schools. Her parents were very privileged. She doesn't seem to be aware of having experienced much discrimination. I'm not sure how to read it. My other friend grew up in Vallejo and Fresno—again, in predominantly white spaces. Some of their response is probably just personality.

LT: Personality and lack of negative experiences. I think if you're lucky enough not to have something smack you personally yet, maybe you can have a different experience. Sometimes, I get frustrated with young Black kids who've been privileged, who've been sheltered, if they only see the world as this wonderful place full of opportunity. For me, it's very off-putting until I think, "No, you want some of this to happen." You want a next generation who isn't carrying the exact same baggage you carry, because then maybe there will be different reactions that can get us closer to truly addressing social inequities and social injustice.

NB: And yet you want to arm them.

LT: But not scare them.

NB: You do want them to be prepared.

LT: Especially with police interaction. No matter how privileged they might be, they are still subject to a biased system that devalues their lives, their humanity and their bodies, based on nothing more than the color of their skin.

NB: Absolutely. I look at my daughters. When they were young, it felt like we worked overtime to install all kinds of buffers—not to shield them from what it means to be a Black person in this country—we would never rob them of that understanding—but rather, to provide them with the time and space to build up their confidence; to appreciate and celebrate their blackness.

LT: There were layers.

MWS: You did the right stuff for them.

NB: They're young women now, and while they've never had any traumatic experiences, relatively speaking, it's been interesting to see them step fully into everything that being Black women in this country means. They're pretty fierce. They feel empowered and they'll speak up in a minute. It's gratifying to see.

18.

Queen Sugar, Chapter 10

BY NATALIE BASZILE

It was a Wednesday morning, the third week of June. The sun had risen high enough to bake the fields and the air was warm, but still held a little of its coolness from the night's embrace. Charley had just settled into the ratty desk chair and was sorting through old bank statements and outdated copies of *American Truck* magazine when Denton poked his head in the office.

"Come with me."

"Where are we going?"

"I'm going to teach you how to fish," Denton said. "Like I told you that day you came to see me, the time for laying-by has almost passed."

"Laying-by," Charley said envisioning the notes on her yellow pad. "That means cleaning up the rows." She felt like a kid at a spelling bee.

"Correct, and Frasier should have done it way back in May." Denton slid a finger under his baseball cap and scratched his scalp. "But if we work quick and double up on fertilizer, we might be able to catch up." He led her out into the yard. "I found an old disc plow behind the shop. The discs were rusted, but the iron case held up pretty good. I cut up some of that rebar you found in that box of pipes and made us this three-row. It's basic, but it'll get the job done."

Charley knelt before the length of extruded pipe. Denton had welded three metal spikes long as chef's knives along the length of it—one on each end and one in the middle. "I can't believe you made a piece of farm equipment," she said. With the circular patterns on the spikes, and the spray of rust along the extruded shaft, the contraption was more suited for a museum sculpture garden than a cane field. "How do we get it out there?"

Denton pointed to the tractor. "We hook it to the back and pull it through the rows where all the weeds are growing. I spaced the spikes far enough apart so they won't tear up the cane. Frasier should have gotten to the weeds when they were low. Now they done took us. You got stands out there that are tied up from end to end. That's lesson number one, Miss Bordelon. Never let them weeds get out ahead of you."

They rode out to the second quadrant, Denton on the tractor, the three-row clanging like church bells as he rumbled over ruts, and Charley following close behind in his pickup, the sun reflecting softly off the hood's dull paint, the dogs pacing in the truck bed, where they barked at every bird or insect that happened by and lifted their noses in the breeze. She gazed out over her fields. Almost a month, and she was still not accustomed to the way the land looked—no mountains or rolling hills, even, to break up the horizon; the sky lower somehow than it was in California; the land for as far as she could see flat as a sheet of paper—and Charley wondered how long it would be before the place felt familiar, how long before she felt in her bones that she was truly home.

Ahead of her, Denton signaled that they'd arrived. He pulled over, climbed down from the tractor, and stood on the headland. Charley joined him.

"See what I mean about this field being tied up?"

Charley squinted and, for the first time, noticed thin green vines dotted with bright red poppy-like flowers twisting among the cane stalks. "Is that kudzu?"

"Tie vines," Denton said. "Also known as morning glory. And it'll smother your cane if you don't stay on top of it." He walked back to the tractor, lowered the three-row, and secured the hitch. "We'll go up and down the rows, pull up the grass first, then we'll come through with the fertilizer. The trick is to get down to the seeds and the roots so the vines don't come back again. I'll take the first row so you can see how it's done, then I'll turn it over to you."

"But I don't know how to drive a tractor," Charley said.

"Time for you to learn."

As Charley stood by, Denton climbed onto the tractor, turned the engine, and fishtailed back and forth until the three-row, like an enormous comb, was directly behind him, then he slowly guided the tractor into the field, being careful to line the tractor's tires up with the furrows so the cane passed underneath the chassis. He pressed the clutch, gave the engine a little gas, and the tractor lurched forward, the three-row's spikes sinking deep into the earth like a dog bite, pulling up the roots and turning over clots of soil in three rows as it dragged along. Brilliant, Charley thought, and her heart leaped as she watched Denton roll through the field. When he reached the far side, Denton swung around and came back.

"Amazing," Charley called over the engine noise. "Mr. Denton, you're a genius."

But there was no time for compliments. "You're up," Denton said stoically, and shifted into neutral, set the emergency brake. Heart thumping, Charley climbed into the seat. "Now release the clutch." Charley obeyed. "Now grab hold of that lever and switch into first, then release the brake." Denton was patient but firm, and Charley followed his instructions like a schoolgirl—*shift into first, release the brake*—letting out a small cry of delight as the tractor rolled forward. "Now look-a-here," Denton called, walking beside her, "as long as you keep the tires in the furrows, the three-row will do like it should. It'll follow behind like a duckling. Don't be hasty. Turn around and check every few yards or you'll tear up your cane. You get to the other side, swing around wide and come back. Understand?"

"I think so." Charley gave a tentative thumbs-up.

"Remember. Go slow. This ain't the Kentucky Derby." And then Denton stopped walking, stopped talking, and let her go.

Charley was halfway down the row and feeling lightheaded before she realized she was holding her breath. Her hands sweated from gripping the gearshift so tightly. She exhaled, sat back in the seat, glanced quickly behind her to check that the three-row was still there, and was relieved to see that it was, the spikes cutting through the soil, tearing up weeds and roots, the earth folding in on itself like cake batter. Charley turned forward and straightened the wheel to keep the tractor in the row.

From up there in the seat, she had a different view of her fields entirely. Overgrown as they were in places, scraggly and neglected in others, when taken all together, they still held a certain beauty; it was like floating on a sea of green tea, and she felt the tiniest bloom of satisfaction knowing that with a lot of hard work and some luck, she might, *just might*, be able to tease a miracle out of those plants.

When she returned to where Denton stood, he nodded approvingly. "Not bad, Miss Bordelon," he said, squinting up at her.

"Thanks." Charley beamed.

Denton tugged his hat brim lower over his eyes, and Charley thought she saw a smile curl in the corners of his mouth. "Just a hundred fourteen rows to go."

Lunchtime. Back in the shop, Charley and Denton dragged two folding chairs just inside the shop door, where, if nothing else, it was a few degrees cooler.

"Tomorrow, maybe the next day, we'll hit those rows with nitrogen," Denton said. He peeled the top slice of bread off his sandwich, which Charley had picked up on her way in, and regarded the remaining layers of sliced turkey, cheese, and tomato with disappointment.

"Do you not like it?" Charley asked, thinking she should have ordered the plate lunch.

"I remember when I could eat for twenty-five cents a day," Denton said. "Ten cents for a piece of ham thick like this." He held his thumb and forefinger a few inches apart. "Fifteen cents for a soda water. Now it's ten dollars and you can't even see what you got." He looked across the road where afternoon sunlight leached through the gathering clouds. "Truth is, everything cost more, nowadays. Labor done doubled. Insurance done tripled, fuel done tripled. Meanwhile, the price of cane's been the same for the last seven years. You couldn't have picked a worse time to get into this business, Miss Bordelon."

Charley felt an ache spread through her gut. Her mother, too, was a straight shooter, often brutally so. "It's a cold world out there, Charlotte," her mother had said. "You have no idea. You go down to Louisiana trying to be a sugarcane farmer, all you'll be is a pretty face."

She turned to Denton. "Maybe," she said, "but anyone who tries to stop me," and here she thought of Landry, with his slick smile and flashy sedan, "anyone who thinks I can't do this, can go to hell."

Denton turned to look at her, and for a few seconds he didn't say a word, just stared. Then he smashed the top bread slice back on his sandwich and took a bite. "I like that you're willing to work hard," he said. "May turn out to be good at fishing after all."

Ten straight days of clearing the morning glories, and tearing out johnsongrass, and spraying double doses of fertilizer. Ten straight days of dirt and dust and sweat from places Charley never knew she could sweat. Ten straight days of rumbling up and down the rows—up and down, up and down, up and down—while the sun blazed overhead and heat rose from below, and finally, *finally*, Charley's second quadrant, and then the rest of her farm, was neat as a pinstriped suit. The cane was still stunted, much to her dismay, and in some places looked worse than it had before, but Denton assured her that now that the rows were clear, it had a chance to grow properly.

"What's next?" Charley asked, as they rode to the hardware store late one afternoon. An order of wrenches had come in.

"Time to run your drains," Denton said. "All that dirt we cleared between the rows has piled up on the ends. Have to clear it out or your fields won't drain right, and the last thing you want is for water to get hung up out there. Cane likes to be damp, but it hates to be flooded." He turned left at the junction and rolled down his window. "Good news is, most of your land is the perfect combination of sand and loam. It drains well. Go over it with a piece of equipment, you can hardly see where you passed. It's that Black jack land, all boggy and filled with clay, that'll hold water and tear up your machines."

"Who knew laying-by was so involved," Charley said.

Denton nodded. "It's critical. You're giving the cane your final *Amen*. You're saying, 'That's it. I've done all I can do.' Everything goes like it should, it's the last time you're in your fields till grinding. After laying-by, you stand back and let Mother Nature take over."

From the passenger seat, Charley looked at Denton, and for the hundredth time was overcome with relief and gratitude. It wasn't simply the knowledge that she couldn't have done any of this without him. No, it wasn't simply that. It was the feeling she got in his presence, a sense of peace, a quiet calm, as though she were standing in the shadow of an old redwood. They didn't make them like Denton anymore; she couldn't have asked for a better mentor. She'd noticed that sometimes, whether it was driving the tractor or operating the drill press or mixing a batch of fertilizer, he seemed to hold himself back, forced himself to step aside so *she* could learn, rather than doing the work himself. At least three times she'd walked into the office to find him scribbling on a pad, sketching pieces of equipment he planned to make. And was she imagining things, or did he seem to be walking with a newfound lift in his step?

"So, we run the drains and then we're finished?" asked Charley. They were approaching the little town of Jeanerette, where LeBlanc's Bakery on Main Street had been baking French bread and ginger cakes since 1884. Over the front entrance with its big picture windows, the red light glowed brightly, signaling that fresh loaves had just come out of ovens and were ready for sale; all you had to do was walk around to the side door. The air was heavy with a sweet, yeasty aroma and Charley inhaled. She'd have to pick up a couple loaves on her way home.

"We won't be sitting around eating bonbons, if that's what you're thinking. Still lots to do before grinding." Denton scratched his forehead thoughtfully. "And that's if Mother Nature doesn't throw us a curveball."

"What could go wrong?"

Denton inhaled, as though he, too, was tempted to stop for a loaf and eat it right there in the car, if only they could afford the time. "What could go wrong?" He looked out over the hood then at Charley. "Plenty."

19.

*F*rame

BY ROBIN COSTE LEWIS

There'd been a field, a farm, hobos asleep in the chicken coop,
white people whose dogs chased us every day on our way to the pool.
I never knew what, if anything, they grew. Never knew of a harvest.
Never saw a thing begin as seed, or sow its way to plant, flower, fruit

There was a shack, I remember that, and an old house with an old lady.
She wore a dingy eyelet dress, and paced her porch dry
carrying a shotgun or a broom. Flip-flops, Blow-Pops, Click-Clacks,
Cracker Jacks, we barked Dog Talk with teeth still muddy and black

from Eat the Peg. Soft lime salamanders, fingers a vivid tangerine;
cow hooves grafted to arid grime; date palms with roots so determined
they sucked up all the water from the other things with leaves. We tore
through her property, a whole band of us, day after day, unaware of
the endings

our bright forms would bring. There wasn't just one, but two
farms, across from each other, and another one, long down

the street, past the pool, next to the Victoria Park Golf Course,
where we never saw one colored man walk into.

Farther out, surrounding us, there were other farms too,
which had been worked, but were not working. There was the pool
a liquor store, an old house, the golf course, a koi
farm, our new neighborhood, the bakery from Hawaii,

then the landing field for the Goodyear
blimp. You could live here for years and never
understand: Were you rural, industrial, or suburban?
We thought we were *home*, but our cardboard

was just slender venture on Negro sprawl.
Before that it was law: we could not own property
except in certain codes: South Central, Compton, Watts,
where the construction companies were under contract

with the LAPD to tile or tar our addresses onto our roofs,
so when their helicopters needed to shoot,
they'd know—and we'd know too—
who was what and what was who.

Throughout the whole state, every third person
Was from Lousy Anna: New Orleans,
Algiers, the West Bank, La Place, Plaquemines
Parish, Slidell, Baton

Rouge. We took pies and cakes to anyone new, but never heard
a sound from the farms. They never brought us nothing either.
No milk, eggs, no butter. It was just clear in the dirt
road we took. Somebody somewhere

was striding in time, but not any of us.
The farmers were lost
and hating it. We were lost
and couldn't care less.

20.

America at the Crossroads: A History of Enslavement and Land

BY CLYDE FORD

Opening this book to learn about the work of Natalie Baszile, to read the arresting tales of Black farmers throughout the years, and to gaze on their faces, I am confronted with a history that cannot be told without understanding the relationship between people of African descent and the land.

Fascinated with the origins of such words as "Negro" and the N-word, I consulted dictionaries, which trace them to a Latin root, *negro*, meaning "black," then stop. Unconvinced, I discovered the word can be traced further back to a vowelless Egyptian root, *ngr*, filled with poetry, meaning "water to flow into sand." *Ngr* refers to the Niger River, whose strange U-shaped course convinced early travelers that it ended in desert sands and fertilized the lands around it. The dark-skinned people along this river were called the "people of the water to flow into sand." So, buried deep, even within our words, is this connection of African peoples to the land.

Land is impregnated with deep spiritual significance for people of African descent. In Angola, from which many slaves were taken, there is a timeless symbol of the "crossroad."

Called a *yowa*, or a *dikenga*, this cross, known long before Christianity, can be found to this day etched on the ground, painted in caves, and carved in wood. The very act of drawing a *dikenga* sanctifies the land, makes it holy. This African cross marks the immediate presence of the spiritual—right then, right there—not a pointer to some spiritual center in holy lands far away, from times long ago. And Africans apprehended this personal spiritual center wherever two roads crossed.

True, slavery ripped many millions from Africa. But while a people may be torn from their lands, land and its significance are not so easily torn from people. Centuries later, an ocean away, faint echoes of the *dikenga*, of the sacredness of the land, can still be heard wafting through the plaintiff wails of blues songs, like Robert Johnson's "Crossroad Blues."

Recently, the quadricentennial of the arrival of the first Africans in the American colonies was marked. In 1619, at Point Comfort along the James River in Virginia, these "20 and odd negroes," as Sir John Rolfe wrote in his ledger, were held in chains aboard the Flemish man-of-war *White Lion*, whose crew had captured them from the Portuguese slave ship *São João Bautista*. They had been boarded in Angola, booty from a brutal war between the Portuguese and the Ndongo of Angola. What history records, though many still do not acknowledge, is that these first Africans, while bound to the land, were not bound as slaves but instead as indentured servants.

The present-day state of race relations in America cannot be understood without also understanding the transition from indentured servitude to slavery that took place between 1619 and 1640. More important for the readers of this book, indentured servitude in early colonial America set in motion a series of promises made, then broken, regarding African Americans and the land.

Early American common folk, Black and white, toiled the land without pay under harsh terms that bound them to indentures for seven, eleven, or even fourteen years. After working off these indentures, they were promised "freedom dues." The freedom dues recorded in Maryland laws, for example, consisted of fifty acres, corn, and farming tools. Some combination of land, grain, clothes, and farming tools was widely accepted, particularly in the Southern colonies, as a means of repaying freed servants for their years of service, thus providing them the barest essentials for establishing an independent livelihood in the future.

But many landholders refused to pay freedom dues, especially when it came to giving away land, breaking a promise that set up conflict with their former servants. Occasionally these conflicts wound up in early courts, where former servants sometimes prevailed as judges and juries recognized and acknowledged a precedent that freed men and women deserved some form of reparation for their time worked under bondage.

Landowners worked hard to keep former bonded servants, Black and white, from owning land, which, after all, was the basis of wealth. This separation between the landed and the landless, between those with wealth and those without it, is very much with us as income inequality today.

Colonial landowners further recognized that separating Black workers from white workers was another way to manage and control their land and the labor that worked it. In three short decades, from 1619 to 1640, the landed aristocracy of colonial America chose a path from indentured servitude to permanent indentures to slavery for colonial Africans while retaining indentured servitude for whites. Slavery was not inevitable in America. Slavery, and the racism behind it, was a choice made by the Byrds and Mathers and Winthrops, by the Jeffersons and Washingtons and the other founding fathers of this country. It was a conscious choice to exploit the labor of Africans for the economic benefit of those who owned the land.

Just as the first Africans did not arrive on colonial shores as slaves, the first working-class whites did not arrive as racists. Racism, brewing among European elites, was taught to the white working class here in the colonies. The same laws that enslaved Blacks also circumscribed working-class whites, enforcing what they could and could not do, whom they could and could not love, whom they were and were not better than. From legislatures to churches to newspapers, a racial divide was constructed, and vigorously enforced, in the decades following 1619.

In the face of slavery's establishment, whites who worked the land had a path to freedom that Blacks, working that same land, did not. However hard indentured servitude was, at least white indentured servants could feel with some relief that their lot was far better than that of Black slaves.

Yet, even during slavery, the connection of Africans to the land was highly valued and greatly sought after. Southern rice and peanut farmers, for example, sought out slaves from African countries where rice and peanuts were grown precisely because these Africans better understood how to farm these crops than their white masters did. Sugar plantations in Louisiana and the Caribbean were often run by Africans, under the control of plantation owners, of course, because these Africans knew more about the intricacies of farming and harvesting sugar than did the white owners. During slavery, Africans, once bound to the land for physical and spiritual susten-ance, were now bound to the land for the economic benefit of others.

Even efforts to reduce the reliance of southern farming on slavery backfired. By the late 1700s, the economy of the southern United States, built on slave labor, lay faltering, and the economic wisdom of slavery lay in question. For a variety of geo-graphic and economic reasons, cotton, tobacco, sugar, indigo, and rice, the princi-pal cash crops of the South, all required ever-greater amounts of money to produce and returned decreasing profit to southern planters. In particular, cotton plantation owners found themselves paying more and more for the upkeep of their slaves, with less and less returned from the sale of their cotton. This economic equation changed dramatically with the introduction of Eli Whitney's new technology—the cotton gin—in 1793.

Whitney's gin could process fifty pounds of cotton lint a day, separating cotton fibers from seed. What southern planters now needed was an inexpensive way to grow and pick cotton to feed the hungry new machines, which would produce the raw materials for northern textile mills, which then exported their textiles world-wide. For that labor, the South turned once again to the sale and purchase of slaves. Suddenly, cotton became wildly profitable, and a technology some hoped would save labor and thereby reduce the South's reliance on slavery had just the opposite effect. The 1790 census recorded approximately seven hundred thousand slaves in the South. By the 1860 census, that number had increased to nearly four million human beings held in bondage.[51]

For some Blacks, enslavement to the land was soon followed by alienation from the land. With Emancipation and the advent of automated cotton-picking machines in the later nineteenth century, the need for a huge cotton labor force dwindled. Blacks, eager now for new opportunities and an escape from the brutality of the Jim Crow South, headed for northern cities en masse. These internally displaced people often traded the overt racism of the South for the subtle, yet equally devastating, racism of the North: lack of housing, lack of educational opportunities, lack of health care, lack of jobs—the very same issues that plague race relations to this day.

For those who stayed in the agricultural South, maintaining a connection with the land proved challenging. Abraham Lincoln issued the Emancipation Proclamation on September 22, 1862, to take effect on January 1, 1863. This executive order freed slaves in all southern states that were in open rebellion against the Union. Most northern states had ended legal slavery in the years before. While slavery may have been ended with a stroke of Lincoln's pen, the proclamation contained no provisions for the welfare of newly freed men and women. Lincoln simply encouraged them to "labor faithfully for reasonable wages." Encouragement, however, is no substitute for a solid plan.

The Civil War ended with General Robert E. Lee's surrender at Appomattox on April 9, 1865, and ushered in a period known as Reconstruction. During this time, the die was cast for the future of independent Black farmers—and for the future of Blacks, in general. Would they be provided a path toward income equality with whites? Would the federal government intervene to support the desire of most freed men and women to become independent farmers, or would the government intervene only to help transition former slaves to serve as a labor force for former slave owners? The stakes could not have been higher.

Even before the Civil War was officially over, Union General William T. Sherman and Secretary of War Edwin M. Stanton enacted a bold plan to address the needs of the Black men and women newly freed by the president's proclamation. In the evening of January 12, 1865, Sherman and Stanton addressed a gathering of Baptist and Methodist ministers, all Black, some former slaves, some formerly free, and asked them, as Stanton suggested to Sherman, "What do you want for your own people?"

A Baptist minister, Garrison Frazier, rose to speak. A slave until 1857, the sixty-seven-year-old Frazier made it clear that what African American communities wanted was land. "The way we can best take care of ourselves," said Frazier, "is to have land, and turn it and till it by our own labor." Frazier went on to say that he wanted African Americans to be given such land until they were able to buy it and to live "by ourselves, for there is a prejudice against us in the South that will take years to get over."

Out of this meeting, from the self-expressed desires of men and women long held in bondage, came Sherman's Special Field Order No. 15, accepted by Abraham

Lincoln and subsequently known as "forty acres and a mule." Mules, it should be noted, were not in the original order; Sherman later requisitioned the US Army to lend mules to these new Black landholders.

Coinciding with congressional passage of the first Freedmen's Bureau Act of 1865, the impact of Special Field Order No. 15 was breathtaking: the distribution to newly emancipated slaves of four hundred thousand acres of coastline stretching from Charleston, South Carolina, to the St. John's River in Florida, and extending some thirty miles inland, land formerly belonging to southern white slaveholders. Furthermore, in this area, African Americans would be allowed to organize and govern their own communities. Special Field Order No. 15 represented freedom dues accepted and allocated by the federal government. "Forty acres and a mule" showcased the government at its finest and most decent regarding citizens of color. Nothing like these sweeping reparations has been enacted by the US government ever since. And, sadly, nothing was acted upon in 1865.

Lincoln's assassination came shortly after Sherman issued Special Field Order No. 15. Andrew Johnson, Lincoln's successor, sympathized with the South and overturned Sherman's order in the fall of 1865, returning the land to the Southern slave owners from whom it had been seized.

America nearly took the road less taken—a road leading to a dramatic increase in Black farmers, in Black landownership, in Black wealth, and in the economic empowerment and equality of southern Black communities, a road that would have changed the complexion and complexities of racial dynamics in America forever. Instead, America backtracked after only a few fleeting footsteps down that road.

In the broken promise of "forty acres and a mule," one cannot help but hear Martin Luther King's words spoken one hundred years after the Emancipation Proclamation on the steps of the memorial to the very man who supported that early promise. "In a sense we've come to our nation's capital to cash a check . . . a promissory note," King said. "Instead of honoring this sacred obligation, America has given the Negro people a bad check, a check which has come back marked 'insufficient funds.'"

By the time of the second Freedmen's Bureau Act in 1866, gone were provisions for land redistribution, gone were provisions to support independent Black farmers, gone were a means of breaking up large southern plantations and the class and labor system related to them. In place of Garrison Frazier's vision of independent Black farmers and strong, self-reliant Black communities, the second Freedmen's Bureau Act assisted in implementing a widespread system of economic slavery.

Sharecropping and tenancy farming replaced outright slavery in the South. Blacks still worked in the fields under the oppressive hands of white landowners. True, the Freedmen's Bureau helped establish a network of agricultural and technical colleges throughout the South, the forerunners of many historically Black colleges and universities in existence today. In some instances, Black farmers banded together through joint church membership to devise collective strategies to resist pressures for them to sell their crops cheaply. But such exercise of Black economic power only further enraged white farmers. Then came the presidential election of 1876, which was remarkably similar to presidential elections of modern times.

In 1876, Samuel J. Tilden, the Democratic candidate, won the popular vote by nearly a quarter million votes, but Rutherford B. Hayes, the Republican, won the electoral college. Vote counts in many southern states, including Florida, were in dispute, and the outcome of the election remained unresolved for several months. Finally, the Compromise of 1877 was brokered. All federal troops, which had been stationed in the South to defend the rights of newly freed slaves, would be withdrawn. In return, Hayes would be named president.

Reconstruction was over. Freed slaves had lost. Independent Black farmers had lost. White southerners, no longer under the watchful eye of Union soldiers, were free to return to a system of oppressing and dominating Blacks. During Reconstruction, independent Black farmers (my great-great-grandfather Goodman Brown, among them) voted and held political offices at all levels of government. Goodman, for example, was a member of the Virginia House of Delegates.

But after Reconstruction, after the 1876 election, in the period known as Restoration, voting rights were stripped from Blacks, lynching and mob rule became common practice, and independent Black farmers had little power to fight back. The federal government formally abdicated its role in protecting and ensuring the welfare of newly freed slaves. Still, former slaves had not relinquished their dreams of owning and farming land. With emancipation, white land owners faced a labor shortage but they refused to create economic independence with formerly enslaved people. As a result, the sharecropping system was invented to maintain economic inequality and the system of white supremacy shifted to Jim Crow. White land owners hired former white overseers as newly minted supervisors. Black people, now free, were expected to pay for their tools, seed, fertilizers, food, and clothing. These costs were settled when the crops were harvested, which, in most cases, left Black farmers further in debt to the landowners. The debt ledger had replaced the bullwhip as the method of coercion.

Sharecropping was a direct result of the federal government abandoning a system of land redistribution and ownership for Black people, as proposed by Special Field Order No. 15, in favor of maintaining a system of white landownership that sprang from slavery. Sharecropping was particularly harsh on small Black farmers, even though as slaves they had helped to secure the wealth of those white farmers.

But all was not lost, even during these dismal years of sharecropping, Black codes, and Jim Crow. During these difficult years for Black farmers, and Black Americans in general, land-grant colleges were established. The Port Royal experiment, a land-redistribution scheme similar to Special Field Order No. 15, was attempted, then abandoned, by the federal government in the Georgia Sea Islands. And remarkably, somehow Black land ownership actually rose between 1865 and 1920, when nearly one million small Black farmers owned and operated their land.

During the late nineteenth and early twentieth centuries, a number of experiments aimed at enhancing Black landownership were attempted. The Farmers' Alliance, for example, a significant movement of all farmers, sought to organize farming and produce marketing cooperatives throughout the Plains states and the South. While an attempt was made to create a racially mixed alliance, resistance from white farmers led Black farmers to break away from the organization and establish the Colored Farmers' National Alliance and Cooperative Union (CFNACU) in 1886. A CFNACU cotton strike in Arkansas in 1891 was met with violent resistance by white landowners. And while organizations like CFNACU surely contributed to the beneficial experience of Black farmers with cooperative movements, they also contributed to the resolve of white landowners to harden already harsh Black codes and Jim Crow laws.

Movements organized by Black farmers such as the Farmers' Improvement Society of Texas (FIST), established by Robert Lloyd Smith in 1890 sought to assist Black farmers through cooperative land purchases, cooperative farming and marketing practices, and financial assistance to relieve Black farmers from the peonage of the sharecropping system.

Even the federal government, with the establishment of the Farm Security Administration in 1937, initially became involved in efforts to promote cooperative farming production and land-leasing that benefited small, independent Black farmers. But by the eve of America's entrance into World War II, with cotton farming having collapsed and the devastation wrought by the Great Depression spread throughout the country, these attempts at cooperative farming and land purchasing had essentially ceased. The US Department of Agriculture (USDA) had thoroughly transformed the Farm Security Administration. Where Black farmers once met a patchwork of local laws that thwarted them and associations that worked to their benefit, they now faced a nearly insurmountable federal bureaucracy. The USDA proved to be no friend of Black farmers.

Black landownership has always been an act of defiance and an affirmation of humanity. Owning land, and working it to benefit one's family and community, makes a powerful statement regarding independence and viability—a statement at sharp odds with the dominant white American trope that Blacks are shiftless, helpless, and penniless. During slavery, Blacks were owned by whites in precisely the same way that a person owns any real property. After slavery, Black landownership forced a definitive, and humanizing, distinction between Black people as real property and Black people as owners of real property. Landownership for Blacks was, and still is, a tremendous source of pride.

So, how is it that there were nearly one million Black farmers in 1920 (14 percent of all farm operators), but only eighteen thousand in 1997 (1 percent of all farm operators), rising to a tepid thirty-two thousand (1.5 percent of all farm operators) in 2007?[52] How is it that, during the civil rights era, the equivalent of an area the size of Central Park in New York City (an average of more than eight hundred acres) was lost each day by Black landowners?[53] How is it that, in 2007, Black farmers averaged $28,000 in loans from the USDA's Commodity Credit Corporation, while white farmers averaged $88,000?[54] How is it that, from Emancipation until the present day, an estimated several trillions of dollars of wealth has been transferred away from Blacks through land dispossession?[55] How is it? Because of yet another promise made by America, then broken for Black Americans. This promise came in the form of the US Department of Agriculture's public commitment to help Black landowners.

Franklin D. Roosevelt's New Deal brought the Farm Service Administration (FSA) into being to help the nation's small farmers, who had been battered by the

Great Depression. After Roosevelt's death in 1945, southern conservatives in Congress replaced the FSA with the Farmers Home Administration (FHA or FmHA). Fifteen years later, John F. Kennedy reached out to help farmers again through the Agricultural Stabilization and Conservation Service (ASCS). But these efforts, while largely successful, contained a fatal flaw when it came to the plight of Black farmers and landowners: though created nationally, the FSA, FHA, and ASCS were all run and administered locally.

Whether the land is used as farmland or timberland, access to credit, markets, and good advice is critical to economically viable landownership. Farm service agents, and the elected local committees that oversee their work and approve how federal programs are applied locally, provide just that access. But the system was designed by southern white segregationists to keep that access away from Black landowners.

Throughout the South, disenfranchised Blacks not only were unable to vote for political officeholders but also for local farm service committees. Even when ballots were distributed to Black farmers, joint ownership of farmland by a husband and wife, for example, might garner only one ballot between them, when an equivalent white couple would receive two. Most county agents were white, and they favored white farmers—providing them access to low-interest loans, membership in farming cooperatives, and advice on the best farming practices and crops to grow. Black farmers were systematically denied loans, excluded from cooperatives, and never told about the latest findings in the science and business of farming. When Black farmers attempted to organize their own cooperatives, for instance, local white farmers did everything in their power to cut off access to bank loans and drive these enterprises out of business.

The cumulative effect of federal agencies that were meant to serve farmers but were rife with racism took its toll. From the 1940s through the 1980s, Black farms were foreclosed on at an alarming rate, and the land was then purchased by white farmers or large agribusinesses. The census of Black farm operators in America marks a decline beginning in the 1920s, at the onset of the Great Depression, then accelerating at an alarming rate from the 1930s through the present day.[56] Peer a bit more deeply, and beneath these dismissal figures are traces of broken promises past—Special Field Order No. 15 ("forty acres and a mule") and, before that, freedom dues.

Yet in post–World War II America, a new stirring began. Black Americans, many of them farmers and landowners, had fought and died thousands of miles away for freedoms they did not enjoy when they returned home. The Black Freedom Struggle, or civil rights movement, is too often understood only in terms of social justice bringing about desegregation of public accommodations and the right to vote. But in the South, the epicenter of this struggle, the movement was equally about the retention of land. The right to vote, as noted earlier, meant the right to vote for local elected officials who controlled access to the resources Black farmers needed to survive.

Farming, landownership, and social justice are inextricably linked as the roots of the current "buy local" movement show. Most food co-ops trace their "buy local" efforts back to the community-supported agriculture (CSA) movement, imported from Germany and Europe in the 1980s. While important, CSAs have a much deeper, though less well-known, origin in the work of Dr. Booker T. Whatley, a Black agriculturist, who, as part of the Freedom Struggle in the 1960s, promoted community-supported agriculture to assist Black farmers, to help them retain their land, and to support local Black communities nearby.

Since Whatley's time, others have taken up his call. CSAs have been established in inner-city neighborhoods to fight against "food apartheid" (areas of a city without access to high-quality food, sometimes known as "food deserts"); Black, brown, and Native American youth have been trained to become farmers; reparations for slavery and land grabs from people of color are now being sought in terms of establishing productive farming operations to correct these past injustices; and traditional indigenous farming practices have been employed to return land to productive status without reliance on chemicals.

Black farmers themselves also organized in the face of the long history of neglect suffered at the hands of the USDA. In 1997, Black farmers brought two class-action lawsuits against the agency: *Pigford v. Glickman* and *Brewington v. Glickman*. Ultimately combined into a single case known simply as *Pigford*, the suit alleged discrimination in farm-lending practices from 1981 to 1996. Black farmers reached a settlement with the USDA in 1999, which disbursed over $1 billion to settle their claims.[57]

But many Black farmers did not hear of the *Pigford* settlement in a timely fashion and so missed the filing deadline—so many, in fact, that in the 2008 farm bill Congress made provisions for late-filing applicants. Black farmers filed multiple lawsuits, which were consolidated into a single case, commonly referred to as *Pigford II*. In February 2010, the Department of Justice announced a $1.25 billion settlement of *Pigford II* claims.[58]

Nonprofit organizations have emerged to defend Black landownership, such as the Emergency Land Fund, founded in 1972 to reverse the trend of decreasing Black landownership across the rural American South; the US Endowment for Forestry and Communities, which created the Sustainable Forestry and African American Land Retention Program to stem the loss of Black-owned forest lands; and the Center for Heirs Property Preservation in South Carolina.

Leah Penniman, cofounder of Soul Fire Farm in Petersburg, New York, who also writes in this present volume, is exemplary of a new breed of Black farmers who specifically work the land to supply Black communities with high-quality, organic food as a means of ending racism and injustice in the food system.

But all of these efforts, while essential, are still not enough. The *Pigford* cases, for example, seek redress only as far back as 1981, while the roots of the discrimination against Black farmers go back many generations earlier. For these reasons, Black landownership is at the center of a growing national discourse on income inequality and reparations for slavery, as it should be. Since the beginning of America, landownership has been the basis of creating wealth. Slavery created tremendous wealth for white landowners. For generations after slavery, broken promises and land robbery transferred trillions of dollars of land-based wealth from Black families into the pockets and estates of white families. This present volume shows the impact of these transgressions on the lives of ordinary Black men and women.

Today, America is again at a crossroads. Only the federal government can remedy centuries of discrimination, disenfranchisement, and dispossession of Black landowners, asserting itself through legislative, judicial, and executive actions. From these crossroads, what direction will this country take? Will Black families who own land, and those who once owned land, be subjected to yet another round of broken promises, or does the political and social will exist to bring about the restorative and reparative justice necessary for lasting change in how Blacks own, retain, and derive wealth from the land?

This isn't simply about making amends. It's about reaffirming our values on which this nation was founded: the principles of fairness and equality and opportunity.

—PRESIDENT BARACK OBAMA
ON THE SECOND *PIGFORD* SETTLEMENT

MR. GLADNEY, OKALONA, MISSISSIPPI.
NINETY-FOUR YEARS OLD AND STILL
FARMING.

21

*F*ield Day at the Hill Place

ODIS HILL
Hill Farm
Bonita, Louisiana

As far as small towns go, you'd think you couldn't get much smaller than Mer Rouge, Louisiana. Located thirty miles north of Monroe in Morehouse Parish, Mer Rouge, which means "Red Sea" in French, was named for the way the ripples in the red soil reminded the town's founder of a vast red sea. But drive another thirteen miles and you get to the even smaller town of Bonita. It's a village, really, founded in the early 1890s at the end of a railroad line. On display at the Bonita Museum is an old saddle, a 1930s cash register from Robertson's Grocery Store, and a wooden ironing board that doubled as a "cooling board" for the dead before embalming was invented.

Bonita's street are quiet most days, but for the last two years, on the last Friday in June, hundreds of Black farmers from as far as Virginia and South Carolina pass through Bonita on their way to the two-hundred-acre farm known as "the Hill Place." That's where fourth-generation cotton farmer Odis Hill hosts his annual field day.

It's 8:00 a.m. and well above 80 degrees. The long dirt road leading to Odis Hill's farm ends in a grassy clearing already packed with cars and trucks. Across the way, nearly a hundred Black farmers have gathered under a large white tent, where they socialize and fan themselves against the rising heat. From a distance, the gathering looks like a family reunion, with farmers shaking hands and slapping backs—and in some ways, it is. Being a Black farmer can be an isolating experience, but here at Odis Hill's field day, folks have a chance to reconnect, exchange information, and compare stories.

Hill came up with the idea to host a field day for Black farmers in 2000, just before the Fourth of July holiday when across Morehouse Parish, farmers were blessed with the perfect amount of rain and sunshine. Their fields were nearly perfect. Thrilled at the promise of a good harvest, Hill called two of his fellow farmers to hammer out the details.

Now it's nineteen years later, and Odis begins the morning by welcoming farmers to his property. This is actually the second field day some of these farmers have attended in the last two days. The first occurred just over the state line in Arkansas. Seeing them all gathered here together, you get a strong sense of community, a sense that these people have known and supported each other for years. The farmers assembled here today are as diverse as the crops they grow. Old and young, men and women, some farming as much as twelve thousand acres of commodity crops—soybeans, corn, and cotton—while others farm a few hundred acres of produce. There are even one or two cattle farmers in attendance.

Odis Hill takes the mic and welcomes everyone to Hill Farm. "Good morning to each and every one of y'all. On behalf of me and my wife, Tammy, and our two sons, O'Brian and Denim, my lovely mom, my nieces and nephews, and my auntie all the way from California, we want to welcome you to Hill Farm. We appreciate you all coming."

It's been a challenging year for American farmers. Excessive spring rain has damaged their crops, forcing some to replant their fields. Then there's President Trump's trade war with China, which has dampened prices on the world market. But Odis's demeanor is chipper. He smiles warmly and cracks a joke about patching corn that makes folks laugh, and then he asks everyone to pray for a dry harvest.

An hour later, after announcements and a few speeches it's time for the hayride. Two enormous tractors pulling long flatbeds stacked with hay bales rumble up to the loading area. Odis Hill invites everyone to climb aboard, and under a blazing mid-morning sun, we all set out toward his fields.

Field day is about community, but it's also about business, innovation, and technology. Odis collaborates with Bayer, New Holland, Local Seed Co., FMC, and others to grow new varieties of corn and soybeans. Now, representatives from those companies are stationed at various points across the farm to introduce the farmers to the test crops. The farmers' expertise is evident as they ask carefully considered questions about estimated yields and fertilizers. Two young farmers, brothers from a nearby farm, walk among the rows of soybeans for a closer inspection. At the last stop, a representative from a commercial hemp company espouses the benefits of growing this new crop and hands out crisply folded brochures and tote bags.

Historically, Black farms have been excluded from conversations about the latest inventions and technologies. In 1862, the US government funded agricultural and technical universities across the country, commonly referred to as "1862s," to educate white farmers on the latest techniques and innovations. These colleges and universities include Mississippi State, Louisiana State University, Clemson, Auburn, and Virginia Tech. But it wasn't until almost thirty years later, under the Morrill Act of 1890, that the government funded land-grant colleges and universities for Black farmers. These colleges, commonly known as "1890s," include North Carolina A&T, Alabama A&M, Southern University, Prairie View, and Tuskegee University. For years, Black farmers had to rely on one another to gain access to information about the latest farm practices, so it's gratifying to see these companies catering to them now.

When the hayride ends, the tractors pull us back to the white tent, where local caterers have set up for lunch. Everyone waits in line patiently for servers to pile fried fish, corn on the cob, string beans, and potato chips onto their plates. There's plenty of sweet tea and water to drink, but only a few open seats by the time everyone is served. There are speeches and more speeches. The Louisiana commissioner of agriculture has flown in to offer his good wishes. By two o'clock, field day is over, and it's time to head home until next year.

The next afternoon finds Odis and two other farmers sitting in folding chairs under the tent. They've been cleaning up all day and are taking a break. In the peace and quiet of the late afternoon, Odis shares the history of his family's farm.

ODIS HILL

My great-grandfather Horace Hill purchased this land. We always say he came up from a place called Shelton, northwest of Bastrop. I want to say he purchased this farm in 1910 or 1915. With no education, he bought two hundred acres. He was "The Man." He was a big force. Everything had to come through him. He rode his horse to town and got the mail and issued the mail out to all of his neighbors.

My great-grandfather was real prosperous, and for his time he was smart and self-sufficient. He had a blacksmith shop and a sugar mill. He had it all figured out. In the 1940s he had electricity in a big two-story house. He didn't drive, so he had a son drive for him. He kept a full-time butler. Even now, I don't have a shed to keep my equipment under, but my great-grandfather had a shed big enough to store all of his equipment because he didn't want it to be out in the weather. The older hands stayed around and worked in the garden, and the children worked in the fields. His kids did the work. Everyone made a joke out of it. They said, "Yeah, Horace *should* have been The Man because his kids were sharecropping for him." He never planted cotton until after the second Sunday in May. I guess that was the ideal time. I'm sure the soil was warm then. He died in 1944.

His kids didn't have to pay for land. They inherited land from him. One hundred years later, we're still farming it. I'm not bragging, but I'm going to be honest: didn't but two Hills buy land—my great-grandfather Horace bought land, and I'm buying land now. In addition to the original two hundred acres, we're farming fifty-eight acres in another section and twenty-five in the back. Everyone knows where the Hill Place is. I have cousins who call it Ponderosa, but the original name is the Hill Place.

Originally we farmed cotton. Due to the market and the increase in the cost of cotton, we switched over to grain. This is good soil. They call this "cotton ground," and all my fellow farmers know what's here.

I had no intention of going into farming, but my father had gotten in trouble with the USDA. I came home after I graduated from college, and a couple of my home-boys had gotten into farming, so I said, "I'm here. I have the land." I'd started working at International Paper Company, so I started farming on the side.

My first year farming was 1989 to 1990. The first year didn't go well at all. In the late '80s and early '90s, the money from the Federal Service [Administration] was always late. FSA is the name of the agency under the USDA that lends money.

It seems like it's designed to get you in trouble. That first year, I borrowed from the USDA and was late in receiving a loan.

In farming, you need your money in January or February. You got your weather conditions and other factors to consider. It's not like opening a store. In a store everything is inside—all you have to do is get it open. But farming is a timing thing. It starts in January. But it seemed like the money from FSA never came at the appropriate time. It was a bad situation, and it always kept us Black farmers behind. Products and fertilizer would go on sale in February, but here it would be April when you finally got your money. By then, there'd be a big demand for fertilizer, so you'd have to pay top dollar. You could never buy supplies when it was cheaper or the price was lower. You had to pay the upscale price due to the fact that you didn't have the money. You almost needed a full-time job to get started.

The second year went pretty well, but the USDA didn't finance me. They came to me in June and told me, "You didn't receive the loan." I was supposed to have planted my crop in June. Then a white farmer came and asked, "Are you going to farm?" They pretty much knew what the Hill Farm was all about. But I was able to carry on due to the fact that I had a job. I was able to get my crops fertilized and planted. A bank came out and looked at the crop, and they lent me money. It was a good lesson. It seemed like after that, everything just took off, and I never applied for another USDA loan. I've been borrowing from the bank for thirty years.

Nineteen ninety-four is a year I'll never forget: whatever the white boys were picking, we picked right there with them. They was picking thirteen hundred bushels per acre, and we were picking thirteen hundred—and I beat a lot of them. This land is fertile. Everything went perfect that year. We bought a cotton picker, so we picked our own crops. This normally don't happen, but that year when the cotton went to be graded, our cotton was so good they paid us a dollar per pound when the highest price was sixty or seventy cents per pound.

I came up with the idea for field day around July 4, 2000. It had rained and after the rain stopped the crops were looking so good on everybody's farms—on the Black farms *and* the white farms. I contacted Mr. Armstrong and Mr. Downs and I said, "Somebody needs to look at these crops because they're outstanding." I called Southern University, and they said they would come. I called Dr. Goldmon, who I'd met at a white field day, and I asked him to coordinate our field day. We all met in the little town of Mer Rouge. We thought it was going to be a little old bit of something but then we went to Mr. Armstrong's shop. He had all kinds of equipment. Dr. Goldmon said, "Wow!" From there it took off.

My main goal was to inform the general public that there are still a few Black farmers who are out here doing a great job. We weren't getting the publicity. We weren't getting any free seeds or free herbicides. Field day introduces Black farmers to new technologies, new equipment, new production practices, new varieties of seeds that haven't hit the market. Now we have sponsors. Every now and then they'll raffle off a tractor.

I'm trying to encourage young Black farmers to get involved. If they have the interest, they should try to get with an older Black farmer who can help them out and mentor them before they get too old. My fear is, if we older Black farmers aren't around, the white boys are going to eat the young Black farmers alive. They don't want us out here no way. They're going to do all they can to take Black farmers out.

For Black farmers, the hardest thing about farming is the planting and harvesting. I'll say this: it seems like we Black farmers can grow the crops real well, but we haven't gotten ourselves in a position to go out there and harvest a hundred acres in a day. Some of us can, but not all of us. It seems like we struggle more during the harvest. We don't have the income to purchase that great harvester—it's the same thing with some whites—but most of our equipment is used and worn out.

We can't afford a $300,000 harvester—especially not when harvesting is the only thing that piece of equipment is going to do, when you can't use it nowhere else. You're going to have a breakdown, and then you still got to pay those hands when you're down. I don't harvest no more. I let someone come in and get mine. In three or four days, they're gone. My concentration is getting my crop planted, getting it matured, and getting it ready for harvest.

What I love about farming is the challenge, I guess, especially when you're working another job. I like getting the crop ready to be planted. You've sat up all winter. When it's planting time, I go wild because I want to make sure it's right. I love getting the fields ready to plant and tillaging. It's determining which field to till first and knowing the weather. In some cases, all we have to do is go out there, put some fertilizer on the ground, and row it up. And then there's the smell of the soil—it's just fabulous.

My legacy that I leave on Hill's Farm is irrigation and land leveling. When you have level land, it flows real well. Those are the improvements I've made which increase the value of my property.

If my sons don't want to farm, we won't have no problem leasing this land. We got water. We got good soil. It's irrigated and land-leveled. We can lease the Hill Place for top dollar. We've already been approached by white farmers, who say, "You ought to lease your land to me. We ought to work together." But I say, "No, not yet." We won't have any problem renting the Hill Place.

This has been a good life for me, a fantastic experience. I've had the opportunity to buy land. My wife always tells me, "You steady buying land," and I say, "Well, they ain't making any more of it." I don't think I could have done any better.

22.

*E*qual Ground

WILLIE EARL NELSON SR. AND SONS

Nelson Sons Farm
Sondheimer, Louisiana

According to Google Maps, we should have turned left at the little Baptist church, but now the road has dead-ended and we're surrounded by dense woods on all sides. The levee is straight ahead. If we were to scramble up its grassy banks, we'd be staring at the Mississippi River. Normally, I'd refresh my location, but the words NO SERVICE have replaced the single bar on the signal icon, and I'm afraid that if I call the Nelsons, I'll break the fragile connection to the outside world and we'll be stuck out here with no way to let folks know where we are. The POSTED sign tacked to a nearby tree extinguishes any thought I have of getting out of the car. God knows what's lurking in these woods. A few miles back, we saw a small deer herd nervously bounding along the road, which means there must be an animal out here that's big enough to eat them. In the passenger seat, my photographer Alison has gone quiet, staring through her window. Just like me, she's a city girl, a New Orleans native who has lived in Brooklyn for the last twenty-two years. Between the two of us, we couldn't make a fire let alone fend off predators if we had to spend the night out here.

I'm still weighing our options when my phone rings and I hear Adrain Nelson's voice on the line. In the same gentle tone I've come to know from our handful of phone conversations, he asks me where I am, and I do my best to describe what I see. He tells me to turn around. "When you see the church, make a right and come down the road."

Wedged in the top northeast corner of Louisiana, Sondheimer nuzzles up against both Arkansas and Mississippi. A quick Google search back at the hotel revealed that the population is ninety-seven people. Now, as we double back, I can see how that's possible. Aside from the church, a kudzu-covered house, and a couple of rusty basketball hoops rising randomly at the edge of a field, I haven't seen any evidence of human life since we turned off Highway 65. Just endless acres of soybean fields and a big open Louisiana sky.

Half a mile past the church, we round the bend and see Adrain up ahead. He's dressed in jeans and a bright white T-shirt, and as we get closer, I recognize the black and gray baseball cap that I admired when I met him in person for the first time yesterday at Odis Hill's field day. Stitched in bright red thread, the words "Nelson Sons Farm" arc gently across a bright blue "N." It's a stylish design—bright and youthful without being conspicuous; bold without being pretentious. And as I will come to learn over the next few hours, the cap perfectly symbolizes the Nelsons' approach to farming: intentional and confident. This third- and fourth-generation farming family has a clear sense of where they're going and how they're going to get there.

A tidy, single-story brick house sits back from the road, and an older gentleman whom I assume is Adrain's father, Willie Earl Nelson Sr., stands in the short driveway. A tuft of gray hair—the only hint of his age—sticks out from under his baseball cap. Tinted glasses shield his eyes. He's polite, but not effusive, as he shakes our hands. His reserved manner is understandable considering what he and his family, like so many Black farmers, have been through. He strikes me as a man who stands back and observes before making a decision, who judges folks by their actions more than by their words. You get the sense that an honest day's work is the best way to earn his respect, and sure enough, one of the first things he tells me is that he'd normally have spent the morning in the fields. It's only when I assure him we won't take up his entire day that he finally smiles and relaxes a bit.

Mr. Nelson is a third-generation farmer. He and his four sons are well known and well respected in the Black farming community. Together, they farm over three thousand acres of soybeans, corn, and cotton. In some ways, they are a throwback to the past—to an era when parents and children farmed side by side, when farming traditions were passed by word of mouth, from hand to hand, and farms were passed down through the generations. But there's nothing old-fashioned about the Nelsons. They use the latest technology to manage their crops. There are actually seven children in all, but the three sisters, Connyettia, Comaneatha, and Montana, don't farm. The four brothers, Adrain, Courtney, Shaun, and Willie Jr., range in age from twenty-eight to forty, respectively. They are whip-smart, ambitious, and unapologetic. Like so many Black farmers, they have faced more than their fair share of hardship and discrimination. And like so many Black farmers, they haven't allowed those obstacles to hold them back. They are determined to farm. It's in their blood, as Mr. Nelson confirms as he begins to narrate the family story.

"It started with my granddaddy, Will Nelson," he says. "The way I heard it, he was five or six years old when he was bought off the East Coast near Virginia as a slave. Will and his brother came on a ship on the Atlantic Ocean and then up the Mississippi River to Natchez. They had to walk from Natchez to over there around Hazlehurst. If you look up a map, you'll see a community called Nelson.

"After slavery, Will and his brother couldn't stay on the land, so they built them a little house out over the Pearl River on the side of Highway 28. They fished and drank river water and had everything they needed. But one night the river flooded the land. The flood washed everything away. My granddaddy and his brother had to leave, so they walked east on Highway 28 down to Simpson County, Mississippi. My granddaddy stayed in Magee, while his brother went north as far as Jackson. My granddaddy didn't hear from his brother but only one time after that.

"Will Nelson married a Blackfoot Indian named Ola. They tried to purchase three hundred acres of ground over in Simpson County. They'd made a deal with the landowner, who was a white man. The man told them, 'If you sharecrop with me over so many years, then you can have these three hundred acres.' Down here in the South, cotton was the only cash crop there was. That was the only commodity you made big money off of. You raised corn to keep your hogs, horses, mules, and chickens alive. Will, Ola, and their children, including Earl, my daddy, worked the land until they paid everything off but the last note. Then the white man wouldn't accept their final payment. He throwed them off the land. They had to leave from that area. My grandparents and all of their children, except my daddy, remained in Mississippi.

My daddy felt that he had been cheated; therefore, as soon as the opportunity arose, he moved over here to Transylvania, Louisiana.

"My daddy, Earl O.K. Nelson, was born in 1911. In 1931, when he was twenty years old, he married my mama, Willie Mae Carroway. They worked over in Mississippi with a white man named Herman Johnson. My daddy wasn't sharecropping for Herman Johnson; he was working on the same plantation in Mississippi that Herman Johnson was working on until Johnson packed up and came over to Louisiana. Back then, in the late '30s, the government had land that they were letting people get. The land had belonged to plantation owners who didn't have enough money to pay their taxes, so the government was breaking their land down into forty- and fifty-acre parcels. The government took the land back and made it available to Black and white farmers. Herman Johnson got him a farm. My daddy sharecropped with two or three other white sharecroppers up in northeast Louisiana until farmland came available down here.

"They called the land near Transylvania 'ice cream dirt' because it's so easy to plow. Down here in the southern part of the parish, on the lower ground, the soil isn't as good. Black people were supposed to have gotten land up there near Transylvania; they were supposed to have had first choice, but then the white people talked some of the older Black people into trading with them. The older Black people went and traded, and the white people switched them from up there to down here. I think there were seventy-two houses here. Each one consisted of between forty and sixty acres of land.

"In 1951, my daddy got this 58.6 acres. He worked the place as a homesteader before he received a government loan to purchase it. He had to be on the land for a year, then he just had to go up to the government office and say he stayed there a year and they automatically granted him the land. He was growing cotton. The property came with a 'project house' that the government built. It came with a chicken house and a barn. The original house burned in 1963. They built this brick house in 1964. This property is an eighth of a mile wide and a half mile long. Half of it is surrounded by the blacktop road.

"I started driving tractors when I was six or seven years old. Working has never been no problem with me. I don't mind working. If you want something, you have to work for it. During that time, it would take all day for the tractor to go over the field one time. It would take another day to do the second time. It took a whole week to work up fifty acres.

"I went to school up to my twelfth-grade year. I worked part-time and helped my daddy with the farm. By that time, my older siblings were mostly gone, and my daddy, he couldn't just do farm work to make enough money, so he started working at the lumber mill to help provide for the family. I took it on myself to break up the land while my daddy worked at the mill.

"I left the farm and went to Vegas with my sister in 1973. I got out there and started to make that big money as a dishwasher, but they moved me to a relief worker because of my impeccable work ethic. I was in Vegas from the last two weeks of October 1973 until Ground Hog Day in February 1974. Then I was on the bus coming back to Louisiana because my mother told me that my father needed my help on the farm."

From 1974 until his parents' mortgage was fully paid off in 2006, Willie Nelson worked on the farm, but like so many farmers, he also had to work outside the farm to make ends meet. He got married in 1976 and had his own family to support.

"I was farming for my daddy and working on the side for my own family. Fifty-four acres weren't going to take care of two families. By me working on the side, I saved enough money to increase the land I owned to a little over two hundred acres."

In 1980, his father had a heart attack, and Willie took over, gradually increasing the acreage they rented until he was farming eight hundred acres.

The Farm Service Administration (FSA) is the lending arm of the US Department of Agriculture (USDA). It was created to provide loans and offer programs to farmers. But for generations, the FSA staffed local offices with agents who treated government funds like their private piggy banks and local counties and parishes like their private kingdoms, deciding who gets access to funds and information and who doesn't. For decades, the FSA deployed a variety of tactics to discriminate against Black farmers, depriving them of information and access to the capital they needed to operate their farms and expand. This, more than any other form of discrimination, has been at the root of Black land loss and has contributed to the precipitous decline in the number of Black farmers. And this is why the agency has been derided by some as "the last plantation."

"In 1978," Mr. Nelson continues, "a white farmer named Stokes was going to sell me and my brother O.K. Nelson Jr. one thousand acres of ground. He was fixing as though we could get it. This was around Thanksgiving. We had a good crop that year. I had paid up everything. I had put in for my loan for the next year. The land he was going to sell us had a good cotton base. The money we would have made from cotton alone would have paid the note on the price he was going to sell the land for. I'd approached the Farmers Home Administration [FHA] and turned in the loan information, but I didn't get a promissory note from the seller. I didn't know I had to do that. The FHA wanted to know who the buyer was, how much the sale was for. I was having so much trouble trying to grow my operation around here, I'd decided to move elsewhere. By me going to the FHA, they said they were going to help me. They got all the information, the man's name and everything—and before Christmas, I went to the office to check. They told me, 'Well, it's taking time.'

"I went back in January; they told me the same thing. February, the same thing. Finally, March came around. I'd gotten my ground broke up and ready for planting. I went up there and asked about my loan. They said, 'It's coming.' It still didn't show up. I asked them about my application for the loan to purchase the land. Finally, I decided to go back and talk to the Mr. Stokes who was going to sell me the land. He told me another white man came and asked him about it. He said the man told him I wasn't able to get a loan. The FHA let the other white buyer buy the land.

"I went in to see the FHA supervisor. Every time I'd go up there, he'd stay back there in the office, or he would go out the back door. Once, my brother and I went up there and sat for a whole day. I was at the front door; my brother was at the back. We wanted to ask him why he'd do that. I never did get a chance to meet with him. I haven't seen him to this day.

"That same year, I went to inquire about applying for my crop loan. I didn't get a loan in April, May, June, or July. When August came, they called, telling me to come sign for my loan. What good was that? None. By them not giving me the loan at the first of the year, it stopped me from expanding. I had other little projects, other land that I was supposed to have picked up that year. After I didn't get the thousand acres, I was still going to get some other acreage, but they found out what I wanted to do. They put somebody else on it. The FSA never would have known about the land if I hadn't told them the seller's name and where the land was. Then they came down here and saw my crop already planted. Then they wanted to give me the money."

No farmer can expand without capital, but the FSA and other lending institutions have historically and systematically restricted Black farmers' access, which eventually drives them out of business. Because there are so few alternatives and few minority lending institutions geared toward lending to Black farmers, the FSA has a monopoly on lending.

Black farmers' loan applications are often denied outright. If the FSA agrees to loan Black farmers money, it's often with the goal of burdening them with debt. The agents encourage Black farmers to borrow money for new, more expensive equipment. In return, they require them to put up their personal assets as collateral. In some cases, the FSA requires Black farmers to be over-collateralized, up to as much as 150 percent. They also require them to take out the loans in their names rather than the names of their business entity, which allows the FSA to seize all their personal assets, including their farms, if they have a bad year and aren't able to repay the loan. "If something happens," Mr. Nelson says, "they have your assets as collateral. They come and take everything. Without a tractor, what will you have? You can't work five acres. You'll be completely out. They don't do that with white farmers."

As Mr. Nelson speaks, his four sons take seats in a loose semicircle of lawn chairs in the grass. They are a close-knit family, and seeing them all together it's easy to understand why Mr. Nelson is so proud of his children. The young men project an ease and self-confidence that draws people to them. They are good-natured and industrious, with a clear vision of what they want. Now, they pick up the story. Like their father, the brothers have had their share of problems with FSA agents who have tried to steer them toward trouble.

"It took three months to process my loan," Adrain, twenty-eight, the youngest brother, explains. He graduated from the University of Louisiana at Monroe with a degree in finance. "Luckily, I started in October. We didn't close until the end of December, first of January—after Christmas. I had to show documents that I know nobody else had to show. They gave me the runaround."

"Adrain was almost about to give up," Mr. Nelson says. "He was going back in there for a second time, and the head guy was sending him to another guy and then to a lady. She kept putting him off, too. I said, 'Just go in there and tell them what you want. And then tell them you're going to record them explaining why they wouldn't do it.' Adrain went in there. He asked to see the Big Boss. I was with him. Adrain put his phone right there on the counter. 'I want you to explain to me why I can't get my loan. What is the reason I keep being denied?' The man looked and started turning red. When the man thought he was being recorded, they brought the papers out for Adrain to sign."

At thirty-one, Shaun approaches farming with a focused intensity of a man twice his age. As the family's unofficial spokesman, Shaun isn't afraid to speak his mind. "They try to overwhelm you with paperwork and talk to you like you're dumb. That's my problem with them. They try to throw out words they think you don't know and treat you like you can't calculate two plus two."

He shares the story of how the FSA tried to lure him into borrowing more money than he needed. "We farm a lot of dry land," he explains, which is less expensive to farm than irrigated land. The yields are lower, but so are the costs to make the crop. When the FSA loan officer calculated how much money Shaun needed to borrow, he based his calculations on the more expensive irrigated land, which, in turn, increased the amount of money he suggested Shaun borrow. "This year, they gave me a loan of $290,000. I knew I wasn't going to spend that." Shaun used $190,000 and put the remaining $100,000 aside.

But the FSA office will penalize him for being fiscally responsible and claim that because he had failed to use the entire $290,000 loan, he wasn't meeting his cash-flow projections. On paper, it will look to the officials in Washington, DC, as though the local FSA agents gave Shaun a fair chance. The fact that he didn't use the entire loan will suggest that he didn't make enough money. Next year, when Sean goes back to the FSA to apply for a loan to farm more land, even five additional acres, the FSA will refer back to the previous year's records with calculations that wrongly suggest he wasn't profitable with the land he had. In other words, the FSA creates a false paper trail, then uses it to justify denying him a loan.

A less savvy farmer would walk away thinking that he had been legitimately disqualified, but Shaun and his brothers see the scheme for what it is—a way for the FSA to limit their growth and ultimately drive them out of business. Shaun shakes his head in disgust. "It all comes down to cash flow. They give you just enough to fail."

Another tactic FSA agents have deployed against Black farmers has been to withhold important information about programs that can help them manage their farms. "We've been behind." Shaun says. "The government was paying to level every-body's field for better flood irrigation, but Daddy didn't know about the program until twenty or thirty years *after* the white farmers learned about it. He just learned about it in the last ten years. See how far behind we are? If Dad had been able to purchase that thousand acres back then, probably for $1,000 per acre, he'd be worth $5 or $6 million by now. Our generation would probably be farming ten thousand acres. We're so far behind. Now we have to catch up."

"The local government agents are looking at their buddies," Courtney, twenty-nine, explains. "They're looking at their sons. If we're doing better than them, they don't want that. It's a government agency, but they're still humans."

The Nelsons describe other farming programs that should be available to Black farmers but aren't: community development funds, special disaster loans, and subsidies that white farmers are already receiving.

"The USDA is set up to subsidize farmers," Courtney says. "They have programs to benefit farmers all day long, but they won't subsidize Black farmers." Nor is it unusual for the USDA to build living expenses into loans for white farmers so they're able to be full-timers and not have to have a second job. But historically, Black farmers have been denied.

"You didn't have to pay back the living expenses," Mr. Nelson says. "It was like getting food stamps would be today. The FSA/USDA was doing that for white farmers when my daddy was farming, but my daddy and other Black farmers never received that benefit. If Black farmers got money for living expenses, they had to pay it back. They didn't find out what white farmers were getting until years later."

For all the barriers that the FSA has tried to put in their way, the Nelson brothers are undeterred. With the help of organizations like the National Black Growers Council (NBGC), the Nelsons have figured out other ways to keep farming.

"When we used to go to the seed companies, they would tell us we had to pay for our seeds up front," Shaun says. "The NBGC told us how we could go to the seed companies and get seeds at 0 percent interest for the year. That means we don't have to get a loan. That's capital we can use for something else. We had to find another way around the FSA."

One reason the Nelsons have been able to keep farming is their large family. Between the four brothers, their three sisters, and all their children, they can have as many as sixteen people working on the farm—enough help to easily farm six or seven thousand acres.

"This is what they're afraid of right here," forty-year-old Willie Jr. says, pointing to his brothers. "None of us drink or smoke. We've got level heads, and we want something in life. We know what we can accomplish if we put our minds to it."

The single factor that would change the game for Black farmers is giving them an alternative source of capital. If other financial institutions outside the government loaned money to Black farmers, they would not have to go through the FSA. The Nelsons know how to farm. If they, like so many other Black farmers, had an alternate source of capital, each one of them would be their own boss. They could have their own companies, their own business entities that they could pass down to the next generation.

"It all comes down to capital. It always boils down to money," Shaun says. "We have the know-how. We know the logistics of farming. They say Black people can't farm, but our ancestors did it as slaves. The only difference is the financial side. They played us on the financial side. Even when they gave Black people forty acres and a mule—and from what I understand, we really didn't even get that—they still broke our backs with the money. It's not that Black people can't farm. We've done it our whole lives; our families did it. It's in our blood. Black people built this country. I want to get us from under other people's thumb."

It's almost noon, and there's work to be done. Before we pack up, I ask the Nelsons about their hopes and plans for the future: what would Nelson and Sons Farms 2.0 look like if the sky were the limit?

"I want to be the biggest Black farmer," Shaun says. Then he pauses. "I want to be *the biggest* farmer."

"If Dad would have been a doctor," Willie Jr. adds, "all of us would be doctors. I drive school buses too. I followed in his footsteps. I want to make him proud. I want to make our mama proud. I want to succeed in life and be the biggest farmers we can be."

"I want to own land," Shaun says. "Some older farmers got out of farming and sold their land; they had ten thousand acres. By the time I get up to eighty years old, when we leave here, I want my kids, my grandkids, my nieces and nephews—I want them to be able to say we own land. I want to send my kids to college so they can live a better life than I did. My mama and daddy lived a better life than their mama and daddy. They gave us a better life than they lived. I want my kids to live a better life than I'm living, and I'm living a good life now. I want it to continue. I want intergenerational wealth."

"We just need the land," says Willie Jr. "Right now, we're farming government land. We need to own the land. There's land for sale right now. We've been doing the calculations to figure out how we can use our cash flow to get the loan to pay it off."

Adrain looks at his brother. "We're already an inspiration to so many other young Black people. They're looking at what we're doing, and that's inspiring them. Our nephew is going to college for agriculture. It's time for Black people to come back into agriculture. Doctors, lawyers—all that is good—but there's so much that can be done in agriculture as well. This industry shouldn't be dominated by just one race of people."

"A farmer has to be able to do everything from beginning to end," Mr. Nelson says. "Not just one thing. You have to take care of everything yourself. But I enjoy farming. Once I can get out there and get to working, I'm my own boss. Not everybody can be a farmer. Not everybody can go from sun up to sun down. That's what it takes. From the beginning of the year to the end."

As a final note, Shaun adds, "I have confidence in us. We've got to quit settling for less. We're making progress, but it ain't fast enough. We're still ten years behind. We just want the same thing that everyone else has. Put us on the same playing field. If we get on the same playing field, I think we could do the same thing that some of these other farmers are doing—or better. All we want is equal ground."

23.

*F*earless

BY TIM SEIBLES

For Moombi

Good to see the green world
undiscouraged, the green fire
bounding back every spring, and beyond
the tyranny of thumbs, the weeds
and other co-conspiring green genes
ganging up, breaking in, despite
small shears and kill-mowers,
ground gougers, seed-eaters.
Here they come, sudden as graffiti

not there and then there—
naked, unhumble, unrequitedly green—
growing as if they would be trees
on any unmanned patch of earth,
any sidewalk cracked, crooning
between ties on lonesome railroad tracks.
And moss, the shyest green citizen

anywhere, tiptoeing the trunk
in the damp shade of an oak.

Clear a quick swatch of dirt
and come back sooner than later
to find the green friends moved in:
their pitched tents, the first bright
leaves hitched to the sun, new roots
tuning the subterranean flavors,
chlorophyll setting a feast of light.

Is it possible to be so glad?
The shoots rising in spite of every plot
against them. Every chemical stupidity,
every burned field, every better
home & garden finally overrun
by the green will, the green greenness
of green things growing greener.
The mad Earth publishing
Her many million murmuring
unsaids. Look

how the shade pours
from the big branches—the ground,
the good ground, pubic
and sweet. The trees—who
are they? Their stillness, that
long silence, the never
running away.

24.

*F*our Days in Alaskan Farm School

MELONY EDWARDS

Calypso Farm and Ecology Center
Ester, Alaska

In her Instagram post, Melony Edwards hoists a twenty-pound Chioggia beet onto her shoulder. The vegetable is larger than Melony's face, and its mass of stems and oversized leaves sprouting from its top match the bunch of braids she has gathered with an elastic band on the top of her head. Wearing a gray fleece and white sunglasses, Melony kneels in the dirt. Acres of leafy greens stretch into the distance. The caption reads, "We grow beets this big that are not woody and grow big from the result of LOVE."

Melony was one of the first young Black farmers I came across. She was wrapping up a three-year stint at Willowood Farm of Ebey's Prairie on Whidbey Island off the coast of Seattle. She'd soon be heading to Alaska to attend farm school as a learning sabbatical.

It's 2 p.m. on a drizzly June afternoon when my flight touches down in Fairbanks. Dressed in overalls and rubber boots, her hair in five braids that fall past her shoulders, Melony waits for me in baggage claim. She leads me outside through the sliding doors, where the gray sky hangs low and the air is heavy with the acidic smell of burning wood. For the last two weeks, wildfires have raged across Alaska. An evacuation alert has been issued for parts of Fairbanks. We toss my luggage in the back seat of her VW Jetta wagon and strike out for Calypso Farm and Ecology Center.

One month ago, Melony traveled to Fairbanks from Seattle—a distance of more than twenty-one hundred miles. From Whidbey Island, she headed north to Bellingham, Washington, where she boarded the Alaska Marine Highway ferry. Her aunt had generously purchased the $1,500 ferry ticket, but the additional $500 for a private cabin was beyond Melony's budget, so for three days, she tent-camped on the windswept outer deck as the ferry navigated Alaska's inside passage. She disembarked in Haines, Alaska, and drove for twelve hours, crossing the Yukon and stopping occasionally to photograph moose tracks, snowcapped mountains, and placid glacial lakes.

Melony's journey to farming is as circuitous as the road we're following. Her car chugs along as we climb the foothills to the small town of Ester. Just past a small painted sign that reads CALYPSO FARM, we turn off Old Anchorage-Fairbanks Highway onto a dirt road. It's still drizzly, and across the road, treetops pierce the layer of fog that has settled in the valley.

For the next five months, the thirty-five-acre Calypso Farm will be Melony's home. Founded by Susan Willsrud and Tom Zimmer, this working educational farm and ecology center is nestled into a terraced, tree-rimmed hillside. Here, one can learn everything about how to operate a farm, from sheep shearing and blacksmithing to mechanics and carpentry.

What follows is the story of Melony's journey to becoming a farmer, crafted from conversations we had during my four-day visit as we cooked, harvested vegetables, spun wool into yarn, milked goats, and helped build a log cabin that will eventually become the farm's woodworking shop.

Originally from Ohio, Melony moved to Seattle with her mom, cousin, brother, and twin sister when she was fifteen. Her mom had been offered a job, and the chance to expand her children's horizons in a more diverse state with better opportunities convinced her to make the move.

After high school, Melony took a gap year to figure out what she wanted to do. She loved fashion and briefly considered pursuing it as a career, but she didn't think of herself as artistic. Curious about photography, she worked as a children's photographer. "It was good for me to take that time to think about what I wanted to do," she explains. "One day I woke up and realized I didn't want to work in a mall for the rest of my life. I need to go to school." She'd always enjoyed cooking, so she decided to go to culinary school.

She enrolled in Le Cordon Bleu in Portland, Oregon, where she was trained as a classical chef. "I loved culinary school. At first, I thought I wanted to open a restaurant that fed and employed the homeless, but people told me I wouldn't make any money, which was discouraging." For a while, after graduating, she worked at the Fairmont Olympic Hotel, one of Seattle's best restaurants. But like so many female chefs, she found the male-dominated restaurant culture to be problematic.

"I decided to go back to school and get my hospitality and restaurant management degree. I was twenty-one." Just as her mother had done seven years earlier, Melony packed up and drove across country to Miami, Florida. "It took us six days. We had a flat tire in Chicago, went to Mount Rushmore and the Spam Museum." She got her bachelor's at Johnson & Wales University, after which she worked briefly on a cruise ship with Norwegian Cruise Line in Hawaii. Eventually, she found her way back to Seattle.

It was in Seattle that Melony started thinking more seriously about her health and nutrition. She realized that she and her family were all overweight and began questioning the root causes. "We were so unhealthy. I'd done the Special K diet, I'd done this diet and that diet, and the weight just came back. I started to wonder what was happening. I searched online for information on how people improved their health. I realized the answer was food. Having access to fresh fruits and vegetables was the key. I looked around and realized that no one of color in my neighborhood or at the farmers' market was growing or eating fruits and vegetables." She began to examine the connection—or rather the *disconnection*—between people of color and their food sources. "I had all the questions about food and its production. Why are we afraid of killing a chicken? Why are we afraid of dirt on vegetables? Was being connected to food something that only white people did, and if that was the case, why?" A longtime science fiction fan, she began to imagine what might happen to people of color in her community if something catastrophic would happen. "My biggest question was, What happens if we don't have someone to provide for us anymore? How do we feed ourselves?"

Her first step was to try her hand at gardening. "I bought herbs, but they all died." Her next step was to volunteer at a community garden. Soon, her curiosity pushed her to ask more questions. She wanted to learn about the process of growing food. She worked at Amazon, and then Whole Foods Market. Meanwhile, she began volunteering at a raw dairy farm. "I scooped cow poop and mucked out the barn and collected chicken eggs. I loved it. I'd never worked on a farm before, but it was so nice to be outside, not have to work under synthetic lights."

Finding a full-time farm position was more challenging than Melony had anticipated. For two years, she applied for internships but was met with rejection, which made her question farming. "Some people told me I was too old; that most people who do internships are in their twenties. I was in my thirties. Then they told me I was overqualified. I thought, 'People change careers all the time.' Then they told me I was underqualified or I didn't fit in. I'd talk to people on the phone and they'd be excited, then they would look at my LinkedIn and suddenly I wouldn't be qualified. I was about to give up. I thought, apparently, this is an exclusive career for people who don't look like me."

A farm that had rejected her application told her about Willowood Farm on Whidbey Island, so she applied. After a lengthy interview, she was hired as an intern in March 2016. "I knew nothing. I didn't know what a seed was. I barely knew that things grew from seeds. I didn't know how to transplant or how to weed." At Willowood, she was immersed in farming. She and a team of six people worked the twenty-acre property, growing two hundred named varieties of mixed vegetables that were sold directly to Seattle's top chefs. "I made the decision to work at Willowood because I wanted to learn how to farm in a rural landscape. I wanted to learn to drive a tractor and produce large amounts of food for my people. I wanted to learn agricultural skills so I could bring them back to communities of color."

But it wasn't until she learned about Leah Penniman, founder of Soul Fire Farm, that Melony began to rethink the farming practices she was learning. "I realized I was learning Eurocentric farming practices. There were previously Native Americans on the land, but there wasn't one Native person in the community. There were Chinese immigrants on the very land I was farming, but there wasn't one Chinese person in the farming community."

For a long time, Melony thought she was a first-generation farmer. It wasn't until she was preparing for her move to Alaska that she learned that members of her family had been farmers for generations. "My family on my father's side are from Tupelo, Mississippi. After Emancipation, my forefathers were first sharecroppers who were eventually able to purchase land. Family members still own the land to this day. They have an annual family reunion, which is occasionally held in Mississippi on the property. They call it 'Homecoming' because everyone comes

home to the South. I couldn't believe my dad and my grandmother never told me."

Summers in Alaska mean that the sun never completely sets—which is great for growing but challenging if you're trying to sleep. It's past 9:00 p.m. on our third day together, and the sky is a dusky rose as Melony hauls out the spinning wheel and teaches me how to spin wool into yarn.

Spinning is harder than it looks. It requires a steady hand and a good sense of timing to work the pedals. As she threads a thin piece of yarn through a series of loops and hooks, she shares her ideas for what type of farm she'd like to start. She explains that most farming programs focus on vegetable production, but Calypso Farms is one of the few farm schools to offer instruction in fiber. Interns tend the small flock of Shetland sheep and learn to sheer, card, hand-spin, and dye wool.

"I came to Alaska because Calypso Farm's program focused on skills that the Black community had moved away from: skills like blacksmithing, woodworking, using fiber to create wool, food preservation to extend the season so that once I've grown all the food, I'll know how to preserve it through a long winter season. I remember my grandmother did things like that, but I didn't grow up doing them.

"I'm a person of color in Washington State, which is predominately white. There are a lot of yarn makers, but there are very few people of color. I only know of one other in Washington. I've always had an interest in fashion, just not high fashion. But I don't see a lot of people of color in fiber arts. I think people need to know there are people of color in this space. We knit; we crochet; we raise animals for fiber. This goes back to the idea of relearning lost skills. It's about reminding people that there are people who look like us who do this. I want to work with BIPOC [Black, indigenous, and people of color] fashion artists to create designs that my yarn can be used for. I like wool because it reminds me of my hair, and much like my hair, wool can be transformed into beautiful works of art.

"I want to be independent. I've worked with people and managed people; I don't want to do that anymore. One of my goals is to create my own fiber farm where I raise my own sheep for wool and cultivate an environment that fosters textile art and creativity.

"I want to make sure my farm is a people of color–led space and that we recognize the previous stewards of the land. As landowners, we need to recognize and show gratitude to the people who came before us.

"Last year, at a conference, I met a lot of First Nations people. We were touring some white farms, and the owners kept saying they owned the land. A Native woman on the tour was in tears. When I asked her what was wrong, she said Native Americans don't think about land in terms of owning it. She expressed frustration that people whose farm we were touring didn't recognize that before the white farmers bought the land, other people were there. One of my core values is land recognition—recognizing who was on the land before us. Another core value is getting away from the word 'own.' We live in a monetary system, but we can think about it in a different way. We can talk about being stewards and caretakers of the land. I'm thinking about how to change the language.

"I think this goes back to why I want to create a space for people like me who want to learn from people like me. I still have a lot to learn. I'm not a master by any means. I know that when I start my farm, I'll have challenges and learning curves. But those challenges are what makes you grow. I'm excited for that challenge and the opportunity. I'm ready."

25.

No Better Life

THE BLUEFORTS

Blueforts' Farms
Nesmith, South Carolina

It's harvest time, and all across Williamsburg County, South Carolina, the cotton fields are glowing. We're traveling along a two-lane road under a sun-bleached sky, through the unincorporated towns of Gresham, Poston, and Johnsonville. There's Sam's Quick Stop, which we've heard serves the best hot dogs around, and a juke joint called the Hill Top where, back in the day, folks gathered on Friday nights after work to dance, drink, and feast on fried fish sandwiches and hot sausages. The road stretches away. Cotton fields and more cotton fields whip by in a blur before we finally turn onto Nesmith Road.

The crunch and ping of gravel against our pickup announces our arrival as we roll down the Blueforts' driveway. Three single-story houses, the largest with a wide porch, are arranged in a semicircle around the edge of a sprawling yard. Across the way, under a tidy shed, farm equipment stands waiting. The scene offers the first hint of what this family is like: close-knit and hardworking, with a deep reverence for the land and the people who came before them.

Wardell Bluefort and his three sons—O'Neal (age forty-two), Tremain (age thirty-eight), and Bryant (age thirty)—come out to greet us. They welcome us warmly, and we settle into comfortable conversation. The harvest is going well so far. The cotton looks good, but they hope they get a frost so they can get a move on with their soybeans. It's November and it's still 80 degrees, in the 70s at night. They don't need any more rain or warm temperatures. Soybeans can't stand the heat or the moisture. Too much more weather like they've been having, and the soybeans will rot. There's an ease between them as they explain what it means to farm as a family, a deep love coupled with a mutual respect, and an understanding that they're stronger together than apart.

Eventually, conversation turns to their family story, and we move to the shaded porch. While his sons hover nearby, Wardell, a fourth-generation farmer, takes a seat in one of the two rocking chairs. He slips off his baseball cap and rests it on his knee, then gazes out across his yard toward the equipment shed as he begins.

"It started with my great-grandmama Luiza Bluefort," he says. The tone of his voice is rich as indigo. Its cadence carries echoes of rustling palmetto, the briny fragrance of seawater, and the swirl of a summer tide. "Her husband died, and she had to run the farm. She was farming her own land. She was with family members on 128 acres—some was farmland, and some was woodland. She had a few siblings who were farming. They had their own portion of the 128 acres. The land was divided among six of them.

"My father, Wardell Blueford Sr., came along. He had to stop school to help the farm keep going after his grandfather's death. He was telling me the story of how his grandmama had to plow with the ox and how he had to plow with the ox—how he plowed with the ox and then with the mule.

"My father got married early. He pulped wood a little bit, as they called it back in the day, and he farmed a little bit. Wood pulping is when you go in the woods and cut trees down. They didn't have trucks running the roads. They had to cut the trees, then use the mules and wagons, and then throw the trees on the canal. The trees go to Georgetown to the mill—this is way back. It would take months floating on the water before the trees would get down there. My dad came from all of that.

"Then I came along. I was born in 1956. My daddy taught me to farm. I'd go to school, and when I left school he had my chores that I had to do. Every day I got off that school bus, he made sure I'm here to go to the fields. So, I grew up on the farm. I kind of hated it in the beginning. By me doing it all my life, growing up on the farm, I come out of high school and I got used to it. I job-worked a little while, but I found out job-working wasn't for me. I liked the outside. I guess that's why I did so good with it. I worked part-time but kept coming back to the farm, and we kept growing by the help of the Lord.

"I remember growing up we worked with these little tractors; I'm talking little Massey Ferguson tractors. We sharecropped with some white folks, the Scotts. We got along with them fine until we got established a little more. Then we moved on from them and started working on our own. We kept growing. My father kept adding. He bought some land, but mostly he did a lot of renting.

My daddy died thirty-one or thirty-two years ago. My boys were just little boys. O'Neal, my oldest, had just started to drive a tractor. My hands were full after my daddy's death. Now I had to do two men's work. But I hung in there. As a matter of fact, I added on the same year he died. My daddy, he taught me the ropes. He taught me everything I know. When we were together we were just like brothers. It's just me now. I'm the only son. My sisters grew up on the farm; they did a lot of work, but they're all married and gone."

"I gave my sons a choice. I treated them like my daddy treated me mostly; when they came out of school, they had to go to work. They grew up in farming, so I thought they would like it a little bit. I thought we all could make a living out of it, put some food on the table. They've stuck with me, and I appreciate that. There have been some down days and some up days. It's never been all good, you know. It's been a struggle all my days, but my daddy always taught me, 'You make a dollar, you put a hold to it; you put a squeeze on it. You spend it when you have to spend it. Use it wisely. Don't throw it away.' That's how my daddy brought me up.

"We used to grow tobacco back in the years. We started with twenty-five acres. When my daddy died, we moved up to about forty acres. The year after my daddy died, we moved up to fifty acres. When my boys started getting old enough, we came on up to about seventy-five acres. Things have changed. We really thought tobacco would be the foundation for the farmer, but these companies come along, and now you have to have a contract to grow it. It used to be each farm had an allotment; your farm came under a certain allotment from the federal government, and that's what you planted. You could go out and rent an allotment from different farmers—that's how, by renting, we brought our farm up to so many acres. That's what I mean when I say we added on. It was rented land.

"I invested in tobacco equipment, but after we got established to grow it, the companies didn't want to pay for it. We took a beating on that. You grow it, you invest, you put all that money in—gas to cure it, labor—then you get nothing from it in the end. One year, I said, 'I'm not going to do it. I'm going to leave tobacco.' That was the hard time I was having. I said, 'Let's try tobacco another year,' but my boys, they told me they didn't want to anymore. It was too much expense—all the labor we had to put into it and not enough profit—so we quit with the tobacco. I started growing cotton. I went into cotton to help take the place of some of the tobacco. It was something different. Now we plant cotton, corn, and soybeans.

"They used to farm cotton here way back in the years. Where I'm sitting right here was a cotton field, right here, before this house was built. I remember when I was a little fellow in a little red wagon. They used to put a sheet in there and a pillow for me. That same old rotten tree down there, that's where they would put me under there. I used to watch them walk these fields right here and pick cotton—I mean, pick with their hands—right where this house is sitting.

"I've been through a lot. I just keep going. That's what you've got to do. I started young. I got married young. I got married when I first came out of high school. I believe I was the first in my class to get married. That's why my boys are the ages they are.

"I enjoy having my boys here with me. We all kind of had a struggle in here. We're still here trying to make it—hard work and a little pay in the end. I'm teaching them how to live with what you've got, you know? That's how I came up. It's not *what* you make; it's how you use it. I taught them that, and they kind of obey that and are doing that likewise. That means a lot. Managing what you make, taking it and doing the best with it. You know how it's a struggle to live from one year to the next, and some people can't live from paycheck to paycheck? You sit down and talk with people, and they say, 'Oh, my check from one week to the next . . .' I say, 'Look, what about my check from one *year* to the next?' The biggest struggle on the farm is you've got to live from one year on what you make to the next year. A lot of people couldn't do that. It's not easy; it's hard. You get paid once a year? Most people wouldn't want to do it.

"People don't know what farmers go through unless you go through it. It's something that has to grow into you. With farming, you've got to grow into it from the blood. I watch a lot of young farmers try to get into it. It costs.

"What I've got on the farm has come gradually. It didn't come overnight. It took a while. My boys wanted me to sell some stuff. I tell them, 'Y'all don't know how hard it's been to get what you get. To just up and get rid of it? It just don't work like that.' You work all your life to accumulate certain things, and then all of a sudden, someone says, 'Let's end this'? That's kind of hard doing. Maybe I should have.

"But we keep growing. A few Black folks that had land—the older fellas and stuff like that—we always communicate. I was a good friend to them, and as they got old they introduced me to their farms. They say, 'Well, I'm going to quit.' They wasn't fortunate like me to have boys. They just had girls and they hired their workers, so when they got old, they didn't have no one to carry it on. We got along good; they thought a lot of me, and they said, 'I'm going to quit this year coming. If you want my farm, you can get it.' So, they ended up giving me their two- or three-hundred-acre farms. I took that on, and that's how we managed to keep growing—through the help of my friends. They said, 'Look, you've got young boys. They need to farm.' They admire how we get along together. I guess they see me struggling and trying to make it so it keeps happening. That's all from God. God is good.

"But I didn't think I'd be as large a farmer as I am. I didn't think I would go that high. But every time I have an opportunity, I make it happen. I never quit. I'd be ready to give up at my age if my boys weren't here. We're trying to keep the farm going. It's not a bad thing.

"I think we need Black farmers. It's a lot of kids coming up with nothing to do these days and times. No one's teaching hard work. If you don't have that farming background, you're usually not going to do too good with work. You might be good with the computer and the pencil, but you don't know that hard labor. That hard labor will really make a man out of you. I had kids who helped me over the years on the farm. Every one of them that got a job today appreciates coming from the farm. As a matter of fact, I know some who've gone to the city—went up there and moved on up through work. They have a good work ethic, so the work they were doing up there wasn't nothing for them. They come back and talk about it. So, that's why the farming community needs to stay among Blacks. Keep them out of trouble; give them something to do; teach the kids how to work.

"I think land is power. If you don't have land, where are you going? That's the main thing about it right there. Where are your kids going? Where are my grands going? You don't have land, you gotta move on to somewhere else—Lord knows where—but if you've got land, you've got roots. That's why I instill in my family: don't ever give up land. It is power—which is hard to come by. It's hard to get money to buy it. If you're not holding a dollar, you really can't get it—for me anyway; I'm a Black farmer." Wardell pauses. His voice trails off.

Until now, his manner has been calm and steady. He has spoken quietly, seated in his rocking chair, managing somehow not to rock. It's as if he has summoned his energy, years of patience and reason, and contained it at the center of his being to produce an internal stillness. But as our conversation turns to the challenges Black farmers face, the challenges he and his sons have faced, something in his bearing shifts—a flicker behind his eyes, a hardening in his expression—and I realize that beneath the calm exterior there lies a smoldering anger. Who can blame him? South Carolina has a long history of discrimination dating all the way back to its founding. In 1730, one year after it split from North Carolina and became a separate colony, King George, worried that the Black people outnumbered the whites and fearing insurrection, wrote to Governor Robert Johnson urging him to pass an act offering an incentive exclusively to white indentured servants:

> We have been informed that the number of white men in our said province bears a small proportion to that of the Blacks, which is not only a hindrance to the peopling and settling of the same but may also be of dangerous consequence from the attempts of an enemy and from an insurrection of the negroes. It is our will and pleasure that you recommend in the strongest terms to the Assembly that it pass an Act giving suitable encouragement to all who shall import servants into the province, either men or women; and as an encouragement for white servants to come, we are gracious to allow you to grant fifty acres of land, free of quitrent, to all white servants, men or women, who shall have served their masters the whole term of their agreement, and shall be allowed afterwards to become planters or settlers in the said province.

> —By order of King George to Governor
> Robert Johnson of South Carolina, 1730

This subsidy gave whites an advantage in the pursuit of land and, eventually, wealth. Meanwhile, Black people—free, indentured, or enslaved—received nothing. The result is an all-too-familiar story of disadvantage and disenfranchisement that has lasted for generations.

"Black farmers really need help," Wardell says now. "The bank doesn't want to cut any money loose on you. They give you a certain amount of money, then that's as far as you go; they want to cut loose on you. I look at these folks around me. They put their hands on it and get anything they want to get, but then they've got a limit for me. I don't know why that is.

"I put up collateral and they want something else, and I told them they're not getting it. Anytime you got collateral put up, that's supposed to stand for itself. But that's how the bank treats us. There are grants out there for young farmers, but my boys have never been able to get a grant. I don't think that's right." Wardell sighs wearily, then the quiet returns.

"Man always thinks he's in charge of everything, but he's not; it's God up above. You have to keep going and have faith that things will work out. I always was told they might can slow you up, but they can't stop you. God is always there for you. I believe that. I truly do.

"I still enjoy farming, even through the struggles. I love getting up. I can maneuver like I want to maneuver with the farm—do this and do that. I like watching the crop grow. I like coming back and looking at it growing; seeing it grow pretty and neat. I put in a lot time and effort into keeping it like that until you get it out of the field. To make it in this day and time, in this world today—give me the outside rather than in a factory. Eight or nine hours in a building isn't for me—not when you're raised up doing something different. I get to run across the different scenery. Moving through the day sometimes I run around getting parts from different places, I get to see different scenery, different things going on—it's just more peaceful.

"When you're doing something you like doing, you do your best. That's what I've done. I stick with it. Whatever you do, it stands for you."

O'NEAL BLUEFORT

"Me being the oldest at forty-two, I missed a lot of days out of school being my dad's partner," O'Neal says. "I started working a whole lot earlier than my brothers because I had to. During that time, we were operating a small amount of acres, but we were in the growing stage. It was tough. When I was seven or eight years old, I was operating a uncabbed tractor. I ran that until I was eleven or twelve. At that age, I started operating tobacco harvesters and the combines.

"I remember seeing my granddad when he was dying from cancer. On his deathbed he said, 'I want you to have this and have that in the future.' His last wish was to get me a cab tractor. It was the first cab tractor on the farm—with AC, heat, and a radio. Right then I felt like I had to have been someone special to get such a big gift. I remember him having the companies bring out two or three different models and brands. It was like a special event. He was in the house, knowing he was leaving. Finally, they dropped it off. It was the first cab in the area that anybody Black owned. We still have it. It's that Ford in the back corner. That was back in 1989. For him to have done that, I said, 'There's got to be something to farming, to give your grand something he never gave his son.' That worked out real good; that's all it took to have me sold. That's when I started. I said, 'I'm going to farm.' To this day, I feel like I'm in debt to him. It was an easy decision to make.

"After my grandfather passed, my dad had help from my grandfather's best friend. He was more like our extended help if we needed him. He helped us get established. I wasn't old enough to drive the grain trucks, so he did that while my dad operated other equipment. We kept adding on and adding on and going.

"At this point, I don't know if we'd know when to stop because we don't know if it's feasible to stop growing. We're pushing farther and farther out to live, just to provide for each family. I still think back to what it was probably like for my dad to do so much struggling to give it all up for us. That's a constant reminder of why I farm.

"A lot of landowners are trying to figure out how to hold on to what they've got. Every year it's changing with them because they're losing a lot. They look at us to tell them the answer of how to keep their land. A lot of the older folks passed on and left their land to their kids. I'm seeing people in my generation who ask me what to do with their property. They don't know what they have, and when I tell them, they look at it and they say, 'Well, I'm working a job and I'm in the city. I moved away. I can't afford to pay the taxes.' I give them the best advice. A lot of family members are feuding with each other because of that. It's sad, because they give it up. It's lost.

"I love planting. You watch the soil with nothing on it. You plant and you look at it a few days later, and the ground has turned green behind you. It's like a baby. You babysit it up to a certain age. You babysit it and work it, and then at the end of the harvest season you see what you've done—whether you've picked up your yield or had losses. There's a science to it because the weather changes so fast. There's no correct way to farm because we don't know the weather. We predict it, but every season is different. It's a different challenge. The chemicals and seeds are changing constantly; it's like you're gambling even more. It's still fun. At the end of the year, I think we've done the best we could. We know what we need to do next year so we look forward to the next year when we can correct something.

"I'm thinking that hopefully in the years to come farmers will get the attention they deserve for what they've been doing forever, way before me—that it will be a family business that my son can do one day. With all the technology they have now, hopefully he'll be smarter.

"Being outside has kind of grown on me over the years. I'd rather be anyplace outside. I think everything extends from the sun. I think the day you can't see the sun and be outside, you'll eventually get weak and die like a crop.

"It's amazing to see the seed changes. There are so many different varieties and different soil types. The highlight is to ride by a field and see it clean; not a single low spot. You know the farmers are really working. The field just looks like a garden.

Then you realize you're riding slow, holding up traffic. You can ride from the winter and see the fields that have just been harvested, and you start back in the spring and you see the fields as you plant them. By June or July, you watch the whole world turn green."

TREMAIN BLUEFORT

"The thing I like about the farm," says Tremain, "is there's always a challenge to do something better than my bigger brother. What he do, I want to do it better. Even though I sit back, I'd watch what he does, and learn from him. When we were young, my brother thought I was in the back of the cab sleeping, but I was paying attention so I could take his job.

"There's no better life than farming because you get to spend your days with family. You can't get that in a building with strangers. It pushes you a whole lot further when you're together as a family doing things because no one person does it all. It has to be a team effort. It makes you strong."

BRYANT BLUEFORT

"It's easy for me to make the decision to farm," Bryant says. "This is part of life. You've got 365 days of being with your family. Every day I wake up—it be hard sometimes—but I've got my father and I've got my brothers. We're doing this together. I watched my brother grow into this and become a man. The only thing I want to do is help support. I decided to go to school then come here. As long as I can make a decent living, I'll sacrifice anything to just be with my family. That's a blessing. A lot of people don't get that chance to have the opportunity to stay with their family and see how far this thing can go. I'd do it again."

26

Ancestral Vibrations Guide Our Connection to the Land

BY JIM EMBRY

We are the seeds of our ancestors' dreams.

MY BEGINNINGS

As far back as I can remember, during my childhood in Richmond, Kentucky, my mother, Jean, always planted a big edible garden in our backyard, along with a beautiful and diverse flower garden. These garden areas, as I recall, were full of honeybees, wasps, bumblebees, praying mantises, many types of butterflies and birds, and even grasshoppers that we buried in the ant hill. Since our bounty was so abundant, it was quite acceptable for my siblings, Richard and Marsha, and me to pull and eat tomatoes from the vine or carrots right from the ground as long as we did not waste anything. On most weekends when we visited the farm of our maternal grandmother, Parolee, or nearby farms of extended family members, we would bring home even more delicious food goodies that we picked in the fields or foraged in the wooded areas.

I grew up experiencing the "great outdoors" on our family farms, which contained pastures of crops and animals to tend; fruit orchards and berry patches to pick from; ponds and creeks to swim and fish in; wooded areas and thickets with trees to climb, brambles to get caught in, and squirrels, deer, and rabbits to hunt; and nights with lightning bugs to chase and stars to wish on. We loved being in the "country," as we called these sacred green spaces with the Black faces of so many loved ones.[59]

Even when my family moved north to the Cincinnati area in 1959, as so many African American families had been doing since the Civil War ended, we still had a backyard garden that was shared with neighbors who also migrated from somewhere in the South. For several summers, my brother and I were sent back "down home" to spend several weeks on the farm of our aunt Bessie and uncle Andrew, who were like second parents to us.[60] It was during these weeks of working on the farm that I began to think that our family members who were small farmers seemed to know everything and could do everything. They not only worked in the fields to tend the animals and crops but also seemed to know everything about the flora and fauna all around us. They knew how to use their hands to fix anything that needed attention. They could read the weather of the days ahead, sew clothing and make quilts, build barns and houses, mix up herbal remedies, prepare delicious meals, and tell great stories.

On our return trip home from summer on the farm, our uncle's pickup truck, which we rode in the back of in those days, was always loaded down with various items from the farm—green beans, corn, tomatoes, June apples and peaches, greens, chowchow relish, eggs, country ham, and so much more. Back then, it wasn't called local food or slow food; it was just this amazing diversity and deliciousness of food that came from our family farms. We didn't use any pesticides (or very few), and I had no clue that what we were doing back then is what we now call organic gardening. It was just the way of farming—using animal manures, cover crops, plant diversity, and pasture rotation—that was passed down from the elders who were reading and applying the bulletins of George Washington Carver. For almost all my life, I have felt a closeness with the land, what it produced, those who worked the land, and the natural world around us.

EARLY FAMILY HISTORY

Through our family's oral traditions[61] and additional research, we know that our African ancestors, who were given the names Matt and Hannah, were brought to Madison County, Kentucky,[62] around 1810 from Culpepper County, Virginia, and were enslaved by the Tom Ballew family. Matt and Hannah had thirteen children who all learned the many skills connected with small self-sufficient farms and who were instilled with the love of and commitment to family. Matt, given the responsibility of overseer, used this position to improve living conditions for all those enslaved on the farm, which included receiving permission to establish the Colored United Baptist Church. As church moderator, Matt was able to use Bible study and church services as a platform to increase literacy and allow members to bear witness to their yearnings for freedom.

In 1864, as word spread that enslaved Africans were needed in the war effort and could fight for their freedom as part of the US Colored Troops, two of Matt and Hannah's sons, Jackson and George, enlisted at Camp Nelson, the third-largest Union recruitment center for African Americans. Both listed their occupation as farmer on their muster rolls. Jackson served with the 12th Regiment and died early in the war, while George, as a member of the 114th Regiment,[63] fought in Virginia, pursued General Robert E. Lee, and was present at Appomattox when Lee surrendered.

Jackson's wife, Elizabeth, and their children were among the thousands of women and children who sought refuge at Camp Nelson with the hope of gaining their freedom after the war. While at Camp Nelson, the refugees were educated by John G. Fee, a white abolitionist preacher and the founder of Berea College, the first college in the South to admit women and African Americans.

When the Civil War ended, even as thousands of freed people fled to the North, my great-great-grandmother Elizabeth, needing to provide for and protect her seven young children, two to fourteen years old,[64] chose to return to the area of Madison County, where they had been enslaved. The family worked the familiar fields and homes as sharecroppers and eventually were able to purchase land and become small farmers. For freed African Americans, this postwar transition period was bewildering, replete with disease and poverty and impacted by escalating violence, but still, they much preferred the responsibilities of freedom over the more dehumanizing conditions of slavery. Even though a widow, Elizabeth was able to provide for and protect her children while also instilling in them the importance of education as a pathway to more fully manifest their individual freedom and collective responsibility to help build community. When I think of my great-great-grandmother with seven children in post–Civil War Kentucky and what she accomplished, I am at times overcome with tears of pain for what she surely endured and tears of joy for her tenacity, courage, and capacity to survive. Because she did survive with all her children, I can write this document and share her story.

DON CARLOS BUEL BALLEW

I have often imagined that these could have been the words that my great-great-grandmother Elizabeth would have spoken to encourage her children's education:

> Now, children, your daddy ain't here no more, but we got to hold on to each other and find our way. Remember that nice white man who educated us colored folks at Camp Nelson? Well, I hear he got a school over in Berea that allows colored folks to attend. So in honor of your daddy who fought and died for us to be free, I want you to go to that school so you can teach and help other colored folks.

Following his mother's advice and honoring his father's sacrifice, my great-grandfather Don Carlos Buel Ballew (b. 1862),[65] taught by his sister Harriet to read and write, enrolled at Berea College in 1879. Besides academic preparation, the school also encouraged racial cooperation, service to community, and, especially for the Black students, landownership. After completing his studies at Berea College in 1881, DB, as he was known, returned home to be near his mother and began work as a teacher in the segregated rural schools. Because of his education, he was often called on to write letters on behalf of his mother or other community elders seeking veterans' pensions or legal redress, and to read documents and letters to them. In 1885, DB married Senia Dudley, and within a year they had enough money to purchase land (in her name) to begin farming; as a couple, they joined with others in numerous collective efforts to help develop a thriving, educated, and empowered community.

In 1870, when the Freedmen's Bureau pulled out of the South, leaving behind successes in some areas and impotent failures in others, it left a void in the efforts to provide safety, education, and legal aid for newly freed African Americans. Faced with increased violence, an all-out campaign by whites to restore white supremacy within every institution, and diminished support from the federal government, African Americans across the South recognized that "pulling yourself up by your own bootstraps" was a necessary attitude that needed individual and collective expressions along the perilous journey toward freedom. The outright betrayal of freed women and men by the federal government was used by our ancestors to "pull themselves up and together" in various forms of mutual aid, cooperation, and solidarity that served to enhance their self-determination and self-sufficiency.

DB and Senia were involved in the important and necessary collective efforts to develop schools, churches, businesses, cemeteries, and various other civic organizations during this postwar Black reconstruction period. Working together, the rural farmers and city dwellers living in a small community in central Kentucky, were connected to state and national organizations and movements that served to empower African American communities across the country. "Lifting as we climb"[66] was the attitude and practice of this generation that moved communities from dependence to independence, from powerless to empowered, from landless to landowning.

My mother, Jean, who grew up living with her mother, Parolee, and grandparents Senia and DB, described her grandfather in this way:

> Granddad was a baby slave whose father died serving as a soldier in the Civil War. Because of this granddad said he would 'never again work for white people.' He went to Berea College, taught school for many years, was a small farmer, served as the community butcher. In a back porch room he had a shoe cobbler bench to repair shoes and a barber chair to give haircuts and shaves, and he helped his brother, Jack, in his blacksmith shop. It seemed like Granddad was always working, but he was also an avid reader who loved Black history and studying those farmer bulletins.

HENRY ALLEN LAINE, CHAUTAUQUA, AND CARVER

In 1900, DB began a collaborative friendship that lasted for many years with Henry Allen Laine, another Berea College graduate who also became a teacher in the segregated Madison County schools and a well-respected small farmer. With his interest in teaching and agriculture, Henry was appointed the director of the Black schools in the county, and he insisted that the schools teach agriculture as part of the curriculum. George Washington Carver's bulletins were most likely part of the curriculum materials for agriculture. Laine also founded the Madison County Colored Teachers Association, which he led for twenty years. He became the county's first African American agricultural agent in 1915 and was given the title "county demonstrator for the colored people," a position that was funded by the fiscal court. In 1917, Laine was named by the University of Kentucky as the first "colored county extension agent" in Kentucky to serve the African American farmers in Madison County. In 1920, there were six thousand Black residents in Madison County, with some two-thirds living on small farms. Feeding the fires of what Monica White calls "collective agency,"[67] Henry was able to organize 15 farmers' clubs of men and boys with 235 members, 20 homemakers' clubs with 500 members, and the annual "colored agriculture industrial fair," which attracted more than a thousand people. He also held 32 community meetings with 4,000 people attending, visited 157 farms and 21 schools, and handed out 130 farmers' bulletins.

Even before 1920, my grandfather DB, Henry Allen Laine, and other African American farmers in Madison County had developed a close relationship with George Washington Carver and his teachings. It is quite clear to me now that the farmers' bulletins that my mother said her grandfather was always reading and the bulletins that were being given out to the farmers' and homemakers' clubs were some of the forty-four bulletins[68] that Carver wrote, illustrated, and published over the course of his tenure at Tuskegee Institute. Carver's bulletins were full of practical ideas in a very readable format, and—even though white historians refused to recognize their importance—they laid the foundation for the modern organic farming movement and are still quite useful and valuable today.

Inspired by the Owensboro (Kentucky) Negro Chautauqua that presented Ida B. Wells as the featured speaker, the Madison County African American farmers' and teachers' organizations, both led by Henry Allen Laine, organized the Colored Chautauqua, an event designed to bring cultural, religious, and social opportunities to the African American community. The Chautauqua events in Madison County were part of the national Chautauqua movement, which started in the 1870s and ended in the early 1930s. Madison County was one of very few counties in Kentucky to establish an annual Chautauqua for African Americans.

The first Colored Chautauqua in Richmond was held August 4 to 8, 1915, at the city ballpark and was supported by the white Methodist lay leader and social reformer Belle Bennett. According to newspaper accounts, the Chautauqua event drew fifteen hundred African American participants and about twenty whites. It featured nationally known speakers, including W. E. B. DuBois, Henry Hugh Proctor, and George Washington Carver. The recommended reading list in preparation for the Chautauqua included Black newspapers, Carver's bulletins, books by DuBois, Frederick Douglass, Booker T. Washington, Paul Laurence Dunbar, Matthew Henson,[69] and others. Carver and DuBois returned to Richmond again in 1919 to speak at the Colored Chautauqua that coincided with the Madison County Institute for Colored Teachers.

By the 1900s, whites in Richmond and around Kentucky in general had begun to turn away from their Union identity and to more closely align themselves with the defeated ex-Confederate states. Thus it was a rather significant achievement for these Black men and women to host an event that attracted fifteen hundred African Americans, featured DuBois and Carver as speakers, and garnered lots of newspaper coverage without any violent repercussions from whites. These individuals, who worked the land and organized such events, are best described as agrarian intellectual activists or freedom farmers[70]—terms that describe their work building resilience within community institutions locally and nationally, even amid racial disenfranchisement and violence.

BEREA COLLEGE LEGACY

Berea College, founded by John G. Fee in 1855, was an institution much like Tuskegee, Hampton, and other historically Black colleges and universities in that it provided the transformative seeds of education that gave rise to activists who worked toward racial equality and community empowerment across the state and nation. During its early years, a number of prominent African Americans attended Berea College. They include James Bond, the early Kentucky civil rights leader who was also the grandfather of Julian Bond, cofounder of the Southern Poverty Law Center and a Georgia state legislator; Carter G. Woodson, author, historian, and founder of Black History Month; Julia Amanda Britton, music teacher for W. C. Handy, "the father of the blues," and the grandmother of NAACP leader Benjamin Hooks; and Mary E. Britton, physician, suffragist, and civil rights activist. Even more recently, Naomi Tutu, daughter of South African bishop Desmond Tutu, graduated from Berea College, as did feminist writer bell hooks, who is currently a Distinguished Professor in Residence.

Over the years, numerous other family members and friends have attended Berea College and have gone on to successful careers with civic engagement that embody the founding principles of the college: spiritual values with action, equality of all people, service to others, and mindful living. I continue to live in the same county, and I find various ways to honor these longstanding family connections with this important and historic American institution.

BACK TO THE LAND

About six years ago, my cousins asked me to move to our extended family's thirty-acre farm to look after my ninety-year-old aunt and uncle, Bessie and Andrew, and to care for a vacant, nearly ninety-year-old house that needed considerable attention. This would mean moving back to Richmond, Kentucky, where I was born. At first I balked and said, "Who, me? I don't think so. I left Richmond fifty years ago and am now a city boy with no desire to move back to a small country town."

I didn't quite understand as clearly then as I do now that the voices of my ancestors were speaking through my cousins and providing clues to the paths ahead of me. These ancestral spirits understood that for me to elevate my ongoing work on social and environmental justice, I would need to become more rooted in the land. I would need to live where I could feel the soil beneath my feet and between my fingers, hear and see the birds singing their morning songs, watch the butterflies dancing among the flowers, and be connected to the more visible celestial landscape.

I remembered that my fifty years of food activism—founding natural food cooperatives, developing community and school gardens, studying organic gardening in Cuba and attending Slow Food's Terra Madre in Italy, designing and presenting workshops on therapeutic horticulture, and dismantling racism in the food system—

link back directly to my childhood experiences with my parents and extended family members who connected me to this land. So I heeded the call of my ancestors, just as Matt and Hannah, Jackson and Elizabeth, DB and Senia heeded their calling, and I moved back to the land. Along my journey, this ancestral guidance has also opened doors for me to become even more intimate with the histories of our family so I would have even more stories to share.

Back in 2008, when I first began working with Will Allen, founder of Growing Power, to plan the Growing Food and Justice Gatherings, I would introduce him at Kentucky speaking engagements and say, "Will has some really big feet, and I hope all of us desire the same!" Both he and I knew that when we choose to walk in the footsteps of our ancestors, we develop big feet. If we learn to listen to the voices and tap into the wisdom of our ancestors—the human and animal people, the air and water people, the rock and plant people—then they reveal clues to the answers we are seeking and help us transform our world.

THE WAY FORWARD—TRANSFORMATIONAL CHANGE

Agriculture, which developed some twelve thousand years ago, serves as the foundation of modern human civilization and thus the axis of a much-needed cultural transformation. When we foster radical changes in our agricultural and food systems, we will also be in the creative cauldron of transforming every other institution within our human culture. As we remove the blinders that obscure the realities and interconnectedness of the collapse of ecological, social, and agricultural systems, the ongoing oppression of people of color and other marginalized groups, the mass extinction of species, and the accelerating disturbance of our planet's climate, we see clearly that we have some really big work to do. While this transformation is unfolding, the declining culture will refuse to change, clinging ever more rigidly to its outdated ideas and structures, and the dominant social institutions will refuse to hand over the leading roles to these new cultural forces. The enormity and complexity of the transformation process challenge us to do more than think outside the box; we also need to think outside the barn.

While living in Detroit and working closely with my longtime mentor Grace Lee Boggs as the director of the Boggs Center,[71] I attended and helped organize the State of the Possible retreats sponsored by the Positive Futures Network (1999–

2004). It was at these retreats, summarized in the document *Movement Building for Transformational Change*[72] and inspired by such books as *The Great Work*,[73] that I gained even greater clarity about the nature and purpose of community building for social change, which I have been involved in for sixty years. Our retreat conversations and readings affirmed for me that our collective efforts need to combine at least three necessary, overlapping dimensions that are mutually reinforcing:

1. HOLDING ACTIONS to slow the damage to the earth and its beings—usually called activism or direct action

2. STRUCTURAL CHANGE that creates alternatives, new laws and policies, solidarity economies, and new ways of being together and organizing

3. VISION AND SHIFTS IN CONSCIOUSNESS, which are where we do the work of inner spiritual and psychological transformation and open ourselves into wider spheres of identity with the earth, the cosmos, and the whole of humanity[74]

WE ARE ALL INDIGENOUS

What is the role of indigenous peoples' cultural and agricultural traditions within this movement of transformation in the United States? The First Peoples of North America—Turtle Island—have much to teach us concerning intimate presence to this continent (however and whenever we came here) and how we should dwell here in a mutually enhancing spiritual intimacy with the land. Despite wars, cultural oppression and appropriation, poverty, and diseases, indigenous peoples have maintained diverse communities committed to self-determination, homelands, and ancestral traditions. Theirs is a tragic and long-continuing story that endures into the present. Yet the First Peoples, in the full range of their bearing and in their intimacy with the powers of the continent, have achieved something that guides and instructs all those who have come to live here. Our work on new laws regarding indigenous peoples should model that of Montana, which in 1999 passed Indian Education for All,[75] a law whose primary aim is to strengthen the understanding and awareness of American Indian culture and history.

As part of my work on food justice and food sovereignty, I go every two years to Slow Food's Terra Madre / Salone de Gusto gathering in Torino, Italy. This international gathering brings together eight to ten thousand delegates from 170 countries, all working on various aspects of our food and agricultural systems. Under the Terra Madre umbrella is the Indigenous Terra Madre Network,[76] which brings indigenous peoples' voices to the forefront of the debate on food and culture and which advocates for the continued custody by indigenous peoples of their native lands, so that they can maintain them and the great variety of seeds, animal breeds, fish, bees, and other living organisms they host. It is important that we seek to find appropriate ways to support, help, and protect indigenous cultures, for they can help us reconnect with an ecocentric worldview and with our own ancestral indigenousness. On another level is the notion that we are *all* indigenous, that we are all indigenous to this one planet, that we are indigenous to our home, Mother Earth. In 2009, heavily influenced by a resurgent indigenous Andean spiritual worldview that places the environment and the Earth deity known as the Pachamama at the center of all life, Bolivia passed laws granting all nature equal rights to humans. The law gives nature legal rights, specifically the rights to life and regeneration, biodiversity, water, clean air, balance, and restoration, and mandates a fundamental ecological reorientation of Bolivia's economy and society, requiring all existing and future laws to adapt to the Mother Earth law and accept the ecological limits set by nature. How can the Law of Mother Earth become woven into our outside-the-barn thinking as we fashion alternative structures and project visions for a sustainable world with justice for all our relations?

Back in 1898, George Washington Carver was dropping similar nuggets of wisdom that linked this indigenous view and quantum science view,[77] which is so critical to our work of becoming the "reimaginers" of our food and agriculture system, when he wrote, "The highest attainments in agriculture can be reached only when we clearly understand the mutual relationship between the animal, mineral, and vegetable kingdoms, and how utterly impossible it is for one to exist in a highly organized state without the other."[78]

At this inner edge of a human epochal shift from our industrial growth society to a life-sustaining civilization, as we claim our native earth-ness, how shall we move? Shall we distance ourselves from and lag behind the insightful, revolutionary, and ecocentric traditions of our ancestors, or do we keep them close, move with them, move beyond them, and move on for them, for ourselves, and for our children to transform this nation? How do we move from the winter of darkness and despair to the spring of light and hope? How do we gather all that we have gleaned from the past and move it into the deeper internal spaces of our cells and into our total being?

As the seeds of our ancestors' dreams, we have germinated and have become trees that produce fruit, providing nourishment for the present and seeds for those who are on their way. Our dreams then also become the seeds for future generations. This work of reclaiming our sacred connections to the soil from which we are made, to the air and water that replenish us, and to the plants and animals that are family is a quest much bigger than a single country or continent. It is a journey that will provide a leap in the development of humans as a species. This journey begins anew every single day.

27.

*R*emember

BY JOY HARJO

Remember the sky that you were born under,
know each of the star's stories.
Remember the moon, know who she is.
Remember the sun's birth at dawn, that is the
strongest point of time. Remember sundown
and the giving away to night.
Remember your birth, how your mother struggled
to give you form and breath. You are evidence of
her life, and her mother's, and hers.
Remember your father. He is your life, also.
Remember the earth whose skin you are:
red earth, black earth, yellow earth, white earth
brown earth, we are earth.
Remember the plants, trees, animal life who all have their
tribes, their families, their histories, too. Talk to them,
listen to them. They are alive poems.
Remember the wind. Remember her voice. She knows the
origin of this universe.

Remember you are all people and all people
are you.
Remember you are this universe and this
universe is you.
Remember all is in motion, is growing, is you.
Remember language comes from this.
Remember the dance language is, that life is.
Remember.

28.

*F*amily Ties

ESMERALDA AND ANTONIO SANDOVAL

Del Valle Fresh, Inc.
Roebuck, South Carolina

The black file cabinet against the wall is plastered with photos of Esmeralda Sandoval's kids and farm-themed stickers that read: "NO FARMS: NO FOOD," "EAT FRESH, EAT HEALTHY, SUPPORT A FARMER," and "I'D RATHER BE DRIVING MY TRACTOR." Dressed in jeans, a cotton shirt, and work books, her hair pulled back into a bun, Esmeralda sits at a large oak desk covered with invoices, hanging files, and record books. A picture of Jesus Christ is taped to the side of her computer monitor. We're sitting in the office of Del Valle Fresh, Inc., the farm she and her husband founded in 2010.

"My father is a direct descendant of Joaquin Galan, the Mexican settler who received a royal land grant from the Spanish throne in 1767," Esmeralda says in a voice as clear and twinkling as a winter's night sky. "Joaquin Galan was granted thirty-seven hundred acres along the Rio Grande in Coahuila to build the Villa de San José de Palafox, a community that ran along the southern border from El Paso in what is now Webb County, Texas." Esmeralda discovered her connection to Galan when her uncles took a 23andMe DNA test that confirmed their lineage. "When the Mexicans started fighting against the US, all those people got run off their lands. They got pushed down into Mexico." Her story goes a long way to proving that the current debate over immigration and citizenship—who deserves to live in this country and who doesn't—is far too narrow, ignores important historical facts, and gives new life to the old saying "We didn't cross the border, the border crossed us," which is uttered by so many Mexican families whose legacy is being challenged.

Not long after discovering their bloodline, Esmeralda and her relatives joined six hundred other Galan heirs in a suit against the state of Texas, arguing that the state took illegal possession of their land in 1870. The land sits atop a "sea of minerals," according to Tony Zavaleta, a sociology professor at University of Texas, Brownsville, who surveyed the land for a coal company in the 1980s. The state has been collecting revenue from those mineral rights for the last 150 years. Now, the Galan descendants are demanding their fair share.

Family is the thread woven into every aspect of Esmeralda's life. It's the thing that has driven her and her husband, Tony, forward all these years. Family grounds and inspires them.

Hearing Esmeralda speak of her family's long history as settlers and farmers, it's no surprise that she has followed in her ancestor's footsteps. Even before she learned of her connection to Joaquin Galan, she was already intimately familiar with the family's business—farming—and the opportunities working the land affords.

"My family is from Texas, along the border from Matamoros and Brownsville," Esmeralda says. "My grandpa was a cotton farmer. He had a good hand for corn and cotton. They grew it on dry soil and waited on the grace of God for those crops to come up. My grandfather Andres Galan got naturalized when all you had to do was raise your hand, swear allegiance to the United States on a Bible, and say, 'I do,' and he got to be a citizen. He used to tell me, 'Honey, that's all we did.'

"In the early '70s, my grandfather brought all his seven children, my father included, to the US and got them their citizenship in the same manner. He brought them over to Florida to work out in the farms to earn a living. My father met and married my mother when he was twenty-three and she was sixteen. They earned their living by working alongside other migrant workers and speaking no English. I was born shortly after my mother got with my father. As early as I can recall, I was always interpreting my parents with English and Spanish.

"My parents moved down to Florida when the produce industry was booming. Farmers grew tomatoes, bell peppers—all the vegetables you could imagine. You could go to the fields when the farmers were done with their crops and pick the second-grade produce. We called it 'pinhooking,' and it was like a gold rush. All those vegetables were being harvested out in the field, free and open. Then you could pick them and sell them at the open farmers' market that we called 'the boneyard.' Vegetable pinhooking was a lucrative business all the way through the state of Florida.

"As the harvest season finished, you could migrate up the states. You'd start in Homestead, Florida, then you go up to Immokalee, then you go into Central Florida, Northern Florida, the Carolinas, Virginia, Maryland, and all the other states that hit in the summer time. You just followed the trail. I grew up traveling from Florida to Georgia to Tennessee to North Carolina. I've been up in Michigan picking watermelons, Ohio picking tomatoes. I learned to swim in Nebraska when I was a migrant. We would only be in one place for three or four months before we would have to get up and move again, following the next crop. That was probably until the year 2006. We still move around but not in the same way."

That scrappy upbringing and can-do spirit turned out to be valuable as Esmeralda grew into adulthood. She had developed a solid work ethic, a steadfast pragmatism, and a sense of personal accountability that helped her overcome obstacles when they arose. "I married my first husband when I was very young. We had two little boys. It was a bad marriage, and most of all we were very young. My ex-husband wasn't a workaholic like me. I saw that he couldn't help me. He didn't want to move, and he wasn't willing to work like the migrant workers. He considered migrant labor distasteful, but there's nothing distasteful about it. It's hard, that's all it is. Migrant workers have all my respect. It's one of the most hardworking and rewarding jobs there is. So, I said, 'You're in the way. I'm going to move on. You can stay in Florida.' Then I disappeared with my boys."

Esmeralda picked watermelons in the years before she met Tony, her second husband. She was barely twenty but already had a nose for business. "I had contracts with farmers who needed 150 to 200 acres picked. You have to know how to harvest watermelons in brand-new fields. When the watermelons are ready to harvest, the vines are about knee high and they intermingle with each other. It's beautiful; it's grand. Here's the tricky part: when watermelons come on during the first pick, you can pick them fresh, but they're not ripe. You have to know what you're doing because you can mess up an entire crop for the farmer, and he'll lose money and not pay you.

I quickly learned how to distinguish between a fresh melon and a ripe melon that's ready to cut. People always asked me how I can tell the difference because the field is brand new and all the melons look big. I used to tell them, 'Watermelons like to show themselves off. If you look carefully, you can see the melons popping up when they're ripe.' The ones that aren't ready are still under the leaves. If you ever walk into a field of melons or cantaloupes, that's how you know."

Esmeralda is still giving me a lesson in melon harvesting when Tony walks in, sporting a camouflage cap and a full beard and handlebar mustache. The weather forecast promises rain for the next two days, and he and a crew of employees have been out in the fields picking half runner beans before the storm hits. He introduces himself and settles into a chair beside his wife.

"I'm the only one of my dad's six children who is farming," Esmeralda says. "Even among my dad's brothers, I'm the only farmer—because I *married* a farmer." She looks over at Tony. "Tony's family is from Guanajuato, in Central Mexico, where they grow wheat and corn. He is a workaholic like me. We met when he was thirty-six. We knew each other through working on various farms. I saw him periodically when we would sell produce at the market. I liked that he felt secure about himself. When we finally met up and started talking, it all just clicked."

"I was born in Madera, California, near Fresno," Tony says. He is soft-spoken, with an unassuming manner. "My father worked for a big timber company near Yosemite, but my mother didn't like that way of living, so she took us to Mexico. My father had his own farm there. He grew corn and sorghum. He had milk cows, beef cows, and pigs. I didn't come back to the States until I was sixteen.

"The San Joaquin Valley is one of the biggest places for agriculture in California. I started harvesting vegetables around Madera, Carmel, Firebaugh, and Mendota. When my sister got married, she moved to Florida with her husband. She told me there was more work there. This was in the mid-'80s and early '90s. By then, more immigrants were working in California. It started overpopulating, so I moved to Florida. When I moved from California to Florida, there were hundreds of small farmers. They have all disappeared over time. Now it's just big corporations."

"When we met, things really took off," Esmeralda says. "We managed big contracts down in Florida, picking twelve hundred acres of tomatoes at a time—just the two of us. We subcontracted eighty to one hundred groups of workers who had van-body box trucks to work in. Each truck carried six to eight people. We would pick the tomatoes in the field, then bring them to the packing house already packaged and ready to ship out. It was a great deal because we were paid on commission. There were days when we picked fifteen to twenty thousand boxes. I was twenty-two or twenty-three years old. It wasn't overwhelming because I'd always been in that type of surrounding. The language barrier wasn't a problem. I communicated well with the farmers, and I could interpret for the workers and tell them what we needed to do, how we needed to complete the task in a timely manner. My husband had a vast network of people."

In North Carolina, Tony and Esmeralda worked for a farmer who owned a thousand acres, then returned to Myakka City, Florida, to work a twelve-hundred-acre farm, and then to Immokalee, to work sixteen hundred acres. "It takes a whole season to pick sixteen hundred acres," Esmeralda explains. "When we would start the Florida season, we had a quick window of eight to twelve weeks. The crops are planted in different settings, and you just keep going and going and going." All the while, they were raising their four children. "I wanted to take care of my kids," Esmeralda says. "I couldn't leave them by themselves, and we were constantly traveling. The biggest thing about parenting is attention. Your kids want attention, and they want it from you."

By 2010, the Sandovals were eager to settle down. They chose South Carolina because the growing season was longer and land was more affordable. "We got into farming by sharecropping in the early 2000s. Then we started questioning, 'You know what? We have to grow our own.' We started buying our own equipment. It was a struggle. The money was tight, and we were trying to manage the outsource contracts and the farming, and buying tractors, pumps, and sprayers."

For the next ten years, the Sandovals' business continued to grow. They expanded their operation to three hundred acres and were making steady progress. Then in 2007, one of their customers ran off with half a million dollars' worth of sales. "We delivered our produce, and he disappeared without paying," Esmeralda says. "We fell into a major hardship. We hadn't done anything wrong." Desperate to save their operation, they searched for other funding possibilities, but the grant application process was daunting. Then they suffered three freezes back to back that damaged their crops. For the first time, Esmeralda's confidence wavered. "I told my husband, 'This is hard. I don't know how we're going to make it.'"

That same year, still reeling from their loss, Esmeralda used her marketing skills to help her friends and family in Florida organize a parade for local small farming businesses and agricultural workers. In the course of working on the parade, she met a professor from Hodges University who assisted her in creating a business plan in exchange for her help with the parade. He also introduced the Sandovals to a grant writer in Aiken, South Carolina. Esmeralda also drew on their vast extended family for support. Tony's brother farmed in Florida, Georgia, and North Carolina. His sister farmed in North Carolina. "I started networking with our family so we could have more buying power. We decided to form a co-op."

It's been a slow climb back to profitability. Last year's hurricanes forced the Sandovals to reduced the number of acres they farm this year by half—from one hundred acres to fifty. Yet, they are making progress, inching forward, taking advantage of opportunities where they can. "One of the big things that hit me after that setback with that particular customer who didn't pay us is how are we managing our risk? You're looking at millions of dollars that you put out there in the ground. How are you going to take care of it?"

This year, with risk in mind, the Sandovals decided not to grow as many tomatoes. Although potentially more profitable than other crops, tomatoes also require a larger investment of up-front capital that the Sandovals didn't have. "This was a good year for tomatoes from beginning to end," Tony says, still frustrated at the lost opportunity.

"We had to be careful," Esmeralda says. "We decided we'd would grow a little and spread them out, mixing them in with our veggies. Right now we're growing pickles, cucumbers, squash, and half runner beans and very few tomatoes."

The one constant through all of Esmeralda and Tony's trials and triumphs has been family. Three of their four children are young adults. The youngest is twelve. Their kids grew up on the farm and witnessed firsthand what it takes to survive. They're all students, but they help on the farm as much as they can. "They know how to drive forklifts," Esmeralda says proudly. "They helped me unload the trucks. They drive tractors. You could put them out on the farm and they know how to do everything." But when asked if her kids plan to be farmers, Esmeralda pauses. "My son is thinking about construction and grading. He's wanting something more that is not as risky. I know my daughter wants to be part of this. She sees our struggle. I think she has more empathy for what we do, and she wants to join in. You hear a lot of kids, even from other Hispanics, the kids are scared. They see the struggles their parents are facing. To us, this is what we do, but our children have options."

"The next generation, they don't want to farm," Tony offers. "They don't want to farm because they don't think there's money in it. They prefer to go and make sure they have a weekly check."

"In corporate America," Esmeralda says.

"Several years ago, a lot of people made a living farming," Tony says. "A decent living. All the minorities, they sent people to college. Right now, only the big companies can afford to farm. All the minorities are getting buried. You talk to a lot of minorities, and they tell you the same thing. You want to be farming, but you got to have another job to support the farm."

"You're in survival mode when you're farming," Esmeralda says. "The people that farm, we're surviving off the ground. Managing our own way of life. That's how we were supposed to do it. Whatever we need to do, we figure it out. If there is an obstacle or a problem, we figure out how we are going to overcome it. Every season has its challenges, and getting through that season again and again, you always feel okay, a sense of accomplishment.

"I go back and I think about all the experiences we have lived. I have learned to embrace my age because of everything I have experienced. My biggest reward was when my daughter was about twelve. She had high standards for me. She told me, 'Mom, I want to be just like you.' When she told me that, it was like, 'Okay, this fight was worth it. I did something right.'"

29.

*H*ow to Make Rain

BY KEVIN YOUNG

Start with the sun
piled weeks deep on your back   after
you haven't heard rain for an entire
growing season   and making sure to face
due north   spit twice into the red clay
stomp your silent feet   *waiting rain*
rain to bring the washing in   rain
of reaping   rusty tubs of rain   wish
aloud   to be caught in the throat
of the dry well   head kissing your back
a bent spoon for groundwater   to be
sipped from   *slow courting rain   rain*
that falls forever   rain which keeps
folks inside and makes late afternoon
babies   begin to bury childhood clothes
wrap them around stones   and skulls of
doves   then mark each place well enough

to stand the coming storm   *rain of our*
fathers   shoeless rain   the devil is
beating his wife rain   rain learned
early   in the bones   plant these scare
crow people face down   wing wing
and bony anchor   then wait until they
grow roots and skeletons   *sudden soaking*
rain that draws out the nightcrawler
rain of forgetting   rain that asks for
more rain   rain that can't help but
answer   what you are looking for
must fall   what you are looking for is
deep among clouds   what you want to see
is a girl selling kisses beneath cotton
wood   is a boy drowning inside the earth

30

Miss Rose's Dirty Rice

BY NATALIE BASZILE

It's Easter Sunday, 1984, and Al Jarreau's album *Breakin' Away* is spinning on the turntable. We're back from church. I'm seventeen, my sister is fourteen, and we've swapped our dresses and heels for shorts and T-shirts. The lamb roast my father put in the oven before we left has cooked down, and a gamy aroma hangs heavy in the air. In a couple of hours, we'll gather around the dining room table my mom is setting with her best china.

Normally, I'd linger in my room, sprawled across my canopy bed, flipping through *Mademoiselle*, but we have a special visitor: my grandmother, Miss Rose. For most of my life, Miss Rose *Belle*, as she refers to herself, has been a voice on the phone. She's afraid to fly, which means I've only seen her three or four times in my whole life. I know her mostly from the letters she writes in her loopy eighth-grade cursive, and by the care packages that arrive on our doorstep around Thanksgiving—a trove of Louisiana delicacies packed in a dented cardboard box: the homemade pecan pralines and the boudin, smoked sausages, and dried gulf shrimp my father uses in his gumbo.

But this year, Miss Rose has decided to take the train, a forty-eight-hour journey from her tiny town in southwestern Louisiana all the way out here to Los Angeles. She somehow towers at just over five feet tall, and her hair is styled in candy curls, oiled ringlets that bob as she moves. But don't be fooled. She moves through a room like a five-star general. My dad is the family chef. The kitchen is his domain. But Miss Rose has commandeered it, and right now our new RCA color camcorder is propped on my shoulder as I record her making her signature dish—something she calls "dirty rice."

I've never heard of this dish, and frankly, the name has me worried. Last New Year's Day, Dad got all old-school on us and cooked a brimming pot of chitterlings. In my mind, I had conjured thoughts of the little colorful gum squares in the bright orange box. Chitterlings sounded like happy, smiling children who danced in circles as they sang. I had no idea that chitterlings are pig intestines. I had no idea that for days after he cooked them, our house would reek like an outhouse. If chitterlings could be *that* disgusting, *God knew* what damage a dish called "dirty rice" would do.

Early afternoon light streams through the kitchen window. Miss Rose waits for my cue. I press the record button, and when the light begins to flash, Miss Rose launches into her performance. She's a Black Julia Child—but half the size—with a singsongy southern accent peppered with French. She calls me "Baby" and "Cher" and instructs me to bring the camera in close.

First, she chops a bell pepper, an onion, and celery—known in Louisiana as the Holy Trinity—and sautés it all in a cast-iron skillet. Next she mixes in the ground beef, breaking up the clumps with a wooden spoon. When the meat is cooked through and browned, she drains the fat into an earthen jug we keep by the stove, then empties the meat into the sink, which she had asked me to scrub and where she had already emptied a heaping pot of steaming white long-grain rice and finely chopped chicken livers. She seasons the mixture with salt, pepper, and garlic powder, maybe a pinch of thyme, and mixes it with her bare hands.

As I record, Miss Rose narrates the story of her life. She was born in 1918 and married my dad's father when she was eighteen. She gave birth to my dad a year later, and to my uncle Charles a year after that. Most of her life, she worked cleaning houses for the white folks in her town, but she's also president of the PTA and a founding deacon at her church, Golden Chain. She's lived in Elton her entire life and knows everyone in her town and all the surrounding towns for a twenty-mile radius. And, as I will learn years later when I attend her funeral and watch the hundreds of people file past her casket to pay their respects, everyone knows her.

When my dad tells stories about his childhood, he always says, "We were poor, but we were never hungry." Watching my grandmother now, I see how that was possible. She says that when my dad was a boy she cooked the squirrels and rabbits he hunted in the woods behind their house. She describes the pot roast and potato salad she likes to prepare. Every summer she cans string beans, okra, figs, and even the watermelon rinds, because nothing goes to waste. She promises to teach me how to make something called mayhaw jelly the next time I come to Louisiana. There's a spirit of abundance in the food she describes, and I can see how it would be possible for my dad to have grown up feeling loved and well cared for even though he grew up in a house with a tarp for a roof until my grandparents saved up for wood shingles. Suddenly, I understand why my dad always keeps our pantry stocked; why we have another whole refrigerator and freezer in the garage where he stores gallon-sized bags of cooked collard greens and gumbo. I understand why he didn't get mad when I invited my school friends over to feast on the $17-per-pound Alaskan king crab legs he bought as a family treat. Food is to be shared. If he has it, we all do.

Finally, Miss Rose transfers the dirty rice from the sink to a large mixing bowl and covers it with foil. When I ask how she came to make it, she tells me that she always has, it's just something she knows, and that she doesn't only make it for her family. Word of her cooking has spread, and she regularly receives requests—from Black people and white people alike. She'll make it for anyone who asks. Food is her way of connecting; it's her gift to the people she loves.

A few days later, we drive Miss Rose to the train station. She's fed us every night. She's told her granddaughters about the people and the place we come from. She's left us with gumbo, ham, potato salad, and plenty of leftover rice dressing, and she let us film her doing what she did better and more generously than anyone we'll ever know.

All four of us put her on the train and get her settled with her pink Samsonite suitcase and her big white purse. And of course, we make sure she's loaded down with food for the long journey home.

31.

A New Country

DORCAS YOUNG

Lesedi Farms
Whidbey Island, Washington

It's 7:30 on a Friday morning in mid-May, and the weather on Whidbey Island off the coast of Washington is perfect for farming. From Highway 525 North, Mount St. Helens and the snow-capped Cascades rise hazily in the distance. Dorcas Young has already been in her field for two hours. She moves with a sense of purpose, a focused determination, and an awareness that she doesn't have a moment to waste. Dressed in a T-shirt and zip-up hoodie, with a wide-brimmed hat that shields her face from the sun, she treks up and down the rows of freshly tilled soil, hauling long sections of black irrigation tubing amid recently planted fava beans, herbs, kale, and other leafy greens.

"My husband and I met in 1987," Dorcas says. "He was in the Peace Corps." At the time, she worked as the regional manager of a retail company, doing bookkeeping and accounting, and spent most of her time crisscrossing Botswana. "We lived in Botswana for almost five years. We got married in 1994. He moved back to Whidbey Island in 1995, and I moved in 1996." Before they moved to the United States permanently, Dorcas made an exploratory trip. "I came to the United States because I didn't know where I was going. I didn't want to leave my job in Botswana, and the next thing I know I'm becoming a slave. So, I said, 'Well, let me go see first what's there.'" They stayed with friends in Chicago and visited her future in-laws in the little town of Sequim on the peninsula near Seattle.

"When I moved here in 1996, that May, we already had a project; we built our house. I said, 'I'm not renting.'" In Botswana, Dorcas had always owned houses and understood the value of owning land. She and her husband had five children, but soon Dorcas was restless. First, she went back to school and got a bachelor's degree to teach, but teaching didn't appeal to her.

"I thought, 'I left my job in Botswana. I can't just sit home and be a mother forever.' My husband was a schoolteacher. I thought, 'I'm going to be a farmer. I'm going to create something.' Plus, the food in America was horrible. I couldn't eat hot dogs and cheese pizza all the time."

Some might consider Dorcas's transition from office work to farming to be a wild leap, but she was actually returning to her roots. Her mother and her father were subsistence farmers in Botswana. Both were from the Kalanga people and members of the wealthy Mosojane clan in Northern Botswana. Her father was the son of the chief. Dorcas, along with her sixteen siblings, grew up on a five-hundred-acre farm.

"It was a big job. My father had two wives. My mother had eight children, and

my stepmother had eight or nine kids. We grew everything on our farm: beans, crops, and grain. We raised chickens, herded cattle, and milked the goats. We made butter, which we exported to South Africa. We owned donkeys for hauling the grain from the fields to the silos, where the grain was processed. I learned how to hold a plow behind the oxen at the age of nine years old. We went to school and then came home and worked on the farm.

"In 1978, we had so much grain we sold it to the government, which they took to the national silos." After that, there was a famine for seven years.

Drawing from her farming background, Dorcas went in search of land to lease. She eventually found these acres near Greenbank and christened her land Lesedi Farm, which means 'sunshine' in Sesotho, her native language.

Meanwhile, she raised her five children. When they were grown, she went back to the University of Washington and earned a degree in food science. In addition to farming, she makes salad dressing and sauces available for sale in local markets.

Right now, Dorcas rents organic farmland from Green Barn Farm on Whidbey Island. Her dream is to buy ten acres. "I don't need to go back to the corporate world," she says. "I worked there for fifteen years; I know what that's like."

There's a spiritual component to Dorcas's farming practice. She travels to Africa every year to work with her ministry. Her ministry is also local. She works with Teen Feed, a program for homeless African American youth in Seattle. "Change starts from the bottom."

It's late morning now. Dorcas finishes laying the irrigation pipe and picks up an enormous roll of gauzy white fabric that she begins to drape over her new fava bean sprouts.

"I wasn't born here, but I look at the American system for Black people—what they went through and what they're still going through. Slavery still continues. They took African Americans' skills. I told myself I would never be a horse. I've got my own business, and I'm running it myself. I do every single bloody thing in this business. Mostly it's me and my kids."

Dorcas uses the same farming practices she learned on her family's farm in Botswana, which include leaving the soil as undisturbed as possible. "I don't do a lot of tilling. I plow and then I cover the seeds with fabric."

She is passionate about food and encouraging other Black people to farm. "I want to pull African Americans into farming." In 2010, she took classes at Oregon State University to get certified in food processing. "I was the only Black person in the lab. I wondered, 'Where are the Blacks? Where are they?' If we don't farm we slave for the rest. I feel like I need to make a small dent to let people know we can farm and process food. We can enter the market. We need to know we are not what we are being called. God didn't create us that way. Just because we are dispersed all over the planet, God has not cursed us.

"I came here as a foreigner. I met two young Black women here on Whidbey who want to farm, but right now they are working for other people. I told them, 'Okay, you can work at that farm, but you need your own farm. You need to have something that can't be taken away from you.' I lease the land, but I really don't like it. I went to Africa in 2017, and I bought five acres of land. It's close to the village where I built

a house for my mother." Her family still owns their five-hundred-acre farm, and her brother recently built a processing plant.

"My father always instilled in us, 'Don't bow down and kiss someone's ass. Don't kiss their feet.' That's the tenacity I grew up with on the farm. I'm not bowing down."

32.

*R*aised and Rooted

DERIC HARPER

Harpo's Farms
Sanford, North Carolina

"I come from the small town of Blounts Creek, North Carolina, about three hours from here," Deric Harper says. "We grew up doing a lot of fishing and shrimping." He surveys his twelve-and-a-half-acre farm edged with American holly, longleaf pines, and dogwoods. The coast and a life on the water seem a world away. But the more Deric shares about his life as a farmer, the clearer it becomes that a love of farming and a connection to the land is something you carry with you no matter where you are.

"I come from four generations of farmers on my maternal grandmother's side and three generations of farmers on my maternal grandfather's side. When my grandmother Corine Moore married my grandfather Kelly Moore, her father sold them land in Blounts Creek, North Carolina. They built a house and started farming. They had fourteen or fifteen acres of fresh produce, five or six acres of cucumbers, which they sold at the farmers' market. They also had fifteen to twenty acres of tobacco. My grandmother is eighty-six now. She has downsized since my grandfather died January 2017 but still goes to the farmers' market."

Deric's grandparents were central figures in his childhood. Not only did they help raise him and his four siblings while his mother, Elaine, worked at a local yarn factory, but they introduced him to farming. During the summer, he and his siblings helped "prime" tobacco—a method of harvesting that dates back to the early 1800s and consists of pulling individual leaves off the stalk as they ripen. Done correctly, each tobacco plant produces three opportunities to harvest its leaves: first, at the base of the stalk closest to the ground, then again when the plant has grown and the leaves are knee-high, and a third time when the mature leaves are at eye level.

Harvesting tobacco is labor-intensive. To this day, most of the work is done by hand, with certain tasked performed by men, others by women, and still others by children. "I started out handing tobacco in the stick barn. The stick barn was a shelter built out of wood. That's where all the women worked." Once the men, or "croppers," cut the leaves off the stalk in the fields, they handed them to the younger men, who laid the leaves on the trailer as it moved down the rows. The trailer was hauled to the barn, where children called "handers" passed the leaves to the women known as "stringers," who tied them on long sticks made of hardwood. "The women knew how to tie the leaves on the sticks and twist and flip the stick over. I tried learning how to do it, but the women—you couldn't beat them." Once the leaves were tied to the sticks, young men carried them into the barn, where men hung them in rows across the rafters. The rafters were arranged in descending layers from the top of the barn to the ground. When the barn was full, a low fire was lit, the door was sealed, and the tobacco leaves were dried until they cured. "That was the old-school way. It wasn't like the buck barns we have today," Deric explains.

"I was about seven when I stopped handing tobacco and started driving a tractor. I was so small I couldn't even press the brake. My brother Kelly was younger, but he was a little bit bigger so he would press the brake and I would steer. I'm not going to lie—I ran over stalks. I was young and wasn't always paying attention. I'd look back at the guys priming, and the next thing I'd know, I'd be on top of a row. My grandfather didn't like that because that was money.

"Once we got big enough—maybe eighth or ninth grade—we started priming tobacco. We'd have to keep up with our uncles. My mom and my aunt would be at the barns handling tobacco while we primed it and put it on the trailers. We were getting paid good money. Half of what we earned went to her, and half went for our school clothes. We were low-income, growing up in the projects, so getting away to the farm was like freedom for us."

Like generations of Black farmers before them, when it came to food, Deric's family's direct connection to the land enabled them to enjoy a degree of self-reliance that has largely been lost in the African American community. "After priming tobacco at 1:00 or 2:00 p.m., we had to go out to the fields that evening to pick butter beans, collard greens, and kale for the farmers' market. Honestly, during that time we hated it, but we were able to provide food for our family. My grandmother had a big ole cast-iron fire heater. She cooked beans, hog chitlins, souse meat (also known as headcheese), and liver pudding. She did it all. She processed sausage—she still does that—made souse and liver pudding. We didn't go without. Instead of going to the grocery store for vegetables, we just ran in the back to the cooler, got the vegetables, and she threw them in the pot. She raised chickens, hogs, and cattle. Everything was raised on the farm."

After high school, Deric joined the military. In the field phase of SERE school, training to be a Green Beret, Deric learned survival and navigation skills. "I think being on the farm, having a 'no-quit' attitude, made the difference. That's what you need to have when you're going through a course like that. You do a lot of rucking. You've got a seventy- or eighty-pound ALICE pack, and you're going through the woods. You have to navigate and go through creeks. To me, it was like walking on the farm. It reminded me of when I had to walk the road, pull weeds, and chop tobacco. I was back in my element." All of Deric's farm skills suddenly came in handy. "When you go through SERE training, you have very limited food and water available to you. Most of the guys on the team were city guys or were from northern urban areas. They hadn't seen soybean fields or roadkill. I was like, 'We can eat this stuff.' We found some trash that had a fishhook in it. We wrapped some fishing line around a Coke can, and that was our fishing rod. Back on the farm, we killed two to four hogs every week. I showed them how to do the hog, boil the meat to get the blood out. We'd made a field grill, so we grilled it up, had some barbeque sauce. They were loving it. I had all this knowledge from growing up in the woods. My upbringing made SERE training easy for me."

Deric learned French in the Special Forces and hoped for a deployment in Africa. He was on his way to Kenya when 9/11 happened. He was sent to Afghanistan instead. "Then we got a follow-up mission to go straight to Iraq," Deric says. "I went to Iraq in 2003 and then again in 2005, both tours were for combat. I went

to Afghanistan six times. I had a total of eleven deployments. I served twenty-four years and eight days. When I got out, I didn't want to do any contract work. I didn't want to go back overseas. I wanted to get back to the farming life. It's in my blood; it's what I love to do."

Deric purchased land for his farm in 2012 and retired from the US Army in 2016. "It was owner-financed. Two thousand dollars down, $432 a month. It was something I could manage. I thought that I could work one or two days a week; that income could pay for the land.

"When I bought this land, it was all trees—all the way up to the road. I had a little small tractor, so it was me and my son out here clearing the land an acre at a time—just kind of building it up the way I saw my grandfather do. It's like I'm going back to my roots." He bought post hole diggers and put up all the fencing, paying for the improvements out of his own pocket. He is digging two ponds and plans to build a fish hatchery with the goal of providing sustainable foods to locals in need and to food banks.

Like many small farmers, Deric has been forced to think creatively to keep his farm going. "There isn't always a lot of money in farming, so we offset our expenses with forestry. We harvest timber—which is still agriculture. That's why I have the log truck and trailer. In the off season, I help other farmers who need their land cleared. We go in and clear and cultivate their land and get it ready for harvest or turn it into pasture for their animals." He bought a steamer to keep his farm equipment clean, which he hires out to local farmers.

Deric also raises a small herd of goats and cows on a nearby farm he manages with his friend Johnny. "The demand is there. There's a meat market up in Syler City. The guy there told me, 'I'll buy as many goats as you can raise.' He sells them to the Muslim shops in Durham and Raleigh. Lamb and goat meat sell for $14 to $15 per pound in the local grocery stores. There's more money in goats and sheep than there is in cattle." He also knows Africans and Middle Easterners who want to buy directly from the farm. "I'd like to have a facility where they can come, pick out their animal, harvest it, package it in a facility that's USDA-approved. You see people with money doing that. Why not have it in this area?"

When he retired, Deric was told there were dozens of programs that provided special funding for veterans and believed he would receive support from the USDA to start farming. "I liked the idea of ownership, but I still didn't have enough income set aside to start a small business. They said there was all kinds of money out there to help you get started. You go on the internet to the USDA website; they show all these grants, all this money that's supposed to be available. I read the different business plans people had submitted. I tried to put my stuff together, but it seemed like the process for Black veterans was intimidating. You go into the office, they give you all these forms, and they just say, 'Alright, go fill them out,' but you don't really know what to do. I filled out an application for a grant for a high tunnel, but when I turned it in, I was told there was no money available." Meanwhile, other nonminority farmers seemed to have access to all the resources they needed. "I decided I wasn't going to fool with it. It just got intimidating. I decided I'd go out and work and build what I can build. Grow what I can grow."

To minimize his expenses, Deric performs a lot of his own maintenance and buys used equipment instead of new. "You look at my stuff, it's old. I bought that truck from an auction. I bought my dump truck from an auction. I just bought a tractor from an auction. I'm using my personal income. My wife helps me out. When times get tough during the winter, we stick together.

"I'm not the type of guy who is going to give up. I'm going to keep working. I've got in my mind that I'm going to build what I can build within my scope. I'd love to get a grant so that I could build the farm how I want to build it, but right now, I'm just taking it one day at a time and putting trust in God."

Deric pulls out his phone and scrolls through photos of his son and daughter. His nineteen-year-old son, Deric Jr., helped him cultivate the land and is helping him dig the two ponds. His twenty-two-year-old daughter, Jonacia, graduated with a bachelor of science and is taking a year to finish her prerequisite class for her doctorate in physical therapy. "Believe it or not, she helps me more than my son. He's going to community college for civil engineering and is focusing on his grades right now, and I don't want to pull him away. He comes out on Fridays and cleans our equipment for us. I keep telling my daughter I want her to focus on school, but she says she prefers to be out here. She runs the excavator, the bulldozer, and the forklift. I just had her out here running the chain saw." He smiles as he shows a video of his daughter gripping a chain saw as it slices through a log.

Deric has packed a lot of experiences into his forty-six years and seems content to keep things simple going forward. "Our goal is to eventually have fifty or sixty acres," he says. "Build us a nice house on it, have some animals, and give back to the community."

In the meantime, it's bear season, and he's looking forward to going hunting. The population of black bears in North Carolina has exploded, and hunting helps regulate their numbers. "We're hunting next Saturday," Deric says. He explains that a lot of Wounded Warriors, veterans with PTSD, enjoy the sport. He scrolls through his photos until he finds a picture of the enormous bear his uncle shot last season. He confides that, one year, he cooked bear meat for Thanksgiving but didn't tell anyone what they were eating. "I cooked it like a roast with potatoes, carrots, onions," he says. "It's real lean. You can cook it in an Instant Pot." His face lights up, offering a glimpse of the kid who fished and shrimped with his family and helped his grandmother sell vegetables, the young man who left home to join the Special Forces and see the world. Now he's back with his family and dreams of owning sixty acres and living a long, happy life on his farm.

33.

Making Space

MORETTA BROWNE

Berkeley Basket CSA
Berkeley, California

Walking down this quiet street in Berkeley, the average passerby would never suspect that an entire farm is growing behind a modest wooden fence. But that's exactly where one-third of Berkeley Basket CSA is located, and right now Mo Browne is talking about tree collards. "I feel like anytime I talk with a Black farmer in the Bay Area, somebody is bringing up tree collards. They're a staple—not just in our diet but in our history." Mo reaches for a pale green stalk as thick as a child's wrist. People generally treat collards as annuals, but they can grow year-round. "The great thing about these," Mo explains, "is that you can cut them, stick them in the ground, and they'll re-root themselves. Our good friend Wanda Stewart is a Black elder farming at Hoover Elementary School. She has so many she cuts them and regifts them."

For the last year, Mo has worked for Berkeley Basket, a community garden project established ten years ago by Sophie Hahn, a local farmer and Berkeley city council member. Over the years, dozens of farmers have worked with Berkeley Basket CSA, which provides boxes for thirteen families from its cornucopia of fruits and veggies—winter acorn, butternut squash, kale, lemon cucumbers, artichokes, cabbage, and asparagus, in addition to a variety of greens—all grown in the three residential backyards.

"My first memories are of being outside, working in the soil," Mo says. "Both of my maternal grandparents are from North Carolina, and my mom and I spent a lot of time at my grandparents' house in Virginia when I was young. That's one of the things I remember and miss a lot. I want to give proper thanks to my maternal grandfather, Melvin D. Wittfields. He was a strong southern Black man, and he's the reason I do this work. My grandfather and I would go to the Home Depot, and he would ask me to pick out roses that we would plant together. I was excited that I got to choose. He planted roses because my grandmother loved them. We kept vases of the roses he grew.

"When my mom and I eventually moved to Virginia Beach where I grew up, my grandfather would come down and work in the yard. He would plant the roses, and I would help him. My extended family, including aunts and even my great-grandmother, had lived in the same neighborhood, and he took care of all of their houses. We would walk to my great-grandmother's house, go in the back, and pick muscadine grapes. It felt special that we would pick grapes together. I remember that period when I felt brave and connected. When I got a little older, I didn't like caterpillars or bees or creepy-crawlers, and I stopped wanting to be outside.

"After graduating from college, I started asking questions about food security and exploring what it meant to be a vegetarian or a vegan. I took meat, then dairy, and eventually all animal products out of my diet. One day I read that the only way to know if you're really vegan is if you grow your own food because that's when you have control. You see what's happening to your food. You know because you have the input and you're investing your time and energy into literally making your own food. That was a light-bulb moment for me: I needed to be in control of what I ate. I was like, 'Okay, how do I do that?'

"I didn't know anyone in my family who grew their own food. There was this idea that farming was slave work, this idea that we were out there in the fields. Why did we need to go back? Those comments came up a lot when I talked about growing my own food. People would say, 'You don't have to do that anymore. That's not necessary.' But I was like, 'No, I really want to do this.'

"A good friend introduced me to a nonprofit, Renew Richmond, that grew organic fruits and vegetables and provided the produce to underserved communities. I started volunteering. At the time, 'food desert' was the term people were using to describe areas that didn't have access to fresh fruits, vegetables, or whole grains. I started working with the soil, learning how things grew. I harvested and delivered food to churches and to people in the neighborhood. I was excited that the program was Black-focused. The people who ran the program and came out to volunteer looked like me. The people we were giving the food to looked like me. I was working with and for our people. It inspired me to work at a local health food store.

"The experiences further affirmed that I needed to immerse myself in learning how to grow food. I felt like being a farmer was going to be the only way to be truly self-sustainable. It just so happened that a co-worker at the health food store told me about UC Santa Cruz's Center for Agroecology and Sustainable Food Systems (CASFS). I was willing to do anything to learn, and applied. When I was accepted, I planned to move to California.

"Two weeks before I was supposed to fly out in April 2016, my grandfather passed away. His passing was the first time I felt grief and the loss of knowing that this person who had been in my life since the day I was born, this person who had filmed my birth, the person who had been our family historian and kept us connected, was gone. I'm a person who tries to see meaning in everything. I thought, 'If anybody would get this, my grandfather would be the one. He would be supportive. He would be the one to fly out and walk with me through the farm in Santa Cruz.' I packed a suitcase full of stuff the program recommended I bring, and I got on the plane.

For the next two years, Mo lived in a tent cabin made of canvas and wood on the UC Santa Cruz ground and worked on a thirty-two-acre farm with thirty-eight other participants, learning the farming practices and skills, many of which could be traced back to indigenous communities here and in Africa and Mexico. "When people think of farmers, they think, overwhelmingly, about white people. A lot of the farming techniques that we now use in sustainable farming and organic farming are things that indigenous people have been doing on this continent and all around the world for generations. One quarter of the program's participants were farmers of color who described themselves as the farmers of the global majority. They were activists and organizers and movement builders. I am grateful to instructors like Kellee Matsushita, who had attended the program herself before coming back to teach, encouraging participants to investigate the complex histories of the vegetables and grains like quinoa that they grew. I learned as much from my cohorts, the myriad of people from all over the world who I was working alongside, as I did from the outside experts who were invited to speak. I got schooled up.

"My time at UC Santa Cruz also provided the language to help me talk about what it means to be a queer Black person doing this work. I was introduced to the concept of queer ecology. Southern folks are very religious, and a lot of that homophobia, transphobia, and queer phobia is wrapped up in a religious connotation. Queer ecology is the idea that nature has always been queer biologically and ecologically, and understanding how colonialism and white supremacy has been used against queer and trans people, specifically queer and trans people of color, to say, 'You're not natural,' when actually we are very much part of nature."

After UC Santa Cruz, Mo wasn't quite ready to start their own farm but was filled with the desire to keep learning. They attended conferences and worked on a farm in San Leandro. They had a year-long fellowship with the California Farmer Justice Collaborative, where they interviewed farmers of color around California. When the fellowship ended, they joined Berkeley Basket CSA as the co-farm manager. Now they live a few hundred yards from one of the property owners where they grow food. "There's always a conversation around whether urban farming is legitimate. I don't have acreage, but now that I farm with the CSA, I tell people I am a farmer. Besides, there's a group in Texas farming in backyards. I know people in Florida who farm in backyards. So, my answer is, 'Yes, I'm a farmer,' because I'm out here sun up to sun down. I'll be in the rain, in the smoke, in the wind trying to get folks fed."

34.

Call Me by My Name

BY HARRYETTE MULLEN

AT EIGHTY-TWO YEARS OLD, MISS WILLIE B.
RICHARDSON OF GALION, LOUISIANA, IS
STILL FARMING.

Call me by my name,
the one I was wrapped in
the day I was born.
Call me by that name.
I have no other.
I'd be more than naked
   without it.
For years it hung on me
like my grandmother's coat,
but I kept growing, wanting
to be big enough to wear it,
until at last it became my skin.

35.

*W*heel of Fortune

MARTHA CALDERON

Calderon Produce
Vale, North Carolina

If the saying is true that "luck is what happens when hard work meets opportunity," then Martha Calderon is lucky. Her life story is one of grit and hard labor, patience and determination. She has an appetite for success and the good sense to know how to step through doors when they open. Seated in her office, her glasses propped on her head, Martha has the bearing of a corporate CEO, and it would be easy to assume she's all business all the time. But walk a few yards up the path from her office to her house, and you'll see that profit for profit's sake isn't her motivation. Her front porch is festooned with Halloween decorations. A harvest wreath hangs on her front door. Building a life for her family is what drives her forward, as she confirms as she sips her coffee and begins her story.

"I was born in the United States, but my parents raised me in a tiny town in Mexico, so I didn't learn English. That town was where I met my husband. We grew up together. He has a sixth-grade education, and I have a ninth-grade education. In Mexico, our families were row crop farmers. We farmed corn, sorghum, cows, and pigs.

"Aside from not having a formal education, we only had a background in farming, so when we came to this country, we worked picking oranges in Florida. Let me tell you, that is one of the toughest jobs you could ever do. We picked big tubs of oranges for $7.50 for each, but we were basically paid by the hour. It took a long time to fill the tubs. You would feel like you would never fill them. Every time we were out in the orange groves, I would think, 'I'm not going to do this for the rest of my life. This is not what I want to do.' At the time, I was pregnant with my first daughter.

"My husband was always looking for something different. He found a place that paid $10 per tub, so we started doing that. If you could put two tubs on the truck, you could deliver them to the warehouse. We worked seasonally. Over the winter we picked oranges. Over the summer we worked mainly vegetables. We would pick peppers, tomatoes, and sometimes cucumbers for other farmers.

"When we finished picking in Florida, we migrated to Michigan, but we didn't have a vehicle. My husband had a driver's license, so someone paid him to drive their car to Michigan, but we couldn't drive together. I had to go separately, but not knowing the language I had to rely on other people for everything, including ordering food. Back then, there was no 'No. 1' or 'No. 2' at the fast-food restaurants. You had to order your drink, your fries, or whatever you wanted separately. I didn't like having to rely on other people, but I had to pay an interpreter.

"When we got to Michigan, we started working. We got our first check; my husband told me, 'I'm going to give you $150. You can buy clothes, or you can buy a TV.' In Michigan, the farmer provides his migrant workers with housing, so I told my husband I wanted to buy a TV. One of the ways to learn anything was by watching TV and reading, so I started watching and reading children's books. Every time we went to yard sales, I would buy books. I learned English by reading books for first graders and watching *Wheel of Fortune*—'the car,' 'the boat'—while I was making my lunch or bathing my daughter.

"In Michigan farm workers' camps, you don't have a shower or a bathroom inside your room. We were just a young couple with a little girl, so we lived in a room smaller than this office. We had a stove, but we had to bathe and go to the bathroom down the hall. By the time we left Michigan, I'd learned enough English to ask for food and buy gas. I kept reading books until I mastered the language a little. A lot of our family members came, and they only knew a little bit of English, so I would have to interpret for them. I had to practice.

"The first time we went from Michigan to Florida, we started pinhooking. The farmers sold us the produce that didn't make the grade, and we took it to the farmers' market. We needed to know a little bit of English to ask, 'How much for the boxes?' You made a little more of a return with pinhooking than you made filling up the orange tubs for $7.50.

"We would move three or four times a year, following the work. About ten years into it, my husband said he wanted to see if we could start working here in North Carolina. We loved North Carolina from the beginning. Farmers were selling plants for $1.25 each. We would purchase plants, plant them ourselves, pick them, and sell them. We were sharecroppers for three years. We liked it. It was a really good business. We sharecropped for a number of years, but then my husband said, "As sharecroppers, once the farmers we're working for retire or simply don't want to grow anymore, then where do we go?' Also, our kids were growing. My oldest daughter didn't have problems adjusting to a new school three or four times a year, but I started to notice that when the little kids entered a new school, they did have a bigger problem adjusting. So we decided if we were going to settle down, it's going to be here, in the mountains, in Waynesville, near Asheville.

"My husband said, 'You stay in Waynesville and settle down with the children so they could go to one school. I'll keep going back to work.' The first year he did that, he sent money. But NAFTA was being implemented, and the pinhooking was being regulated. It wasn't worth it anymore. The first year he sent money to me. The second year, I sent money to him from what we had saved.

"In North Carolina, we had already bought our first tractor, but we didn't have any land. We were leasing land and sharecropping. My husband didn't mind because he was learning to fertilize, learning to spray, knowing that in time we would go out on our own. We were two years in North Carolina when we found a buyer called Mr. Wright. He bought 90 to 95 percent of our tomatoes, but we had to travel all the way from the mountains to here. Mr. Wright told us we could grow up to a hundred acres of tomatoes for him and he would buy 100 percent of what we grew, but we had to be closer and we needed to do several settings. In the mountains you have frost, but down here the growing season is much longer, until May 15th instead of April 25th, depending on the weather.

"The first season it was just me and my husband. We traveled back and forth because our kids were in school in Waynesville and we didn't want to move them again if this wasn't going to work out. It's an hour and a half each way. Sometimes we would work until 7:00 or 8:00 p.m. We would get home to the mountains by 9:30 p.m., and by the time we had dinner and a bath, it was already 11:00 p.m. and we had to get up at 5:00 a.m. to come back. My girls were already fourteen, fifteen—maybe a little older. So, we rented a house here. We would stay here on the days when it was too late for us to return to the mountains.

"We started farming fourteen acres on our own. We told Mr. Wright we would honor the hundred acres but that first we had to try it. He lent us fourteen acres. He didn't charge us because he knew we were hard workers. It was just me and my husband. Sometimes if we couldn't do all the work, or were behind on time, or we were doing pruning, we hired local people—but that fourteen acres, that was mostly me and him.

"Sometimes, we were so tired we didn't want to drive all the way back to the mountains. That hour and a half up and hour and a half down—we just wanted to rest. But we didn't have a bed in the rented house. I told my husband, 'I don't know whether I want to be working or sleeping. The floor is too hard.' I told him when we came to the United States I would do anything, but I will not shower with cold water, and I will not sleep on the ground. Those two things I would not do. I don't know where we got a mattress, but at first we put it on the floor. All migrant workers put tomato boxes on the bottom and sort of use it like a base for the bed, so we did that.

"The first year we did fourteen acres, and we didn't move the kids. We did that, and it was really good. We were like a novelty around here because there weren't a lot of Mexicans in this area, but they saw how hard we worked. There was a guy who wanted to sell sixty-three acres, and he would owner-finance it. He was only asking for a $10,000 down payment, and he would sell the land for $2,300 per acre, which was really cheap. We got those sixty-three acres and started to grow on them. We moved our three youngest kids, and the girls stayed in Waynesville for one more year until they finished middle school.

"The next year we did a season of about forty to fifty acres. It was going to be good. The third year we grew more acres, but there was a big flood and we didn't have crop insurance. When a farmer doesn't have the right kind of crop insurance, that could mean being in business or being out of business. The only thing that saved us was we had a really good market afterwards, so we were able to at least break even.

We got crop insurance, but we noticed that every year, farming was getting more and more difficult.

"We knew the difference between just farming the land with a tractor and a plow, and agribusiness. We had to make that transition. I had to start learning how to manage the business, and my husband did more of the farming part. That's how we've been able to grow and survive. When the kids left school and started being independent, I thought we'd start seeing more money come in. I thought, "Okay, this money we're going to save," but I don't see that happening. We continued to do good—we made this house from scratch—but not as good as I thought it was going to be. It's getting harder: the market, the competition, and the weather. The weather has played a big part. Especially in the last four years, we haven't gone below 72 degrees. It's just too hot. The plants don't like it. Other times it's so humid and hot, your plant is basically cooking. You try to do your best, you do cover crops, you try to rotate. Last year we swapped land with a farmer—he grew corn on our land and we grew tomatoes and peppers on his—just so we could give our land a little rest. But it's tough.

"The best thing about our farm is we were able to put our five kids through school, through college, without any student loans. I always wanted to go to school—always. But educating a woman back when I was raised in Mexico—it was more important for my parents to have someone feed the pigs and the cows and help them. My husband used to say, 'I don't want our kids to struggle like we did.' We're here and God has helped us. We were in the right place at the right time. Maybe, as the industry changes, our kids might not be as lucky as we were, so we tell them, 'You have to go to school. You have to do well in school.' When we saw the chance to give them an education without having all that debt behind them, we wanted to do that. That's not only for them; that's for us because if they do good and they're independent, then we're going to be good. We're able to keep the family in a better financial situation than we were.

"I like to think that all my kids could say, 'I know my mom and dad tried to give us a really nice childhood.' We never told them, 'The market is good, the market is bad; we have money, we don't have money; we've got problems.' They never knew any of that. We tried to raise them so that when they leave home, they say, 'I'm homesick. I miss my mom and my dad.'"

36.

*E*xceeding the "Yes"

MARVIN FRINK

Briarwood Cattle Farm
Red Springs, North Carolina

"If you can meet me right there," Marvin Frink says as he swaps his cowboy boots for a lace-up pair, "I'm going to move them over."

"What's involved in moving them over?" I ask.

"I'm going to call them, and they're going to walk behind me. Then I'm going to release them into the next field."

By "them," Marvin means his Black Angus cattle, and right now most of his herd is grazing in the distant pasture. He points to a neat stretch of electric fencing a few yards from where we're standing, beyond which sprawls another wide-open field. It's a little past four o'clock on this late-October afternoon. The wind is picking up, the sun steadily dipping toward the tree line.

It's hard to look at Marvin Frink, standing tall in his cowboy hat, crisp plaid shirt, and dark jeans, surrounded by all this open space, and not think you've stumbled into a classic Western. But there's nothing make-believe about him. He possesses a studied calmness, a presence that is utterly commanding. The gray in his beard suggests years of experience and hard-earned wisdom, and yet there's a gentleness emanating from him, a kindness you see in his eyes and hear in his voice.

For the next few minutes we stand by the fence exactly where Marvin told us to, watching as he heads out across the open ground, past the hay bales and the farm equipment. The wind carries birdsong and the sound of Marvin's whistle, followed by his cattle call. Sure enough, his herd falls in line behind him as he leads them through the gate separating one pasture from the next. Once the task is completed, the herd scatters. Marvin strides back along the fence, his head down, his hands wedged deep in his pockets, the sun glinting off the brim of his cowboy hat.

When he rejoins us, Marvin apologizes for the interruption, explaining that he does something called "sectional grazing"—the daily practice of moving his herd from pasture to pasture to save time, preserve his pasture, and reduce his feed costs. I've only been on Marvin's farm for fifteen minutes, but I've already sensed that he is a man who keeps his word and respects people's time. "In the military," Marvin says, "if you say you'll be there at 9:00, *we're* there between 8:30 and 8:45 to respect the 9:00. Time is based on your integrity. Now that I'm on this side of the fence, it's a different story." He pauses for a moment, then adds, "Time is a big deal you're when dealing with PTSD. I try not to let time stress me out anymore." This is a startling admission, one few people would be willing to share with someone they've just met. But as I will come to find out as the afternoon unfolds, Marvin Frink is willing to put himself on the line if it means forging a deeper, more meaningful connection.

"My father and my mother both came from farming families and grew up farming," Marvin says. He has invited us into his home, and now we're sitting in his family room, which opens onto his kitchen, where everything is in its proper place. "I come from farmers on both sides, but no one in my generation farmed. My mom is from Georgia, and my dad is from right here in Whiteville, North Carolina, but neither of them farmed as adults. They met in Florida. That's where I was born.

"Most people look at Florida and think of Jacksonville at the top, Orlando in the middle, and Miami at the bottom, but they totally forget about driving down Highway 95. Farming was engrained in me because it was all around us. There's nothing but grassland along the right-hand side of Florida; nothing but cattle, peanuts, orchards, and orange groves everywhere. Florida is nothing but farmland. My first adventure as a little kid in elementary school was visiting farms. I was attracted to cattle from the very beginning. I'd come home and talk about them with my parents."

Marvin graduated from high school with an academic scholarship to the University of Miami, but he got into some trouble, which left him with the option to join the military. He served in Desert Storm. By 2011, he was home from a deployment, stationed at Fort Bragg, and haunted by memories of the war. "I was dealing with a lot of nightmares. I was distancing myself from everybody. There were times when I couldn't even tell my wife who I was. I still have a grocery bag full of meds in my house. They're no joke; they'll knock a horse out. But that's what they give us. This is what all of us veterans deal with. We've been to places and done things, and now what? Now they've sent us home, and the VA doesn't always want to help us out. Sometimes it feels like they value us being equipment over being human beings."

Sensing that his son was in distress, Marvin's father called and asked him to come home. "I stalled for two weeks," Marvin says. "In the middle of those two weeks I almost committed suicide. I finally went home to Florida on a Friday. My dad and I talked for a long time.

"The next morning, he wanted to go to his friend's farm. The farm was old, but his friend was a veteran and cattle farmer. We lifted things, and I helped with the feed bags. He had me walk around with the grazing cows, which was intimidating and exciting at the same time, being close to such big and impressive animals. I could feel their strength. Each cow had a personality, a character. Unexpectedly, I started talking to them. I felt like I was part of something, like I was part of a team, a platoon, a family.

"There are two key things that help vets deal with PTSD. The first is working with our hands. We have to do something with our hands—it keeps us busy. The second thing is the time. When vets wake up in the morning, our minds are hungry. We have to do something. If we can do something and work with our hands, we're okay."

When Marvin went back to his father's house, his father immediately noticed the change. "He saw that I was smiling again. That same night I found out my dad had cancer. It's a bittersweet story, but it was okay. I didn't know it at the time, but my dad was preparing me. A month later, my father called me again. This time, he gave me a yellow legal pad. He told me to open it and read it. He'd drawn out the whole plan for me to have a cattle farm.

"I'm from a neighborhood in Melbourne, Florida, called Briarwood, that's heavily infested with drugs and crime. When my dad gave me the yellow legal pad, he said, 'I want you to take the name Briarwood, a name that's negative here, back to North Carolina and make it positive. That way you'll never forget where you come from.'"

After the experience with his father's friend, Marvin threw himself into learning more about farming. He went to his local extension agent's office hoping to meet and connect with other farmers. But finding mentors proved to be more difficult than he expected. "There's a big gap between the older and younger farmers. Sometimes the older farmers don't want to talk to us. They kind of view us, the next generation, as competition. Farming can feel like a fraternity that you have to get into. If you look at the ratios, you'll see that a lot of farmers were military. You've got to remember, they had to earn their way up through the ranks, and they feel like you have to earn your way up through farming. Here I was, someone they didn't know, asking for techniques and secrets—which was their everyday living, their way of bringing in money. I was the new guy. They didn't know me or trust me. They didn't know what my agenda was."

Eventually, Marvin found three mentors. The first was a former battle buddy, a sixth-generation farmer and James Beard semifinalist for Best Chef in the Southeast, Matthew Raiford. Matthew, along with his sister, Althea, a Navy veteran, owns Gilliard Farms, an organic Century Farm in Glynn County, Georgia. Gilliard Farms was started by their great-great-great-grandfather Jupiter Gilliard, a freed slave, in 1874. "Matthew and I last saw each other in Korea," Marvin says. "He didn't want to deploy with us to Saudi Arabia. He said, 'Hey, I'm done.' To have a family farm in one family for one hundred years is hard to find. When Chef Raiford left the military, he farmed and went to chef's school at the same time. I had 'X' number of years in the military; that's all I knew. I didn't know who to talk to." Chef Raiford introduced Marvin to the Farmer Veteran Coalition, an organization that helps retired vets and active-duty personnel find resources to help them get started in farming.

When we first arrived, Marvin showed us a tractor parked just behind his house. Now our conversation circles back to it. "I'd been asking around, looking for a tractor for a good three to five years. I needed what's called a 'cab tractor,' which is enclosed, to help deal with my health issues. But a tractor is expensive, and the price is steadily going up. For a guy like me who was trying to get started, I was willing to settle for something less that still got the job done. We didn't have the money to buy a tractor outright, and we couldn't afford to finance one."

When hay-cutting season rolled around again, Marvin and his wife, Tanisha, found themselves in a tough spot. They'd changed the grass in their pasture to Ozark grass, which is good for cattle but expensive. The grass hadn't taken root the first time, so they had to replant it. Now it was time to cut it, but all the people who'd said they could help pulled out, claiming they didn't have time to help cut it or wanted to charge too much for their services. "One Saturday morning, I practically gave up. I didn't want to farm anymore. I felt like I was letting my family down. I didn't know what to do." That's when Marvin's close friend and fellow veteran, Annette Stevenson, came up with a plan. She emailed every veteran, congressman, and senator she knew. The next week, Marvin and his wife were invited to participate in the North Carolina Veterans Business Association conference in Raleigh. The organizers asked Marvin and Tanisha to sponsor door prizes, which they did, gathering their modest funds to offer three gift bags.

But the day of the conference, all the politicians and businessmen who had promised to help suddenly couldn't be bothered. "When I met them in person, they acted like I wasn't that important. I would talk to them, and they would walk off. I can't do malls. I can't do movies. It's hard for me to go out to dinner with my wife, and I struggle with that because I love her. When I go out—and you'll see this with vets—I need to sit a particular way so I can see the door. I need to see what's coming in because I've been in situations where some bad things happen at the door. So, there I was at the conference. I had finally stepped out of my comfort zone, put myself in a larger crowd, asked for help and opened up to them, but they all blew me off. I got home, and honestly, I was so depressed."

In every town there's one breakfast place where the farmers gather. In downtown Raeford, that place is Edinborough Family Restaurant. The weekend after the conference, Marvin went there for breakfast. That's when his luck changed, and he met his second mentor.

"As soon as I walked in, I saw all the farmers there. Everyone was speaking to each other. There was a guy in the corner I'd never seen before. Immediately, I felt in my stomach that I needed to get to know him. I decided to pay for his meal. I got up and was getting ready to pay for his meal when the farmers at the table next to me asked me a question. Before I knew it, he'd done got up and was walking out the door.

"I left Edinborough and went down the street to my friend Papa's place. He sells barns, and my wife and I wanted a particular size. When I got there, out of the blue Papa said, 'Marvin, there's a guy down the road you need to meet. He does pasture-raised cattle and chickens—the same thing you're doing. You should go meet him.' Papa gave me directions.

"I never just pull up in front of somebody's house if I don't know them, but when I got there, I knocked on the door and the same guy from the restaurant answered. I said, 'Sir, I know you don't know me.' I introduced myself from a distance. The next thing I knew, he said, 'Come on in, son. Let's talk.' I said, 'I saw you in the restaurant. I wanted to pay for your meal.' He said, 'No, son, you're good. Sit down and talk to me. Tell me what you're doing.' His name was Mr. John Counsel. He's an African American farmer. He was 2009 or 2011 Farmer of the Year."

Marvin told Mr. Counsel about his cow/calf and chicken operations. "Mr. Counsel stood up, adjusted himself, picked up his cane, and said, 'Come with me in the back.' He had *six* barns. We went back and he opened one small barn and said, 'This is where I do my chicken processing.' He'd made his barn into a processing plant. It had concrete floors and stainless steel sinks—it was exactly what my wife and I wanted to do. It was exactly why I'd gone down to Papa's place.

"He asked me what I needed, so I told him I needed a tractor. When he asked me what kind of tractor I was looking for, I said I needed a tractor that can cut hay because I couldn't find anyone to cut it for me. I told him I had a tractor, but it's only 35 horsepower. Hay equipment is 55 horsepower and above. We walked into another barn. Inside was that blue tractor. It's a Ford 5000. It was in two pieces. It had been that way, sitting in his barn, for ten years. It needed a seal around the gasket that needed to be replaced, but he couldn't find anybody to help him put the tractor back together. The brand-new seal, the screws—everything—was sitting on the seat. Mr. Counsel said, 'I'll tell you what, son. If you can put this tractor back together, you'll have the tractor you need.' He told me to come back tomorrow so we could start working on the tractor. I was mesmerized. I kept thinking this was some kind of joke. The same day I met Mr. Counsel, he was giving me everything I needed—education-wise, tool-wise—plus a tractor. I wasn't looking for this at all."

For the next three days straight, while Mr. Counsel sat in the garage, Marvin worked to reassemble the tractor. "He'd say, 'Son, move this over here. Move that over there.' We were trying to slide it back together, put bolts in it. The tractor weighed ninety-five hundred pounds. I had to get more people to come help us. When we pulled it out of the barn, it hadn't seen sunlight in ten years." Marvin hauled it to the local Ford dealership for repairs. "Now my wife and I are sanding it down so we can repaint it. We're giving it a new life. I'm trying to find a sticker to go on the side of it so I can dedicate it to Mr. Counsel. When I show it to him the next time, I want the body to be painted dark blue and the wheels painted white. I want it to look like it's supposed to so he'll know how much I appreciate his help. He's that farmer I was saying I was looking for, that African American farmer who is my resource. I see myself in him, and he sees himself in me."

As his operation has grown, Marvin has drawn on the wisdom of Black farmers in various ways. When he needed fencing for his twenty-five acres, a potentially massive expense, his father suggested he use telephone poles to cut his costs. Marvin purchased two eighteen-wheeler loads of old telephone poles from the phone company, then cut each thirty-foot pole into three ten-foot sections. "They already had creosote on them and were already USDA-approved to go in the ground. In the African American community we have a history of fixing things up, putting our touch on them, and making them special. We're gonna call that 'swag.' I took something old and made it look good. I cut my cost by thousands of dollars. All I had to do was buy a chain saw and blades."

His third mentor and father figure is a retired Air Force veteran, Harrison Campbell. At eighty-six years old, Mr. Campbell—or "Daddy Campbell," as Marvin calls him—taught him time-tested traditional farming practices and strategies for analyzing soil. "Mr. Campbell always carries a mason jar and a small shovel with him," Marvin says. "He will dig up some soil, put it in his mason jar, fill it with water and shake it up. Then he lets it sit. He can tell by the layers of the soil what's in it: if you've got more sand, more clay. It's a quick way to do a field analysis. He told me those are techniques that Black farmers used when they couldn't afford to pay for soil samples. I've been with both Mr. Counsel and Mr. Campbell, and they'll walk up to land—I'm talking *straight dirt*—and they'll say, 'You need lime here and minerals over there.' I'll say, what is it you're looking at?' They're old-school farmers."

Mr. Campbell also inspired Marvin to give part of his harvest away. "When you're in the military, traveling around the world, you see that food is a big deal. It's the number one source of security. Part of Mr. Campbell's agro-therapy is to load up the back of his truck, pull up somewhere, and give away the produce he grows: corn—shucked and everything—peas, whatever. He tells people to come on and get what they want. Now, every time we process a cow, we call someone and ask if they know someone who needs food. I don't want to know who they are."

Recently, Marvin had an opportunity to purchase the fifteen-acre farm next door, which would allow him to expand his operation. "The owner was going to give me a good deal. My credit is good, and our finances are fair. My wife is the financial person. She keeps us under our budget. We wouldn't try to reach for something if we couldn't handle it." But when he applied for a loan, he was denied—not once but twice—first by a bank and then by a government program backed by the US Department of Agriculture. The agent told Marvin he didn't have enough equity in his existing property, even though the money he had already invested to improve his farm—clearing the cornfield and creating a pasture, installing cross-fencing, building his home, to say nothing of the value of his cattle—has more than doubled its value. "There's not another property like this in the surrounding three counties. If we had access to capital, we could explode."

Despite his disappointment at being denied a loan, Marvin continues to contribute to his community. He invites veterans to bring their horses, goats, and even a python snake to his farm so kids from the community have an opportunity to interact with animals. "I want to show them a different possibility. They don't feel valued. I know because I was that same kid." Realizing that his pasture, with its wide-open fields free of overhead power lines, could serve as a perfect emergency staging area, he offered his pasture to local law enforcement as a helicopter emergency landing zone. "Because it's not just about the money," Marvin says. "You have to be a certain kind of person to want to be out here. You have to be with someone who loves this life. To us, it's precious. What you're hearing here—the wind, the birds, the peace and quiet—people pay for a vacation spot with this kind of quiet, but we have it right here. Cattle do it for me. My home, my farm—it's peace of mind. That's why I'm out here—for the peace and quiet."

37.

Swarm

BY TONYA FOSTER

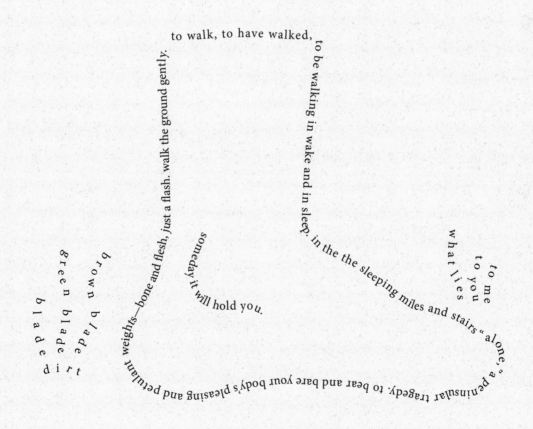

to walk, to have walked,

to be walking in wake and in sleep.

walk the ground gently.

weights—bone and flesh, just a flash.

someday it will hold you.

in the the sleeping miles and stairs "alone,"

to me
to you
what lies

a peninsular tragedy, to bear and bare your body's pleasing and petulant

brown blade
green blade
blade dirt

38

A Brief History of Tobacco

BY NATALIE BASZILE

In a barn somewhere in Caswell County, North Carolina, 1839, Stephen Slade, an eighteen-year-old enslaved blacksmith, woke to discover the small open fires he'd lit to cure his owner's six hundred pounds of tobacco had died down during the night. Panicked that the fires would go out completely, Stephen revived them with charred logs from his nearby blacksmith shop. The charred logs produced an intense, dry heat that cured the tobacco leaves quickly and turned them a bright, spotless yellow. Little did Stephen know, but his accidental innovation, "flue-cured" tobacco, would alter the course of North Carolina agricultural history for generations and impact farmers, especially Black farmers, for the next 160 years.

Through the seventeenth and eighteenth centuries, most smokers preferred flavored pipe or chewing tobacco, but the nineteenth century witnessed a trend toward Turkish tobacco-filled cigarettes that had become popular in Spain but proved expensive for American and British smokers. Stephen's discovery of "flue-cured" or "bright leaf" tobacco, which his owner, Captain Abisha Slade, refined, offered a cheaper alternative. Suddenly, North Carolina's sandy soil, which many considered worthless for large-scale cotton and rice farming, was regarded as perfectly suited for growing tobacco. Within a decade of Stephen's discovery, North Carolina had evolved into a tobacco-producing powerhouse. While large farms grew the majority of the state's tobacco, even smaller farmers, capitalizing on demand, entered the market and found tobacco to be a profitable crop. After Emancipation, as formerly enslaved people forged new lives, many farmed tobacco as tenant farmers and eventually as landowners.

But when the Great Depression began in 1929, an already unstable tobacco market was further destabilized as farmers, desperate to compensate for falling prices, grew more tobacco and flooded the market. In the 1938, ninety-nine years after Stephen Slade discovered flue-cured tobacco, the federal government created a price support program to assist tobacco farmers who had saturated the market as they struggled to survive through the Great Depression. The government devised a quota system based on a farmer's acreage, which limited the amount of tobacco an individual farmer could grow and sell, the rationale being that by limiting the supply, tobacco prices could be controlled and stabilized.

For the next six decades, the price of tobacco remained predictable. The federal policy kept many small farmers, including many Black family farmers, afloat. Farmers knew that if the big tobacco companies like Phillip Morris, Marlboro, and R. J. Reynolds didn't buy their crop at auction, they could rely on the government to purchase it. By 1950, the top five tobacco brands sold more than 300 billion cigarettes in the United States. North Carolina yielded 850 million pounds of tobacco. The government even allowed farmers to purchase quotas from other farmers, which enabled them to expand their operations. For many Black farmers, tobacco farming was the path to prosperity. Tobacco paid for their children's school clothes, cars, and college tuitions.

But by the late 1980s, the nation's concern over the dangers of smoking had taken its toll on Big Tobacco. The number of American smokers had steadily declined. By the late nineties, large manufacturers were forced to lay off workers, close factories, reduce production, and shift their focus to overseas markets.

Then, in 2004, Congress voted to withdraw from the tobacco industry and eliminate the support program. Recognizing that the change would cause upheaval, the legislation included a $10 billion aid package known as the Tobacco Transition Payment Program (TTPP), which would provide farmers with a series of payments spread out over a ten-year period from 2005–2014. Known commonly as the "tobacco buyout," the funds came from assessments on tobacco manufacturers and importers. But without the quotas, restrictions, and subsidies, tobacco was only profitable for the largest producers. Many small farmers, including many Black farmers, realized they couldn't survive. In 2004, there were eight thousand tobacco farms in North Carolina. By 2014, that number had dropped to sixteen hundred.

39.

*A*fter Tobacco

THE WRIGHTS

Happy Land Farms
Bladenboro, North Carolina

Mr. and Mrs. Wright, owners of Happy Land Farms, are one of the many Black farming families whose livelihood was adversely impacted by the tobacco buyout. After years of relative prosperity, they saw their community disintegrate as tobacco manufacturers and other small businesses that depended on the industry left the area.

HAROLD WRIGHT

My grandfather William Wright came over here in the late 1800s. He bought four hundred acres of land, which he paid for by logging in wintertime and farming in the summer. His seven children inherited his land. Out of his seven children, six of them farmed. My father, Luther, was born in 1910. He and his brother Frank farmed together. They farmed tobacco, cotton, corn, and peanuts. He farmed in the summer and hauled logs in the winter, just like my grandfather. My daddy had about a hundred acres.

My father divided his land between his thirteen children. Of my siblings, my baby brother, Donald, and I were the only farmers.

The first couple of years, I farmed my father's hundred acres and my aunt's land. My third year, I started renting land, and around 1972, I bought another ten acres. A guy came to me wanting to sell it. He told me to go to the local bank to finance it, but the local bank refused, so I put the money together anyway. The owner financed it for us, and I paid for the land in six months.

I had another experience when I tried to buy seven acres of my grandfather's land. The white lady who owned it told me I didn't need any more land; I had enough land. I told her I didn't appreciate her telling me what I needed and didn't need. Two years later, her daughter came and sold it to me.

In 1974, we bought twenty-one more acres, and in 1976 we bought thirty-five more acres. I had an opportunity to buy a lot more land, but I didn't want to tie myself up and not be able to pay for it. I only bought what I knew we could pay for. I tried to keep from getting loaded down with debt. Later on, I bought another five acres.

Whenever you bought land, you had a tobacco quota with it. Say you bought fifty acres. You'd have a quota of twenty-five hundred pounds of tobacco that the government would guarantee to buy at a certain price. Before the tobacco buyout, the government promised to pay $8 per pound to the farmer who produced the tobacco and $2 went to the landowner. If you owned the land *and* you farmed the tobacco, you got $10 per pound. Tobacco was the money crop.

When we had the good government support price, you took your tobacco to the warehouse. In order to get paid, the tobacco companies like Philip Morris, R. J. Reynolds, or Marlboro had to put a grade on it. If the tobacco companies didn't want it, the government would put a grade on it, and you'd get paid.

But in 2004, the government stopped the subsidy program. Farmers couldn't grow tobacco and count on government support. You could contract with the tobacco companies, but if they wouldn't put a grade on it, you had to bring it home. Your crop was lost because you didn't have a guaranteed buyer. When the government stopped putting a grade on tobacco and buying it, it drove a lot of Black farmers out of growing tobacco.

Then the tobacco companies said they were dealing with too many small farmers. They only wanted to deal with farmers who farmed a hundred acres or more. That wiped out a lot of Black farmers because those who didn't have enough acreage couldn't get a contract.

You take a town like Clarkton, where they had three warehouses. The population was growing, buildings were popping up. People would come in the summertime and be all over the place. People would set up mobile homes for the workers to stay in and would make money on rent because they knew people were coming.

After the buyout, warehouses were falling down, and people left town. It trickled right down—the car dealerships left town, the general stores closed up, eating joints closed. There was no money to circulate. Fairmont was the biggest tobacco community in North Carolina. I bet they had ten warehouses down there. They all failed; there was nothing but empty buildings left.

We had to find some other way to keep our income, so we started in the trucking business. We're doing day care, trucking, and still farming two hundred acres of corn and soybeans. Our grandchildren are at North Carolina State and are interested in farming.

I love farming. I love the fresh smell of the dirt and seeing the crops grow. I love to see the combine going through the field, harvesting.

ANN WRIGHT

I have prayer, faith, and the intention of never giving up—I don't give up easy. I'm always trying to figure out a way that we can make it. I have to keep going. My five children are grown, our grands are growing up. I want to show them that you can't give up. Because if we don't keep pressing on and everybody sits down, there won't be any Black farmers. I talk to a lot of Black farmers, and I say, "Don't sell your land. Please don't sell your land. We've got to have something to leave our children, grandchildren, and great-grandchildren."

AUSTIN WRIGHT

When I was small, I knew I had a strong passion for farming. I would see my grandfather working in his shop. I wouldn't want to go home. That's pretty much how I came to farming. Once I got older, after I graduated from high school, I knew that I needed an education to get where I wanted. I graduated from North Carolina State this past May with a degree in agribusiness and land management. Since then,

I've been on the farm, taking care of the animals, growing crops—anything—you name it. For planting, I do soybeans and corn. My day starts at 5:30 a.m. I come out here, check on the chickens and the cows, the hog—all that. I feed them, then come back and start the day with my grandfather. We work until 5:00 p.m. I love the hands-on and the hard work that comes with farming. It taught me that life isn't easy; you have to work for what you want. I would say it's good for everyone to have a little hand in farming. Everyone needs to know where their food comes from and who produces it.

40.

Yellowjackets

BY YUSEF KOMUNYAKAA

When the plowblade struck
An old stump hiding under
The soil like a beggar's
Rotten tooth, they swarmed up
& Mister Jackson left the plow
Wedged like a whaler's harpoon.
The horse was midnight
Against dusk, tethered to somebody's
Pocketwatch. He shivered, but not
The way women shook their heads
Before mirrors at the five
& dime—a deep connection
To the low field's evening star.
He stood there, in tracechains,
Lathered in froth, just
Stopped by a great, goofy
Calmness. He whinnied
Once, & then the whole
Beautiful, blue-black sky
Fell on his back.

41.

*H*ome Games

KELLYE WALKER AND WERTEN BELLAMY

Rafters Point at Freedom Farm
Heathsville, Virginia

It's a balmy Monday evening in San Francisco, and the waiter has just taken our orders when Werten Bellamy, who is in town for business, mentions that he and his wife, Kellye, recently purchased a one-hundred-acre farm near Heathsville, Virginia. "The closer we got, the smaller the roads became," Werten says, describing how he and Kellye felt the first time they laid eyes on the property. "We ended up on a winding road, and as we turned into the gates and started down the tree-lined driveway, we were overwhelmed with the power of our need for space. I looked over and Kellye had her arms outstretched. When we came onto the property, we realized how long it had been since we'd had space. Most people can't remember the last time. As dusk settled in, we started feeling a real connection with our ancestors. We realized our people—Black people—had been there for hundreds of years. There are sounds you hear in the night in rural spaces. We realized our ancestors heard those same sounds, saw the same sunset. We realized how rare an experience we were having. It was a total full-circle moment."

Located on Virginia's northernmost peninsula, on the western shore of Chesapeake Bay, and nestled between the Potomac and Rappahannock Rivers, the five counties of Northern Neck—King George, Westmoreland, Richmond, Northumberland, and Lancaster—are steeped in history. Eight Native American tribes were the region's first inhabitants. The first enslaved Africans and white indentured servants arrived in 1619. In 1687, enslaved Africans in Westmoreland County conspired to kill the white colonists and destroy their property—the vast estates and tobacco plantations that accounted for the region's prosperity. The following year, in April 1688, an enslaved man named Sam, who "had several times endeavored to promote a Negro insurrection in the colony,"[79] was found guilty, along with his co-conspirators, of plotting another rebellion. As punishment, he was whipped and ordered to wear a four-pronged metal collar for the rest of his life. The region was also home to free Black people, many of whom fought in the American Revolution. Northern Neck is the birthplace of three of the first five American presidents.

Kellye and Werten are advocates for Black farming and landownership. A lawyer and a talent development consultant, neither one of them farms, opting instead to lease their land to a local Black farmer. Still, they both come from farming families and appreciate what it means to reconnect with the soil.

KELLYE WALKER: I grew up in the small town of Arcadia in North Louisiana. On my father's side, there were many cousins and extended family who owned land and owned farms. I didn't think of it as farming. We just had people who lived in the country. They had big gardens. They had cattle and horses. That's where I spent my summers when I was young. That's where I learned to drive a tractor and watch things like calves be born. It's where I learned how to feel comfortable around animals and how to grow food and eat what you grow. I remember my relatives literally lived off their land. They sold their cattle for the meat. The garden was for the house, but selling the animals was part of how they earned their living.

WERTEN BELLAMY: On both my parents' sides, you only have to go back one generation to find people living on farms. Overwhelmingly, the people on both sides of my family were farmers.

I've been bitten by the Ancestry.com bug. When you start to look at census reports and they list our people, you typically see us listed as one of two things: as housekeepers or farmers.

Our journey to get to our farm was really a process of thinking about two things: what would be a setting that would be a source of fulfillment for Kellye and I in the next season of our lives, when we're no longer working out of necessity and have some discretionary time? We knew we weren't the type of people who wanted to set up in some resort community in Phoenix or Florida, where we would be guests—only there because we had the financial wherewithal to be there, but not for any other reason. We weren't interested in that. The other thread of our thinking was watching our children move into adulthood and asking ourselves what kind of setting would lend itself to family connection, understanding that our kids, like most kids, are going to end up wherever their aspirations take them. What could we do to continue to have a home for them?

We were curious about properties that had land, properties that could accommodate a family. We wanted to find a place that was within driving distance of our home so that we could actually start using it. It turns out that in the very state where we live, Virginia, there's a rich farming community called the Northern Neck of Virginia. It's actually where George Washington was from. It's very much a farm and water type of community. Some of the biggest fisheries around the turn of the century and some of the biggest plantations weren't very far from where we are.

KW: This whole thing pricked both of us in our hearts for a couple reasons. When we got married, one of the things Werten and I talked about was, What's home base? We have busy lives, we travel—all that—but as we thought about our kids, that notion of a home place for them was really important to us. Having land and being able to look out and say, "All that you survey belongs to you"—it's sort of a joke now; whenever we go to the farm, I do this waving thing with my arms—but that's actually the beauty of it, having the physical and visible manifestation of this notion of home. It's important.

WB: This notion of home is important particularly for current and future generations of Black people. To use a sports analogy I use when I train professionals of color, I tell them that from the moment we put our children into academic settings, to the types of work settings they find themselves in upon graduation, they're always playing "away games." You can't get to the championship if all your games are away games and you don't have any home games. We wanted a place where our kids, friends, and family could play a home game—a safe environment where you can just be. I believe those places are increasingly scarce because the lives we live and the communities where we live—it's very difficult to find space. We had our first Thanksgiving here as a family. It was remarkable, not because of anything we did differently but because of where we were.

I just spent three days on the farm with my eighty-five-year-old father. He's a lover of land and can identify all the trees. We were in the car together looking for a place to have lunch in the neighboring town of Reedville, and as we're driving over my dad remembered that he had an old friend who he thought had relocated there. We googled his name and got his address. We got off the road and drove down this graveled path *way* deep, I mean *deep* in the woods. We got to this house; my dad got out of the car while I kept the car running in case we had to make a hasty exit, and next thing I see are these two eighty-five-year-old men in a warm embrace. Think about it. Where else in America could you, without any notice, go up to someone's house who you haven't seen in fifty years? They talked about how they double-dated to prom together in the early '50s as if it were yesterday. To be able to drop in on people without an agenda, without having to bring anything, without any pretense—to be able to just be you and have them be delighted to see you . . . ? We're trying to recapture that. We're trying to get a bit of that back, to have a space where our kids might see what our best selves look like.

KW: Werten and I both have experienced the feeling individually and together. We get to the farm and we feel all the masks and the armor we wear in our daily lives melt away. Being there, feeling a connection with what's around us in a way we don't feel when we are in what I call our normal everyday lives—I fundamentally believe the farm allows us to reconnect with who we are. We feel a connection with the space, with the land, in a way that frees us. It is really amazing.

WB: Maya Angelou writes about what happens to Black people as we have lost touch with our history and our connection to the past. So, I guess what I'm saying is, this farm is the embodiment of our connection with our past. Because all you have to do is a little research, and unless your people came straight from Africa, you don't have to dig too deep to discover they were on a farm somewhere. That's just a fact. And so, what does that mean? It means that, at our core, we're connected to something deeper than the activities that consume us today and to the things we consume.

We wanted a place where our kids could be contemplative, where they could fellowship on their own terms if they wanted, without disruption. It's very difficult to get cell service out where we are, so some of the distractions of the outside world go away very quickly.

KW: When we initially told our kids we bought a farm, they did not get it. But as we continued to talk to them and then they got there, they were awestruck. It was an immediate connection. We walked the whole perimeter of the property and talked about the importance of landownership, keeping it for generations. Each one of them, in their own way, I think, was humbled and proud. They felt connected. They were out walking around saying, "We can do this; I wish I could bring my friends here."

WB: Our son was outside at midnight. I thought he was crazy, but he was like, "Dad, it's so amazing. At night you can see all the deer out." I think deep down inside, our kids continue to want home. So the question is, How can you give it to them, understanding that they're not likely to move back in the house with you? You've got to redefine where is the place where they can, as they grow, return to something familiar and safe.

KW: If you tie all this back into what we were saying earlier about home games, I do believe that we are built to be connected with the land. We continue to chase the smoke and all the accoutrements of this society, all that's pulling us farther away. That's an away game. The more we can try to connect with the land—having land, owning land—and what that does to the soul, the best of who we are will come out.

Recently, I was talking to a guy, and I happened to mention the farm. He was an African American guy, and he told me *he* grew up on a farm. We started reminiscing about shelling peas. His family had cattle. Now he wants to buy a farm. He wants to get back to that. This whole notion of getting back, having that sense of connection to home, I just think it's deep for us. It's more than "Oh, let me come back to, as Werten calls it, that box in the away game and that gated community."

WB: Black people are running out of space. If you don't create some space for yourself, then you've got to confront all the challenges that space- and time-constrained people confront.

We reject this thesis that Black people are tied to dysfunctional communities. If you think about the way Black people are portrayed, when you hear the phrase "Black community" in the media, typically it's tied to something dysfunctional. But we know that's not our truth. Things get dysfunctional when people get tight—that's true for Black people, white people, yellow people, and red people. If you get people too tight, it gets challenging. If you have been blessed to be able to elect where you spend your discretionary time, we believe there's no better place than to do so on land and in space. Period.

KW: Something feels good about being able to change the narrative of what has happened to Black people and to start to reclaim, in our own little way, that which has been taken from those who look like us. We want to change the narrative so that others begin to desire to reclaim land. We want to bring anybody and everybody we can, who we care about, to see and experience this so that maybe they will begin to reclaim that on behalf of those who, in recent years and years before us, have found themselves subject to the ugliness that has happened in this country. That changes the narrative about what it means to be the Black community. It changes the narrative about understanding and appreciating landownership.

WB: This farm is the first time I've lived in a place where I am incredibly wanting my friends to come. Kellye and I are private people. We don't do a lot of stuff out and about, but right now, we want everyone who is important to us to share this space with us. Isn't that what community is about?

If you gave me truth serum, I'd wish that everybody I know who is Black and had the means would go get themselves a farm. I really do. If I could start a movement where we began to restore what we had in the beginning, that would as a result be restorative for our people, I would be all for it.

A lot of Black farmers are under financial duress because the farming industry has fundamentally changed, and it's changed in a way, like a lot of industries, where the people who are benefiting are the people who were advantaged to begin with. If you're on the margins, there's no relief. At the same time, what is interesting for Black people with means is that the one thing that I believe they need the most is more available than ever—and that's land.

You look out over the bay, you see how the moonlight hits the water, and you're like, "My ancestors saw the same moonlight, the same water, the same space." Last week I saw a bald eagle in my own yard. I'd never seen that before. Up the road is a two-hundred-year-old Black church. The whole street to get to our farm is all Black homesteads. I was at our farm during the week and saw twenty or thirty Black men hunting together. I'd never seen that before. Ever.

If I could do it, I would open up the calendar and just have people come through. Just book a weekend and see for yourself. Sit outside and look out over the water and listen.

KW: The historic name of our farm is Rafters Point because part of our farm goes out onto the point in the water. The previous owner traced the history of the property. In 1640, the first African American on our land was an enslaved woman named Venus. We know for a fact our ancestors walked this same land. They lived on this same farm and made lives for themselves along these same waterways. As we walked the land and thought about what it meant to us, we wanted to honor the history. We knew Venus was on this land. We wanted to honor the history of this historic name, but also honor the legacy of our ancestors, so we called the farm Rafters Point at Freedom Farm.

WB: When friends call, I answer the phone by saying, "You want to be free? Are you seeking your freedom?"

42.

Butter

BY ELIZABETH ALEXANDER

My mother loves butter more than I do,
more than anyone. She pulls chunks off
the stick and eats it plain, explaining
cream spun around into butter! Growing up
we ate turkey cutlets sautéed in lemon
and butter, butter and cheese on green noodles,
butter melting in small pools in the hearts
of Yorkshire puddings, butter better
than gravy staining white rice yellow,
butter glazing corn in slipping squares,
butter the lava in white volcanoes
of hominy grits, butter softening
in a white bowl to be creamed with white
sugar, butter disappearing into
whipped sweet potatoes, with pineapple,
butter melted and curdy to pour
over pancakes, butter licked off the plate
with warm Alaga syrup. When I picture

the good old days I am grinning greasy
with my brother, having watched the tiger
chase his tail and turn to butter. We are
Mumbo and Jumbo's children despite
historical revision, despite
our parent's efforts, glowing from the inside
out, one hundred megawatts of butter.

43

A Love Letter to Future Generations

BY NAIMA PENNIMAN

1.

A flower comes before fruit

Love precedes a child

Someone was dreaming of you
with a womb full of water and seeds and stars
a drum skin stretched over a full moon

One heart beat becomes two

One seed becomes a hundred

You are the result of countless love stories
and unnumbered feats of overcoming

Can you hear your mother
humming you to sleep
while hiding out on escape routes
to an implausible freedom

     you made her believe in

2.

Every seed braided
into the crown of messengers
before uncertain passages

     a love note to future generations

a grain of hope
     somewhere somehow
     there would be soil
     that would open
     to receive our prayers

and multiply

3.

We are descendants of futurists
who did not give up on the possibility

     at least one seed would survive

the endless tides of
transatlantic crossing
auction blocks

monocrop cotton
razor sharp sugar
the harvest of salt
the scalding sun
and burning crosses

hidden propagation in forbidden gardens
generations of dehydration and bondage

summoning softness from the clouds
our bodies are made of water

    and promise

4.

Our mother's mother's mothers
did not give up on the possibility

    at least one seed would make its way

through layers
of cold hard rocky silt
    and sand
        and clay

and in the face of great danger
soften its shell
    open its hull
        extend a tender root
            find water and food

trusting

there is light somewhere
            enough to bloom

A flower comes before fruit.

Love precedes a child.

Someone was dreaming of you.

44

*I*nside *Queen Sugar:* Jason Wilborn Reflects on His Years in the *Queen Sugar* Writers' Room

BY NATALIE BASZILE

I first met screenwriter Jason Wilborn on a rainy April afternoon on the *Queen Sugar* set in New Orleans. The crew was filming episode 103, and having written the episode, Jason was on location to oversee the script. When the production paused for a lunch break, Jason and I sat together and discovered all the ways our lives overlapped. Three years later, Jason and I met for lunch in Los Angeles, where he shared the story of how he brought his personal history into the *Queen Sugar* writers' room.

My parents both grew up in the Jim Crow South. My mother is from Houston, Texas, and my father is from Dallas. Each summer when I was a boy, my parents shipped me and my brothers from Southern California, where they'd settled, back to my paternal grandparents in Dallas. My grandfather was a jack-of-all-trades. He made a great impression on me as a hardworking, salt-of-the-earth guy. He had a shoe repair shop and a moving company. Rather than living in Dallas, my grandfather would rather have lived in the country and been a farmer. He had a farm in a little town called Giddings, about forty-five minutes from Austin, which he'd inherited from his father, my *great*-grandfather Papa Johnny. Papa Johnny was one of the larger land-owners of his era and had amassed almost five hundred acres of land. After his death, the property was divvied up among his heirs. There was still family living there, so we would go to a couple of different little spreads visiting relatives. My grandfather's spread wasn't a working farm, but we'd ride around on the tractor. He also had cattle—just enough that he had to go out there once or twice a month to take care of them. There was also the house that my father had grown up in.

Early in 2015, I read in the trades that Ava DuVernay and Oprah Winfrey were developing a project. That September, I saw Ava at a dinner, so I approached her and introduced myself. I said, "My name is Jason Wilborn. I'm a drama writer. I've heard about your project, and it sounds fascinating." I knew the project's general subject matter and its tone, but I didn't know where it was in its development.

In November 2015, I was coming off writing for the show *Underground*. My parents had been retired eight or nine years by then and had moved back to Houston. I was at their home getting ready for Thanksgiving, surrounded by my entire extended family, when my agent called saying that Ava DuVernay wanted to meet with me about this show called *Queen Sugar*. I've always thought it was serendipitous that I got the call, not for the job, but just to meet about the show while I was surrounded by my extended family.

After Thanksgiving, I returned to Los Angeles and met with Ava and Melissa Carter, whom Ava had hired to run the show day-to-day. I don't remember whether Ava shared the script during that initial meeting, but she asked me about my background.

The writers' room for the first season of *Queen Sugar* opened around the first week of December 2015. I came onto the show at the very beginning, and we began breaking the episodes for the season. I knew Anthony Sparks, one of the other writers. We felt a sense of brotherhood as the only two male writers on the staff. I'm happy to say now there's a growing number of African American male drama writers in the industry.

Once I got the job, I read the novel *Queen Sugar*, which the series was based on, and loved it. But it was made pretty clear up front that the script was going to be a major departure from the book. In the writers' room, we took what was in the novel, the clay that was there, and molded it. Ava had written the script for the first episode; it was pretty tight. We realized there were characters whose genders had changed and that other characters like Nova were made up out of whole cloth. Davis and Charley had really been changed and evolved. And Remy was a *very* different person.

Writing for the show was a great experience. The book and the script both spoke to me; elements of each character's experience felt rich. Charley had been living in a white world and had sort of figured out how to navigate the pitfalls—or at least *thought* she had. She had an aspirational quality. Then there was Davis, her husband. Putting aside everything that happens to him in the story, I could relate to his character. I played football at Cal Berkeley, then briefly for the Seattle Seahawks. Just the whiff of that element in Davis's character made me think, "That's a vessel for me; there's a vein that affected my life." I saw Ralph Angel as a young Black father. And then, when I read the script version of *Queen Sugar*, Ernest Bordelon felt like my grandfather. All these tendrils spoke to me.

When I was a kid, I loved to sit around and listen to my father, who is a wonderful storyteller. As a writer, I feel like I'm born of that African American oral tradition, which I loved as a kid. My dad told stories about growing up in Dallas and growing up on the farm, stories about Papa Johnny, my great-grandfather, who wore all black and rode a horse. I had all this rich material that I could channel into the first season of *Queen Sugar*. I came into the project thinking there would be a lot of contemporary things we'd be able to write about, but at night in my little office, in my house, I thought, "I'll write about my family."

Writers' rooms need to be safe places. I've been in a lot of rooms that weren't safe. They can be dog-eat-dog and full of ego—maybe because of the hierarchy or because of the subject matter, or maybe it's the personalities—but none of that was part of the *Queen Sugar* writers' room. It was a safe place for everyone. You want the chemistry to be right because you sit with people for twelve hours a day. I thought it was great that Ava hired Melissa Carter to run the writers' room and the show day-to-day. Melissa is a white woman from the Midwest who walked into a writers' room that was basically all Black, save for one writer, Denise Harkavy, who is Iranian. Anthony Sparks was born and raised in Chicago. Tina Mabry was born and raised in Mississippi. Kay Oyegun is Nigerian American. Melissa basically said, "What do I need to know?" She's a good writer, and she radiates a kind of openness. She'd written other shows like *Queen Sugar*—a family drama with political elements—so her résumé spoke to that. She wanted to hear about us and what happened in our families.

As we started thinking about the series, we had the road map of the pilot. It was pretty tight, but it wasn't locked up. We did some small things here and there, but we really began in earnest working on episode 2. We had to figure out what an episode of *Queen Sugar* looked like. One of the first things we did was get to know each other and talk about the characters as they had been developed in the pilot and what their journeys were going to be. We started asking ourselves, "How do we give ourselves as writers the space to explore these characters?" We knew that Ernest had died. We knew we were going to have a funeral. All that work happened before we began to break episode 2. Then we put up a grid of all thirteen episodes, added the characters' names along the side, and began to plot where we thought things would happen to them. As we pitched out things we thought we might want to have happen or stories that seemed to have legs and momentum, we slotted things in. We put "Charley's moving for sure," in there. I remember conversations about how quickly Charley realizes she's going to stay in Saint Josephine. We couldn't arbitrarily decide that would happen in episode 3—that felt weird and crazy and compulsive. We started to realize Charley wasn't going to decide until episode 5 or 6. It felt real to us that Micah would want to go home, but we wanted it to be a difficult decision for Charley to stay. For a long time we felt that we needed to get to the harvest by the end of season 1. That first week or so, I bet we put the harvest in episode 13. I remember feeling liberated when we realized we didn't have to put the harvest at the end of the first season. We struggled to figure that out.

We started talking about the character Nova, who I know was created as a kind of entity that could be political. We started thinking about the contemporary stories and the historical issues that we could give life to through Nova. That's how we decided to deal with all the contemporary issues like police brutality and Black Lives Matter. Conversations about her character were where we began to transition in the writers' room, asking, "What do we want to say about this? How do we want to explore these issues?" Charley was touching all kinds of pots. For me, she was about assimilation. And again, I had lived that growing up in Orange County, California.

For Davis, I was concerned about what we were saying about the Black male ath-
lete. I wanted to be mindful of the stereotypes about Black men and aggression. I also
felt that since Davis wasn't the only male character, that since there was a breadth of
Black male characters being portrayed, Davis could be flawed. He could have shades
and dimension. He didn't have the responsibility of representing all Black men. I
knew that over the course of the seasons we had Ralph Angel, Hollywood, Remy, and
Prosper Denton, and that we would explore the breadth of Black manhood through
each one of them. Rightly or wrongly, I felt that as a writer on the show, I was pro-
tective of Davis, but I also had other avenues to explore what it is to be a Black man.
I didn't have to battle to save Davis as I might have in another environment. There's
the scene when Micah gets arrested and Davis goes to the cops—that's an example of him being a good father. We decided we were going to explore tenderness in
Ralph Angel. I had tears in my eyes as I wrote some of the scenes with Ralph Angel
and Blue. We wanted to use Hollywood to explore a character who is a hardworking,
blue-collar guy who does everything right. In terms of portraying Black men on the
show, I felt we had an embarrassment of riches in what we could explore.

Then there were the big global conversations about the show and the characters
and the things they'd experience along the way in addition to the nuts-and-bolts
work of figuring out how to build an episode. I can't tell you how the pieces fell into
place, but I remember realizing we were telling a long story of the saga of this family.

Sometimes you go into a television show, and there's a pilot to look at. We had
the novel, *Queen Sugar*, which was tangible in that it gave us a sense of the community and the world, but it became clear we wouldn't be able to go to Louisiana. I felt
pressure and certainly wanted to be authentic to New Orleans, but in terms of my
own personal experience, I remembered the way my great-grandfather's house looked
and smelled. Tina Mabry's first feature was set in the South. Anthony was from Chicago, but his family moved north during the Great Migration, so he had a sense of
that oral history in his family. I think Melissa grew up in a rural environment. So,
we drew on those experiences. Also, while we had departed from the characters, the
novel was in the writers' room and it was dog-eared in places that described what
something looked like or how Louisiana smelled. Those were things we held on to
when we tried describe what Saint Josephine and Louisiana sugar farming were like.
I didn't know a damn thing about sugarcane farming but—this is a terrible term,

I hate to say it this way—I knew what a "Black farm" looked like. I had nothing to do with the decision—kudos to Ava and our production people—but what turned out to be the set of *Queen Sugar* looks exactly like my grandfather's farm. Rightly or wrongly, I approached the show and the subject matter feeling comfortable. In terms of what we were writing about, I'd lived a lot of it.

We also felt certain there would be angst and anguish and power dynamics around the land, that the characters would struggle over it and what it meant to each one of them. Early on, I talked about my father. My dad always talked about how every generation of Black families starts at zero. It's not entirely true, but so many Black families start that way. This was a story, in my mind, about a family that *didn't* start at zero. So, what does that mean? My paternal grandfather had been one of seven or eight siblings for whom the land was very important; it meant something to him. Over the years, he bought back and cobbled together land that my great-grandfather owned. My aunts, his sisters, have sold off most of their land. I think there's a little core piece of about eighty to a hundred acres that the house is still on that my dad still owns. But no one ever goes there anymore.

Queen Sugar was a character-driven story. And just by the nature of who Ava is, by her writing staff, we knew we'd be political. But the question was how to be political and not too heavy-handed. That's a challenge for a lot of shows. One of the things that was unique to this show was Ava saying from the jump, "Yes, we need act-outs—something that pushes the momentum forward—but the show should feel novelistic. It should be about the texture of our people and our community. We should talk about anything and everything." I'm not saying she said this in some big speech, but she intimated that whatever TV tropes or things we'd thought about, we could shirk those off. She wanted us to come to the room and write, and if our scenes are however-long, then so be it. Sometimes, we'd ask ourselves, "Was there any conflict in that scene? This is a scene about people just talking." But conflict was never the end-all and be-all. Oftentimes, conflict was unearthed as we edited, but we didn't go into the room every day thinking there had to be conflict in every scene.

We were doing that and still trying to tell those smaller stories about Violet as a Black woman of a certain age, about Hollywood. . . . But that's what we do as writers. That's what we love to do. That's the challenge of it.

Anthony Sparks said something, and I'm paraphrasing, but he said, "For the first time in my life as a television writer, I'm able to write with both of my hands." That always resonated with me as a metaphor. There's a moment in season 2 where Charley is with her mother, and they're talking about how her mother tried to raise her. Dawn-Lyen Gardner (who plays Charley) called me about the scene, and we talked about it. I don't think it's a perfect scene, but what I thought as I wrote it was, "I get to write a scene that, hopefully, if I can get anything through, my daughters will see it one day and think, 'This is what my mom was trying to say to me.'" To have had that kind of opportunity to write those kinds of scenes—I'm blessed. It was really a blessing.

Writing for *Queen Sugar* was a magical journey for me. I can barely remember some of the details of the episodes, but I remember the feelings. Seeing what the actors—Kofi, Dawn, Rutina, Timon, and Omar—brought to their work . . . they're incredible. But first it's the feeling of channeling. That's what I'm so grateful for. I don't know where I'll go in my career, and I hope I have a lot more to do, but I've gotten a chance to channel some part of my own family. The older I get, the more I do this, the more I'll appreciate what *Queen Sugar* really is, because it's rare. And that's why I can't tell the story without telling the serendipitous part about where I was when it happened. As a screenwriter, you look for those opportunities. You're always asking, "How do I make this mine? How do I make it me?" *Queen Sugar* was one of those opportunities where it just seemed like wherever I turned, I could take something my mother said or grab some small piece of my family story. The show gave me a chance to honor my history. I had a great experience working on that show. I wish Anthony Sparks, the new show runner, and the new writers the very best. I hope the show continues to have great success.

45

The Boudin Trail

BY NATALIE BASZILE

It's two o'clock, a Thursday afternoon in early May, and the air inside the New Orleans airport smells like fried shrimp, mildew, and a hint of the Gulf. It's a comforting smell, at least to me, and every time I fly down here from California, the first thing I do stepping off the plane into the terminal is inhale deeply.

If I were here by myself, I'd be on the road by now, easing into the Crescent City or flying down Highway 90 toward New Iberia where my friends live. This trip, though, is different: I'm on a mission. I'm meeting my mother, my dad, and my sister Jennifer, to whom I have just started talking after a two-year estrangement. I'm taking them on a drive along the Boudin Trail.

We have a lot to heal on this trip.

Jennifer's flight from Connecticut is scheduled to arrive twenty minutes after mine. We've agreed to meet in the baggage claim area. The carousel has just lurched to life and suitcases are sliding down the black conveyor belt when I spot Jennifer at the top of the escalator. For years, we both wore short Afros. People assumed we were twins. Three years ago, Jen decided to grow pencil-thin dreadlocks, and now they cascade across her shoulders. I can't help but stare. Even in jeans and a v-neck T-shirt, she looks downright regal.

It's odd to think of my mom and my sister being here in this place I've laid claim to. Louisiana is mine, and I'm not eager to share it. I cringe at the thought of having to show them around the city, taking them to the restaurants and shops I frequent, the out-of-the-way spots most tourists know nothing about. I'm being selfish, I know. If my Louisiana friends had been this closed-hearted with me, I'd still be a tourist, wandering down Bourbon Street with a fishbowl filled with green alcohol hanging from a cord around my neck.

Unlike my dad, who was born in Louisiana and hated most things about it, I love the heat and the crumbling buildings overtaken by kudzu. I love the endless hours my aunts, uncles, and cousins spend in church. I love Louisiana's earthiness, her accents, and her twisting bayous. I love it all—or mostly all.

So while I wait for my bags, I give myself a little pep talk—*Come on, Baszile, lighten up. This will be fun.* By the time Jennifer steps off the escalator, I'm feeling generous.

"Hey, Wench," I say and hug my little sister.

"Hey, Wench," Jen says, hugging me back.

This is our standard hello, the way we've greeted each other since we were teenagers. But we haven't used the greeting at all lately, and I can tell Jen is as nervous and relieved as I am to say the words. We used to be close, calling each other every day, sometimes *two or three times* a day, and then suddenly, two years ago, we stopped speaking. At the time, I was struggling to write my novel, going to grad school, and raising kids. Jennifer was divorcing her husband, writing a memoir, and leaving her university job. I don't remember the details of the argument, only that one day, neither of us picked up the phone. Days stretched into weeks. Weeks stretched into months. We didn't speak when her book was published or when my oldest daughter delivered her middle school graduation speech. We didn't speak when my dad's cancer came back a second time.

It was only after my dad landed in the hospital with failing kidneys that we finally reconciled. *It would be a shame if you two reconciled over your father's deathbed.* That's what my husband told Jen when he called to intervene. She called me a couple of days later to say she was coming to San Francisco for a conference. She asked if we could meet. I drove to her hotel near the airport and saw her through the plate glass windows in the lobby. Before I could park, she was outside, standing beside my car.

An hour later, my mother arrives, dressed in pleated pastel slacks and white patent loafers, a black quilted carry-on slung over her shoulder. She greets us with her signature beauty contestant wave and flashes a toothy smile.

"Here they are," she says, standing on her toes to kiss us. "My two girls." She runs her hands through Jennifer's dreads, fingering the tiny cowry shell dangling from one of them.

"Where's Dad?" I ask.

Jennifer messages her temples. Her tone is somber. "I can't believe we're doing this."

"Got him right here," Mom says, patting her carry-on conspiratorially.

A trip along the Boudin Trail was my idea. Three years ago, a friend sent me an article listing all the types of boudin—the mix of seasoned pork, beef, or crawfish and rice all stuffed into a sausage casing—in South Louisiana. The article linked to a website showing every grocery store, restaurant, gas station, and roadside stand along the two-hundred-mile strip between New Orleans and Lake Charles. If you planned right and had the stomach for it, the article said, you could hit every establishment in a single weekend, three days tops. The moment I finished the article, I called my dad.

"How'd you like to take a trip along the Boudin Trail?" I asked.

My dad was into slow food and "nose-to-tail eating" decades before the life-style became fashionable and trendy. *Black folks practically invented slow food*, he liked to say. As a kid growing up in South Louisiana, he hunted raccoons, possums, and squirrels in the woods behind his house, then brought them home to his mother, who cooked them in stews. Sometimes, he shot an animal just to see how it tasted. Once, he shot and ate a crow.

"Let's do it," he said. "I'd like to get home one last time anyway." He'd just been diagnosed with leiomyosarcoma for the second time.

Instead, he spent most of the next two and a half years cycling through hospitals and rehab centers, growing frailer every month. Until the cancer, he'd never spent a night in a hospital. By the end, he couldn't walk from the family room to the kitchen, couldn't hold a fork.

Now, it's just the three of us: my mother, Jen, and me. Mom transferred some of Dad's ashes from the urn she has at home into a small wooden container no bigger than a pack of cigarettes. That container is now safely zipped in a plastic sandwich bag. We're going to sprinkle his ashes along the Boudin Trail.

* * *

We've just tossed our suitcases in the trunk when Jennifer notices my food bags—two oversized, insulated empty totes with heavy-duty zippers and straps wide as seatbelts.

"You've got to be kidding," she says.

"What?" I sound defensive. "Someone has to do it."

Dad always brought his food bags on our road trips so he could stock up. He bought boudin but also crawfish and the andouille sausage he used in his gumbo. We'd stop in a handful of towns on our way back to my grandmother's house, and by the time he purchased what he needed, we could barely zip the bags, each of which—between the food and the ice packs—weighed nearly fifty pounds. Dad treated his food bags like they were his children. He requested hotel rooms close to the ice machine, monitored the bags' internal temperature to make sure the contents stayed cold, and carried them on the plane rather than check them as luggage.

Jennifer looks at me skeptically. "Do you even know how to cook gumbo?"

"That's not the point." I fold the food bags and tuck them in among the suitcases.

We're hurtling down I-10 when we spot Don's Specialty Meats, our first stop along the trail. Don's used to have a single location off Highway 49 in Carencro. Recently, they built a huge operation in Scott, just off the interstate frontage road. The building looks like a casino with its enormous neon red sign and sprawling parking lot. We pull between two monster trucks.

Mom takes the Ziploc bag out of her carry-on.

How *do* you sprinkle someone's ashes in a store without alarming the proprietors or the customers? The question hasn't occurred to us until just now. We step inside Don's and feel the rush of air-conditioned air against our skin. The place is packed. There's a long line of people at the counter ordering boudin to go; another dozen shoppers plunder the deep freezers and banks of refrigerators along the wall. I see no way to do this without someone noticing. And suddenly, all I can think of are the sanitation laws we're surely breaking. I'm about to chicken out when Mom comes up behind me gripping a plastic spoon.

"I got this from the girl at the counter." She grins.

Jennifer posts herself near the front counter and keeps watch while Mom and I wander to the back corner. Mom opens the Ziploc, lifts the lid off the wooden box, and scoops out a quarter teaspoon of what looks like tiny bits of gravel and grit. She bends low and sprinkles the cremains of my father under the last refrigerator, back far enough that no one will notice. They look pale and gray, almost like silt, against the dirty white floor tiles.

I'd never seen Dad's ashes before. I think back on all the years I heard Mom scold him for being overweight, and how he loved to walk barefoot through the garden we planted behind my house because the feel of his feet in the soil reminded him of his Louisiana childhood—and my mind can't compute. I can't reconcile those memories with the spoonful of dust.

Mom dips the white spoon into the bag again, then looks at me. "I think we should say something."

Her suggestion catches me flat-footed. Until now, the tone of our trip had been easy and lighthearted. We cracked off-color jokes and reminisced about the time Dad glided right off the treadmill and broke his arm. We shook our heads in wonder at the time he took twelve Aleve tablets in one sitting. It's gallows humor, we knew, but it's our way of coping. *Why are we getting serious now?* I wonder. Besides, Jennifer's the better public speaker. Three years my junior, she has always possessed a seriousness, an intensity that makes most people assume she's older. She delivered the eulogy at Dad's memorial that had everyone in tears.

"Well, Dad," I say, fumbling for words. "I guess this is it."

But it isn't it.

As I stand there listening to the refrigerators hum, I think about how, before he got sick, people often mistook him for Muhammad Ali. It was easy to do. He had the presence and personality to match. If he were here now, he'd be sauntering down the aisles, his arms loaded with frozen packages of smoked boudin and andouille sausage, never bothering to disabuse staring onlookers of their belief he might be the real prizefighter. Now, standing under the fluorescent lights in the bustling store, I thank Dad aloud for letting me tag along on all those road trips. I tell him about my book. I tell him Mom's going to be okay and that Jennifer and I are talking again.

When I finish, Mom grabs my hand and squeezes.

We give Jennifer the signal—two thumbs up—and the three of us walk back to the car.

Two more stops and we've established a rhythm. The Best Stop Supermarket. Billy's Boudin & Cracklins. My mother keeps the plastic spoon. We have our good-byes down to five minutes. We pass through St. Martinville and scatter cremains in the parking lot of Joyce's Supermarket. Rabideaux's in Iowa doesn't sell boudin so it's not officially on the trail, but we swing by anyway because Dad swore they made the best andouille in South Louisiana. It's a tiny shop with a counter and a single display case. In a place this small we'd get busted for sure, so we mix ashes into the soil of a potted palm near the door.

The Walmart Supercenter in Jennings is our last stop before we call it quits for the night. The place is larger than three football fields, and it takes us a while to find the outdoor/sportsman section, which is where the insulated food bags are sold. As far as Dad was concerned, you couldn't have too many, so we pick out one we think he would have liked and place it on the bottom shelf. And since we're less concerned with sanitation, we scoop out a heaping spoonful of cremains and sprinkle them lib-erally underneath. The cleaning crew will mop this aisle by this time tomorrow. At least we've paid our respects.

The next morning we drive to Elton, Dad's hometown. When Dad was a kid, he planted an oak sapling in his front yard. The house he grew up in has long since been razed, but the sapling is now a massive oak tree—four stories tall with roots so thick they've buckled the sidewalk.

Here is the scene: Two sisters stand at the base of an enormous oak—a tree their Dad planted sixty-five years earlier. They are surrounded by twenty-five people—aunts and uncles and cousins; their great-aunt Dell, who just turned ninety-three; and a few of their father's childhood friends. Their cousin Antoinette steps forward and sings the first verse of "At the Cross"—their dad's favorite hymn. Her voice is crisp and clear, a siren's voice that rises into the oak tree's highest branches. And when the rest of the crowd joins in the singing, the sound carries down the street and out to the road. The group sings two more hymns, both a cappella, the way Black folks in the South used to sing when the girls' dad was a boy. The moment has an old-timey feel.

When the singing stops, the sisters hold hands. They watch their uncle Sonny dig a hole between the tree roots. Their mother places the little wooden box inside, and then their uncle Charles fills the hole with concrete and places a small marble headstone over the spot.

It's done. Their dad is home.

It's a long drive back to New Orleans. Jennifer and I are speaking easily, a gift of my father's illness—but no one has much to say. We pass all the boudin joints we visited along the way, but this time we don't stop.

I don't realize how different, how sacred, a trip this has been from what I expected till I get to the airport and see them again: my food bags.

They are empty.

*B*lack Harvest Fund

Before *We Are Each Other's Harvest* was published, Natalie Baszile established the Black Harvest Fund at the San Francisco Foundation. Some of the proceeds of this book are being donated by the author to the fund. If you would like to donate to the fund, please visit Natalie's website, www.nataliebaszile.com/black-harvest-fund, for more information.

Natalie would like to thank the following seed funders for their generous donations to the Black Harvest Fund:

Ruth Bartron; Janet Baszile; Dylan Landis Baquet; Joan Binder; Tanum Davis Bohen and Sean P. Bohen, MD, PhD; Arlene F., Henrik Jones; Chip Koch and Tricia Stone; Brad Stone; Sarah and James Manyika; Dale and Gordon McWilliams; Roosevelt Mobley; Diane and James Staes; and Laura and Melvin Williams.

The San Francisco Foundation is a registered 501(c)(3) tax-exempt organization
Employer Identification Number (EIN) #01-0679337

Acknowledgments

A very special thanks to the farmers who continue to inspire us with their tenacity and irrepressible passion.

Thank you to Warrington Parker for your love and unwavering support, and to Hyacinth and Chloe.

Thanks to my editor, Tracy Sherrod, for offering the path, and to my agent, Kim Witherspoon, for encouraging me to take the ride.

Eternal thanks to my poetry editor, Tonya Foster, for sharing her library and for being a friend of my mind.

Thanks to photographer Alison Gootee for her keen eye.

Thanks to photographer Malcom Williams for his skill with the camera and for stepping up just in time.

Thanks to Sade Ayorinde for help with archival research in the early stages.

Thanks to Archie Hart for his wisdom and for the history lesson.

Thanks to Dr. Dewayne Goldmon, Nickolaj and Crystal Morris, and the members of the National Black Growers Council for the warm welcome.

Special thanks to Darrell Tennie for being an excellent guide and for reminding us that everyone up north has southern roots.

Thanks also to Michelle Powell for her patience and expertise and to Rebecca Tezi and Herlena Herndon.

Notes

1 Isabel Wilkerson, *The Warmth of Other Suns: The Epic Story of America's Great Migration* (New York: Knopf Doubleday, 2011).

2 Will Allen, *The Good Food Revolution: Growing Healthy Food, People, and Communities* (New York: Gotham Books, 2012).

3 John J. Green, Eleanor M. Green, and Anna M. Kleiner, "From the Past to the Present: Agricultural Development and Black Farmers in the American South," in *Cultivating Food Justice: Race, Class, and Sustainability*, ed. Alison Hope Alkon and Julian Agyeman (Cambridge, MA: MIT Press, 2011), 47–64.

4 On how poor whites sometimes lose white privileges, see Matt Wray, *Not Quite White: White Trash and the Boundaries of Whiteness* (Durham, NC: Duke Univ. Press, 2006).

5 Pete Daniel, *Dispossession: Discrimination Against African American Farmers in the Age of Civil Rights* (Chapel Hill: Univ. of North Carolina Press, 2013), 194. For treatment on the impact of New Deal programs and especially the power of county ASCS committees, see Pete Daniel, "The Legal Basis of Agrarian Capitalism: The South Since 1933," in *Race and Class in the American South Since 1890*, ed. Melvyn Stokes and Rick Halpern (Oxford: Berg, 1994), 79–101.

6 Daniel, *Dispossession*, 6.

7 On the creation of committees, see Gladys L. Baker, Wayne D. Rasmussen, Vivian Wiser, and Jane M. Porter, *Century of Service: The First 100 Years of the United States Department of Agriculture* (Washington, DC: US Department of Agriculture, 1963), 159–61. On how committees came to represent the white elite, see Robert Earl Martin, "Negro-White Participation in the A.A.A. Cotton and Tobacco Referenda in North and South Carolina: A Study in Differential Voting and Attitudes in Selected Areas" (PhD diss., Univ. of Chicago, 1947), 242ff.

8 Memorandum to Paul W. Bruton, n.d.; Margaret S. Bennett, memo to Paul W. Bruton, March 7, 1934, Cotton, Landlord-Tenant, Records of the Secretary of Agriculture, Record Group 16, National Archives and Records Administration. Hereafter cited SOA, RG 16, NARA.

9 William R. Amberson to Paul Appleby, November 21, 29, 1934, Cotton, Landlord-Tenant, SOA, RG 16, NARA.

10 See A. B. Book, "A Note on the Legal Status of Share-Tenants and Share-Croppers in the South," *Law and Contemporary Problems* 4 (1937): 542–45.

11 *Jackson v. Jefferson* et al., 158 So. 486–87.

12 *Dulaney et al. v. Balls et al.*, 102 S.W. 88–90.

13 Wilmer Mills to Henry A. Wallace, March 28, 1935; C. H. Alvord to Mills, April 4, 1935, AAA, Rice, Records of the Agricultural Stabilization and Conservation Service, RG 145, NARA. Hereafter cited ASCS, RG 145, NARA.

14 Linda Flowers, *Throwed Away: Failures of Progress in Eastern North Carolina* (Knoxville, TN: Univ. of Tennessee Press, 1992), 59.

15 See especially *Fulford v. Forman*, 245 F.2d 149.

16 David Westfall, "Agricultural Allotments as Property," *Harvard Law Review* 79 (1966): 1188–89.

17 See Brainerd S. Parrish, "Comment. Cotton Allotments: Another New Property," *Texas Law Review* 45 (1967): 734–53; *Fulford v. Forman*, 245 F.2d 145, 151, 152n20.

18 Daniel, *Dispossession*, 66; "The Federal Agricultural Stabilization Program and the Negro," *Columbia Law Review* 67 (1967): 1121–36.

19 D. P. Trent, memorandum for C. C. Davis, December 28, 1934, AAA, Production Control Program, Landlord-Tenant, 1933–38, ASCS, RG 145, NARA.

20 Ward Sinclair, "Lying Laid Down the Law, but Is the USDA Enforcing It?" *Washington Post*, September 21, 1987, A13.

21 Pete Daniel, *Breaking the Land: The Transformation of Cotton, Tobacco, and Rice Cultures Since 1880* (Urbana: Univ. of Illinois Press, 1985), 65; see also G. L. Crawford to Boswell Stevens, February 12, 1953, Boswell Stevens Papers, subject files, general, Mississippi Farm Bureau Federation, Mitchell Memorial Library, Mississippi State University.

22 For insights on possibilities for meaningful reform, see Jess Gilbert, *Planning Democracy: Agrarian Intellectuals and the Intended New Deal* (New Haven, CT: Yale Univ. Press, 2016), and Sarah T. Phillips, *This Land, This Nation: Conservation, Rural America, and the New Deal* (New York: Cambridge Univ. Press, 2007).

23 Medgar Evers and Mildred Bond to Gloster B. Current, January 23, 1956, Mississippi Pressures, Relief Fund, 1956–63, NAACP III, A 233, National Association for the Advancement of Colored People Papers, Manuscripts Division, Library of Congress.

24 *Equal Opportunity in Farm Programs: An Appraisal of Services Rendered by Agencies of the United States Department of Agriculture* (Washington, DC: US Commission on Civil Rights, 1965), 93; *The Decline of Black Farming in America: A Report of the United States Commission on Civil Rights* (Washington, DC: US Commission on Civil Rights, February 1982).

25 Daniel, *Dispossession*, 4–5.

26 Daniel, *Dispossession*, 89–97.

27 Daniel, *Dispossession*, 61.

28 Daniel, *Dispossession*, 82.

29 Daniel, *Dispossession*, 90.

30 Daniel, *Dispossession*, 100. The 1964 COFO effort to win ASCS seats is covered on pages 58–99.

31 Daniel, *Dispossession*, 133.

32 Daniel, *Dispossession*, 58–132.

33 Daniel, *Breaking the Land*, 9–10; P. O. Davis to H. H. Williamson, June 16, 1950, Alabama Cooperative Extension Service (ACES) Papers, Record Group 71, box 58, Archives and Manuscripts Department, Auburn University. Hereafter cited ACES Papers, Auburn.

34 See, for example, Carmen V. Harris, "The South Carolina Home in Black and White: Race, Gender, and Power in Home Demonstration Work, *Agricultural History* 91 (Summer 2019): 477–501; Daniel, *Dispossession*, 156–215.

35 John B. Jordan to J. R. Otis, February 29, 1948, box 358, ACES Papers, Auburn.

36 Clipping, *Pittsburgh Courier*, December 15, 22, 1951, General Correspondence, 1940–55, box 3, Negroes, SOA, RG 16, NARA. On 4-H clubs, see Gabriel N. Rosenberg, *The 4-H Harvest: Sexuality and the State in Rural America* (Philadelphia: Univ. of Pennsylvania Press, 2016).

37 Daniel, *Dispossession*, 205–10.

38 Ibid., 156–95; *Willie L. Strain v. Harry M. Philpott*, 331 F. Supp. 836 (1971).

39 Greta de Jong, *You Can't Eat Freedom: Southerners and Social Justice After the Civil Rights Movement* (Chapel Hill: Univ. of North Carolina Press, 2016).

40 Joe Henry Thomas to Fay Bennett, January 25, 1963, box 41, Alabama Appeals for Help, folder 25, National Sharecropper Fund Papers, Walter Reuther Library, Wayne State University. Hereafter cited NSF Papers.

41 James Franklin Estes to Dwight D. Eisenhower, April 6, 1960; K. L. Scott to E. Frederick Morrow, May 12, 1960; H. C. Smith to Scott, June 6, 1960; Scott to Morrow, June 29, 1960, farm credit, loans, box 339, SOA, RG 16, NARA.

42 Richard M. Shapiro and Donald S. Safford, interview with Fred Amica, Marshville, Georgia, March 9, 1964, box 1, CFLID, US Commission on Civil Rights Papers, RG 452, NARA.

43 Ira Kaye to Fay Bennett, February 9, December 18, 1962; January 7, March 4, 1963, box 46, folder 44, NSF Papers.

44 T. T. Williams, interview with John S. Currie, Jackson, Mississippi, May 13, 1964, box 46, folder 44, NSF Papers.

45 William Seabron to J. William Howell, October 29, 1965, box 4254, Civil Rights, GC, 1906–76, SOA, RG 16, NARA.

46 Statement of Cato Lee, Lowndsboro, Alabama, n.d., box 57, Alabama, folder 35, NSF Papers.

47 Orzell Billingsley Jr. and Harvey Burg to Robert C. Bamberg, July 20, 1965; "The Substance of Reverend McShan's Testimony Offered to Alabama State Advisory Committee of the US Commission on Civil Rights," July 10, 1965, box 4255, Civil Rights, GC 1906–76, SOA, RG 16, NARA.

48 Daniel, *Dispossession*, 216–45.

49 On female farmers, see Judith Z. Kalbacher, "A Profile of Female Farmers in America," Economic Research Service, USDA, Rural Development Research Report Number 45, January 1985; Daniel, *Dispossession*, 246–64.

50 Daniel, *Dispossession*, 92.

51 Campbell Gibson and Kay Jung, "Historical Census Statistics on Population Totals by Race, 1790 to 1990, and by Hispanic Origin, 1970 to 1990, for Large Cities and Other Urban Places in the United States," working paper no. 76 (Washington, DC: US Census Bureau, 2005).

52 National Agricultural Statistics Service, selected years 1920, 1997 (Washington, DC: US Department of Agriculture).

53 Joe Brooks, former president of the Emergency Land Fund, cited in Vann R. Newkirk II, "The Great Land Robbery," *Atlantic Monthly*, September 2019, https://www.theatlantic.com/magazine/archive/2019/09/this-land-was-our-land/594742.

54 Census of Agriculture (Washington, DC: National Agricultural Statistics Service, 2007).

55 Darrick Hamilton and Dania V. Francis, cited in "The Grand Land Robbery."

56 National Agricultural Statistics Service.

57 *Pigford v. Glickman*, 182 Federal Rules Decision 341 (US District Court for the District of Columbia, 1998).

58 Settlement Agreement, In re Black Farmers Discrimination Litigation, No. 08-mc-0511 (February 18, 2010, revised and executed as of May 13, 2011), available at https://www.blackfarmercase.com//Documents/ SettlementAgreement.pdf.

59 In recent years, I have been labeled as being "black and green," as if being close to the land and caring for the natural world were a white thing.

60 My sister, Marsha, died in 1952 because the segregated hospital did not provide the proper care for her pneumonia. Our mother experienced a "nervous breakdown" and spent time on the farm with her mother to heal from the trauma of losing her only daughter. Inspired by my mother's healing, I have spent many years providing therapeutic horticulture programs to groups that serve "women at risk," as outlined in these articles: "Greenhouse 17 Combines Gardening, Business and Healing for Survivors of Domestic Violence," www.kentucky.com/living/home-garden/article44613195.html; and "From Family's Farmland, Jim Embry Brought Knowledge, Passion to Lexington's Community Gardens," www.kentucky.com/living/home-garden/article44614398.html.

61 Our family members who are great storytellers in the African griot style assembled this oral family history into a written document for our first Ballew Broaddus Simpson Noland Family Reunion in 1942. As we have done additional research in various archives, we have simply corroborated our oral historians.

62 This region of Kentucky, which sits at the foothills of the Appalachian Mountains and is part of the Kentucky River watershed, was the ancestral homeland of the Shawnee, Cherokee, Chickasaw, and other native peoples for thousands of years before the colonial period.

63 We retrieved from the National Archives the military records of Jackson and George, which contained not only military service records but also names and birthdates of their children.

64 The seven minor children were Ann, Mary, Harriett, Sophia, Lyman, Don Buel (DB), and Jackson.

65 We always wondered why our great-grandfather had such a long name. As I was doing research for articles in the *Encyclopedia of Northern Kentucky*, I read that Union Army General Don Carlos Buell served in Kentucky and was known for not confiscating and destroying property of the farms in the South and for court-martialing pillagers. DB's owner, George Ballew, was evidently pleased with the general's policies and most likely named the next born on his farm after General Buell.

66 "Lifting as we climb" was the founding principle of the National Association of Colored Women, organized in 1896 with chapters in Kentucky. Core members, who were educators, entrepreneurs, and social activists, believed that by elevating their status as community organizers and leaders, black women could improve the public image of black women, bolster racial pride, and elevate the status of their entire communities.

67 Books by such authors as Monica White (*Freedom Farmers*) and Jessica Gordon Nembhard (*Collective Courage*) describe these intentional efforts of building community through farm cooperatives, mutual-aid societies, and other forms of solidarity and collective action.

68 The bulletins were published between 1898 and 1943; see https://www.tuskegee.edu/support-tu /george-washington-carver/carver-bulletins.

69 The *Daily Register*, Richmond, Kentucky, June 30, 1920.

70 Monica White, *Freedom Farmers: Agricultural Resistance and the Black Freedom Movement* (Chapel Hill: Univ. of North Carolina Press, 2018).

71 I met Jimmy and Grace Lee Boggs in 1974, maintained a close personal and organizational relationship with them over the years, served as the Boggs Center board chair for six years, and moved to Detroit in 2000 to serve as its first director. See Boggscenter.org. See also Curt Guyette, "Down a Green Path," *Detroit Metro Times*, October 31, 2001.

72 Frances Korten and Roberto Vargas, *Movement Building for Transformational Change* (Bainbridge Island, WA: Positive Futures Network, 2006). These retreats included such luminaries as Vincent and Rosemarie Harding, Danny Glover, Belvie Rooks, Tom Goldtooth, Drew Dillinger, Joanna Macy, and Fran and David Korten.

73 Thomas Berry, *The Great Work* (New York: Three Rivers Press, 1999).

74 I explore this more in my article "Transforming the Heart of Agriculture," *Biodynamics Association Journal* (Fall 2018): 8–13. Leah Penniman shares a similar framework in "Movement Building," chapter 15 in *Farming While Black: Soul Fire Farm's Practical Guide to Liberation on the Land* (White River Junction, VT: Chelsea Green, 2018).

75 "Indian Education for All," Montana Office of Public Instruction website, https://opi.mt.gov/Educators /Teaching-Learning/Indian-Education-for-All.

76 "About Us," Slow Food, https://www.slowfood.com/our-network/indigenous/about-us.

77 Through the lens of quantum science and spirituality, Barbara Holmes dissects white supremacy, the cult of whiteness, and the acceptance of reason/logic and western scientific methods as superior to intuitive indigenous practices for obtaining knowledge. Barbara Holmes, *Race and the Cosmos: An Invitation to View the World Differently* (Harrisburg, PA: Trinity Press, 2002).

78 George W. Carver, "Nature Study and Garden for Rural Schools," *Bulletin of the Tuskegee Agricultural Experiment Station*, no. 18 (1898): 3.

79 Anthony S. Parent Jr., *Foul Means: The Formation of a Slave Society in Virginia, 1660–1740* (Chapel Hill and London: Univ. of North Carolina Press, 2003).

Credits

Contributors

Dr. Analena Hope Hassberg is a scholar, activist, and educator committed to organizing low-income communities of color around food justice and environmental justice. She earned her PhD in American studies and ethnicity from the University of Southern California before becoming an assistant professor of ethnic and women's studies at California State Polytechnic University, Pomona. Dr. Hassberg is a Ford Foundation predoctoral and dissertation fellow and an active member of several community-based organizations in South Los Angeles. Her research investigates and complicates notions of food security and food sovereignty and situates food as central to freedom struggles and liberation movements.

Pete Daniel, a historian of the US South, has published seven books, including *Dispossession: Discrimination Against African American Farmers in the Age of Civil Rights*. He spent twenty-seven years as a curator at the Smithsonian National Museum of American History after working briefly for a US senator and teaching university courses for a decade. He has served as president of four historical organizations, including the Southern Historical Association and the Organization of American Historians.

Jim Embry comes from a long line of social change agents that extends back to the Civil War. Three members of his family fought with the US Colored Troops during the Civil War, and one was at Appomattox when General Lee surrendered.

His maternal great-grandfather, DB Ballew, used his father's Civil War pension to attend Berea College from 1879 to 1881. Embry was born in Richmond, Kentucky, a grandson of small farmers who were also social activists. In 1971, inspired by his friendship with Dick Gregory, Jim became a vegetarian and food activist and joined with others to found the Good Foods Co-op in Lexington. Inspired by his work in Detroit, Jim returned to Kentucky in 2005 and founded Sustainable Communities Network the following year.

Leah Penniman, cofounder, codirector, and farm manager of Soul Fire Farm, has over twenty years' experience as soil steward and food sovereignty activist, having worked at the Food Project, Farm School, Many Hands Organic Farm, Youth-GROW, and farms in Ghana, Haiti, and Mexico. Leah cofounded Soul Fire Farm in 2011 with the mission to reclaim our inherited right to belong to the earth and have agency in the food system as Black and brown people. Her areas of leadership at Soul Fire include farmer training, international solidarity, food justice organizing, writing, speaking, "making it rain," and anything that involves heavy lifting, sweat, and soil.

Michael Twitty is a food writer, independent scholar, culinary historian, author of the book *The Cooking Gene*, and historical interpreter. He is devoted to preparing, preserving, and promoting African American foodways, including their parent traditions in Africa and the Diaspora's legacy in the food culture of the American South. Michael is a Judaic studies teacher from the Washington, DC, metropolitan area, and his interests include food culture, food history, Jewish cultural studies, African American history, and cultural politics. His blog, *Afroculinaria*, highlights and addresses food's critical role in the development and definition of African American civilization and the politics of consumption and cultural ownership that surround it.

*P*hotographs

p. 32   Natalie Baszile.

p. 34   iStock.com/SimonSkafar.

p. 38   Natalie Baszile.

p. 42   Alison Gootee.

p. 53   LC-USF33-030584-M4. Library of Congress, Prints & Photographs Division, FSA/OWI
         Collection. Photo by Marion Post Wolcott.

p. 54   Alison Gootee.

p. 62   Alison Gootee.

p. 65   Alison Gootee.

p. 68   Natalie Baszile.

p. 88   Natalie Baszile.

p. 90   Alison Gootee.

p. 98   Natalie Baszile.

p. 104   Brenae Royal.

p. 113   Natalie Baszile.

p. 114   Alison Gootee.

p. 123   iStock.com/Katsuhiro Kojima

p. 126   LC-USF33-012145-M5. Library of Congress, Prints & Photographs Division, FSA/OWI
         Collection. Photo by Rusell (CK) Lee.

p. 145   Natalie Baszile.

p. 146   Natalie Baszile.

p. 183   Natalie Baszile.

p. 184   Alison Gootee.

p. 192   Alison Gootee.

p. 206   LC-USF34-040609-D. Library of Congress, Prints & Photographs Division, FSA/OWI Collection.
         Photo by Jack Delano.

p. 208   Natalie Baszile.

p. 213   Natalie Baszile.

p. 214   Natalie Baszile.

p. 216   Alison Gootee.

p. 223   Alison Gootee.

p. 241   iStock.com/KanKankavee.

p. 242   Alison Gootee.

p. 256   Natalie Baszile.

p. 258   Natalie Baszile.

p. 260   Natalie Baszile.

p. 262   Alison Gootee.

p. 266   iStock.com/slowmotiongli.

p. 270   Natalie Baszile.

p. 275   Alison Gootee.

p. 276   Alison Gootee.

p. 282   Alison Gootee.

p. 294   LC-USF3301-012133-M2. Library of Congress, Prints & Photographs Division, FSA/OWI
Collection. Photo by Russell Lee.

p. 296   Alison Gootee.

p. 300   Alison Gootee.

p. 302   Malcolm Williams.

p. 315   Alison Gootee.

p. 318   Natalie Baszile.

p. 326   Natalie Baszile.

p. 334   Alison Gootee.

p. 336   iStock.com/Andrew Robins.

p. 338   LC-USF33-012148-M3. Library of Congress, Prints & Photographs Division, FSA/OWI
Collection. Photo by Russell Lee.

p. 344   Natalie Baszile.

p. 352   iStock.com/dndavis.

About the Author

Natalie Baszile is the author of *Queen Sugar*, which has been adapted for television and coproduced by Ava DuVernay and Oprah Winfrey. Natalie has an MA in Afro-American Studies from UCLA and earned an MFA from Warren Wilson College's MFA Program for Writers. Her nonfiction work has appeared in *The Bitter Southerner*, *O: The Oprah Magazine*, *Lenny Letter*, and numerous anthologies. Natalie is a resident at SFFILM. She is a member of the San Francisco Writers' Grotto. Natalie lives in San Francisco.

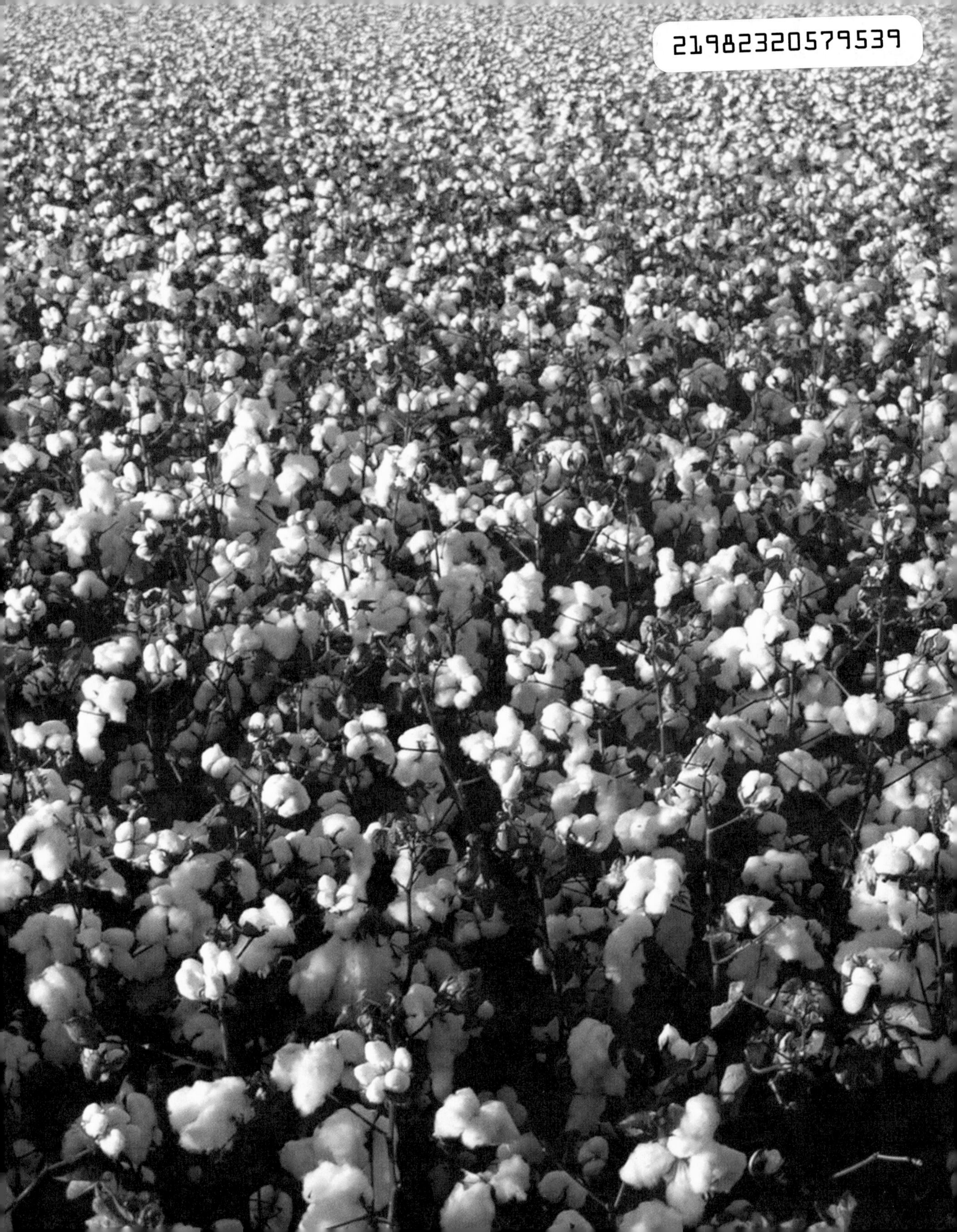